German Life in WWII and Beyond

How Civilians Survived and Rebuilt

Dr. Ilse-Rose Warg

Genre
Library Solutions

German Life in WWII and Beyond: How Civilians Survived and Rebuilt by Dr. Ilse-Rose Warg

Copyright © 2024 by **Dr. Ilse-Rose Warg**

E-book: 979-8-3302-7302-7
Paperback: 979-8-3302-7301-0
Hardback: 979-8-3302-7303-4

Printed in the United States of America.

Genre Library Solutions
300 Delaware Ave. Suite 210,
Wilmington, DE 19801
www.genrelibrarysolutions.com
(315) 367-7314

My book is dedicate to the women
who cleaned and rebuilt the torn landscape
after the war. They kept traditions
and the Christian Faith alive.

ACKNOWLEDGMENTS

My appreciation goes out to all the students and professors with whom I remained in contact after my retirement, for their encouragement to write a revised version of *To Cope and To Prevail*. I thank Dr. Horst Strohbusch, who kindly gave me permission to quote from his book "Das Licht kam aus der Kirche: die Wende in Meiningen 1989-1990.[1]" For my account of the GDR after 1953, I relied on phone calls with him, Eberhard Fleischer, Horst Bollmann, and interviews with my relatives. My cousin Ingrid Thiel (née Oswald) shared her memories of events that occurred after most of my family members' farms had been confiscated in 1945-46.

Many thanks to my siblings: Ernst Höfer, Hildegard Steinbömer, and Dr. Reinhold Höfer. They and my other relatives refreshed my memory and permitted me to mention them freely throughout the first edition and again for the new version.

Especially helpful was my cousin Hermann Georg (Hermjörg) Oemler. In 2006, he drove me to Klostermansfeld, Eisleben, Edersleben, and Sangerhausen. He also provided valuable photos that enrich this new version.

I thank my husband, Jamison B. Warg, PG, and my daughter, Sonja Chestnut, for helping with selecting maps and encouragement. I am greatly indebted to my son, Ernst Bernhard Warg, for his invaluable technical skills. Last but not least, I thank him and Carol Ann Moore (retired teacher), for their corrections and input when editing the manuscript.

Ilse-Rose Warg, PhD

---

1   "Das Licht kam aus der Kirche: die Wende in Meiningen 1989-1990," English translation: The Light came from the Church: The Turning Point in Meiningen 1989-1990.

CONTENTS

FOREWORD

"The Cold War reared its ugly head after 1948. It developed into a monster until 1989, when it died with the tearing down of the Berlin Wall." This statement is in chapter five of my book *To Cope And to Prevail, Growing up in Germany in 1930-50s,* which I published in 2012.

Now we know that the Cold War only went dormant until a new dictator, like Stalin, woke it up again. In 2014 Russia attacked Ukraine. Vladimir Putin, in search of a harbor on the Black Sea, succeeded by taking hold of the peninsula Crimea. Eight years later in early spring of 2022, he attacked Ukraine again with the intent of ruling the whole country. Not being able to perform a blitzkrieg, he ruthlessly ruins cities and the countryside where the roads lead to the Black Sea. Now Ukraine is entangled in a war with Russia. But Ukraine has the help of NATO and the European Union. Both of these establishments came about after WWII mainly because the West feared the Cold War could develop into another World War. My grandmother, Oma, would think *See how out of evil God brought about unification not only inside of Germany, but also unification among many European States.*

Originally, I wrote my book to dispel misconceptions about Germany's history and culture that I found among my students who took the diversity course German 200: *The History and Culture of Modern Germany.* I could find no suitable book, covering Germany's turbulent time from 1923 through the 1950s, which could serve as supplemental reading at the Pennsylvania State University, Altoona Campus.

To Cope And to Prevail[2] is not written in the conventional style of textbooks. My goal was to stay away from political and military events as much as possible, and rather acquaint the reader with the different

---

2   Ilse-Rose Warg, PhD: To Cope and To Prevail: Growing up in Germany in 1930-50's. AuthorHouse, Bloomington, IN 47403. 2012

reactions of the common people who had to live in Germany through these years.

The book was well received by students, faculty, and their assistants. For instance, after I retired, Dr. Steven C. Andrew still used it for his Holocaust course. But these readers also suggested revising my book by adding maps and pictures to supplement and substantiate the reports about the cultural, political and economic changes in Germany, which took place during the Nazi regime, the Allied occupation, the Cold War and its split into two politically and economically separated German lands.

In the revision at hand, I kept my own observations as I grew up and, of course, the actual events. The rather novelistic style was added through a tradition in German culture called "Stammtisch," which, in my book, is a group of fictional characters representing the lower to higher middle classes. They discuss major political, economical, or cultural events from various perspectives. Their lively conversation gives my book the different approach. In certain paragraphs, the book almost reads like a drama with humor and tragic moments intertwined. I continue to show how people overcame the devastation of their country as many inhabitants of the countryside helped evacuees, fugitives, expellees and other homeless fellow men.

It is inevitable that the women and children in particular held on to their traditions and Christian beliefs to overcome their bleak circumstances. Authors of history books often neglected to give credit to those who were the enduring force in the war, as Trümmerfrauen[3] cleaning up the shattered towns and standing behind the rebuilding of the torn country during its occupation and after.

Teaching at the university level, I thought I could not express my Christian belief in a textbook. I had to consider the beliefs of some students being brought up in different religions, i.e. Buddhist, Islamic, Jewish, Hindu and others. But now in my retirement, I wanted to show how God

---

3   This word was coined by writers mainly meaning the women of Berlin. I find it is time to apply it to all the German women in the big cities as well as in the countryside.

delivered Germany, and with it my family and myself, from a regime that had turned into satanic destruction.

I had more time to revise the book. I wanted to change its title, *To Cope And to Prevail: Growing up in Germany in 1930-50's,* which seems to concentrate too much on a child's experiences. Now the book is aimed more to the general reader. Occasionally I show how I, as a Christian, see God's purpose in bringing down the Hitler regime, and His hand in the recuperation of Germany. I often leave it up to the reader to discover God's guidance in those turbulent times of WWII and its aftermath. Bible verses head each chapter. I hope they aid in discovering how God's wisdom and care is reflected in the course of the events described.

I changed little in the first 6 chapters, save for dropping quotes I had used before. Now, the text points further ahead toward the reunification of East and West Germany in 1991. After more than 30 years many wounds between the "Ossies" and "Wessies" have healed, although I know that it will take still more time before the two politically separated Germanies' cultures and attitudes are overcome. My favorite Professor, the late Dr. Rio Preisner of the Pennsylvania State University, was a refugee from Czechoslovakia. He told me, out of his deep wisdom acquired during a turbulent life, that it takes 75 years or three generations before wounds created by wicked actions are forgiven.

WWII lasted six and a half years. I hope and pray that Ukraine can push back the invader in a much shorter time. May this book give us hope, and the Ukrainians confidence and strength to last and rebuild their beautiful country.

May the words of C.S. Lewis be an encouragement for the readers and a beacon for my work.

Even in literature and art, no man who bothers about originality will ever be original: whereas if you simply try to tell the truth (without caring twopence how often it has been told before) you will, nine times out of ten, become original without ever having noticed it.[4]

---

4   Quoted here from a Collector's Edition of C. S. Lewis' book Mere Christianity, Book IV Chapter 11 pg. 226. The Easton Press, Norwalk, CT. 2002

Germany after 1991

https://www.germany-insider-facts.com/german-states.html

Translation of the above legend:

Mainz ✳ capital of the state (Rheinland Pfalz)

Fürth ⊙ other towns/cities

✳ cities with more than 5000,000 inhabitants

Klostermansfeld is in Sachsen Anhalt (central in map above) WNW of Halle

CHAPTER 1

"But take care and watch yourselves closely, so as neither to forget the things
that your eyes have seen nor to let them slip from your mind all the days of
your life; make them known to your children and your children's children."
Deuteronomy 4:9.[5]

New Regimes for Germany

Klostermansfeld[6] is a middle-sized village located in the center of
Germany. It developed around a former cloister founded by Benedictine
monks circa 1140 AD. In the 16th century, in the course of the Reformation,
the cloister was dissolved. The Count of Mansfeld confiscated its fields,
gardens, and buildings, and granted the old cloister buildings and the
land to a close friend of Martin Luther[7]. The new owners farmed the
rich soil and during the following centuries, their heirs converted the old
monastery buildings into a stately farmhouse, flanked by stables and a
barn. It was in this environment that, about 400 years later, in December
1930, Herbert Edmund Gottlob Höfer and Ilse-Paula Oemler married in
the protestant church of the village. They had met while he was an intern at

---

5   Unless otherwise stated, all Biblical quotes are from *The New Oxford Annotated
     Bible, New* Revised Standard Version, New York, Oxford University Press,
     1991.

6   If Klostermansfeld were on the map on page X, you would find it in Sachsen
     Anhalt and in the middle of the BRD (Bundesrepublik of Germany). In its
     southern part, you'll notice the town Halle, which is about 20 miles ESE from
     Klostermansfeld.

7   Martin Luther's friend was Nicolaus Oemler. Martin Luther was born in
     1483 in Eisleben. His parents moved to Mansfeld when he was a young boy.
     Although in his adult life, Luther traveled throughout Germany and taught in
     Wittenberg, he stayed affiliated with the Mansfeld district throughout his life.
     He died in Eisleben in 1546.

the "Domäne"[8]. Herbert's father had told him sternly that, being the eldest son, he needed to study agriculture in order to farm their land in Thuringia. Ernst Höfer, Sr. was well known as the leader of the Thüringer Landbund since its foundation in 1919. A framed print from a woodcarving depicts only his head. He looks up slightly. Underneath is an inscription, which reads; "Staatsrat Ernst Höfer: *Die Hand am Pflug den Blick zu Gott.*[9]

Originally, only professional farmers belonged to the Thüringer Landbund. In 1930, under Ernst Höfer Sr.'s leadership, it had developed into the strongest political party in Thuringia. By now, their members not only included owners, renters, and workers of farms, but also businessmen, industry workers, artists, craftsmen, shop keepers, pastors, and teachers. Its strongest support came from the rural areas in Thuringia. Although they were powerful, they were neither able to stop the advancement of the National Socialist party nor the progress of the Communist party. These two parties opposed each other on everything except for one common goal: pursuing the destruction of the Weimar Republic[10].

Ilse-Paula's father had died not quite a year before her wedding. He had suffered from diabetes and succumbed to the disease. He never was a strong man, and farming was not his passion. He would rather work on scientific endeavors, especially chemistry. He liked to create beauty creams based on finely ground almonds and flower fragrances for his three daughters. His third child, Paula[11], seemed to have been his favorite. She loved literature, poetry, and music and had an open mind for all the arts. Paula liked instructing her younger brother in mathematics. Also, she seemed to be the most athletic in her family. Paula attended

---

8   Manor, usually a large estate formerly owned by nobility, or by the state. Usually men who graduated from a German agriculture academy oversaw these huge farms. They supplied internships for students of agriculture and for future farmers.

9   "The hand at the plow, the eyes on God."

10   The Weimar Republic was founded in 1919, as a democratic government to rule over Germany.

11   Although her legal name was Ilse-Paula, her family and friends called her just Paula.

several years of the high school in Halle on the Saale, but when Germany experienced uncontrollable inflation in 1923, her father, like many middle class Germans, lost almost all of his money. Now he could not afford a higher education for his daughter. She had to decide where to finish her studies without obtaining a degree from an Academy. She chose to go to East Prussia to learn how to manage a big farm household. In the 1920s and 30s, East Prussia was separated from the rest of Germany by the so called Polish Corridor, created by the victorious Allies after Germany had lost the Great War—later named WWI.

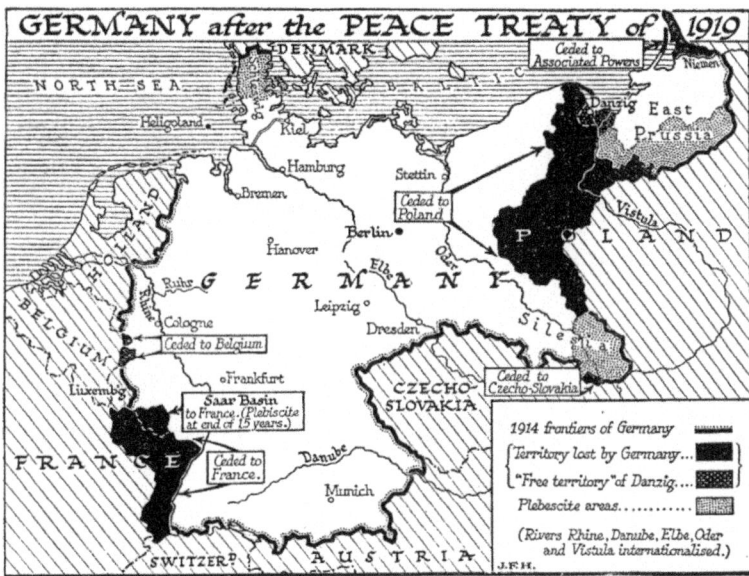

GERMANY after the PEACE TREATY of 1919

https://www.google.com/search?q=germany+map+treaty+of+versailles&client=firefox-b-1-e&

The black area between Germany and Poland was called the Polish Corridor. East Prussia still belonged to Germany. The black area in the southwest is the Saar Basin ceded to France.

Relatives and friends of Paula Oemler thought she had to be a strong fearless young woman to travel so far away from home and to pass through a hostile foreign country to reach her destination in East Prussia. She stayed with a Mennonite family at their huge estate, and grew especially fond of their beautiful garden and park. She liked their outlook on life, and soon they became dear friends to her. After completing her education, she returned to Klostermansfeld, where she met Herbert Höfer. Paula, a petite, pretty redhead of twenty-four years, and he, a very charming, tall young man of twenty-five, married according to their family traditions.

Herbert's father owned a smaller estate in St. Bernhard in Thuringia. When he, as the first Chairman of the Thüringer Landbund, had to be away from home, his wife Frieda took care of the fields and stables with the help of her second son, Hans, hoping her eldest could take over soon, since he would inherit the farm. But when her husband died in 1931, Herbert revealed that he did not intend to be an agriculturalist.

Ernst Höfer, Sr. had succumbed to a severe flu with complications. His doctors ordered him to relax and visit a spa to rehabilitate. He chose Heiligenberg in the southern part of the Black Forest. On June 13, while on a walk with his wife near the spa, he suddenly stumbled and fell. A doctor was soon at the scene, but although he was transported promptly to a nearby hospital specializing in cardiology, he died the next day. He had suffered a heart attack. His widow and a nurse returned to Thuringia by train. As was customary at that time, they loaded the casket with the deceased's body onto the same train, so Chairman Höfer's funeral could be conducted near his farm in Thuringia.

Ernst and Frieda had selected a beautiful spot in their forest for their burial place a few years earlier. Tall oak trees still stand guard over them[12]. Many people attended his funeral. Among his friends were the members of his Thuringia Farmers Party and representatives of all other political parties of Thuringia. Only the National Socialist party did not send members to pay their last respects.

Although Herbert inherited the farm, he preferred to work as an insurance agent and was glad that his mother and his brother, Hans, could continue to take care of the fields and livestock. Sometimes Hans had help from their much younger brother, Horst, who was still attending school.

---

12   After the farm was confiscated in 1945, the leaders of the Communist party in
       Thuringia kept the burial place as a culturally historical site.

Unfortunately, in 1942 Hans had to give up the heavy work, because he suffered from epilepsy. He told Herbert that he was forced to seek employment as an office clerk. He actually was very gifted as a painter, but freelancing as an artist was out of the question for him. He had married and needed to support his wife and their two children.

Herbert, not wanting to give up his thriving insurance business, made arrangements to rent the farm and house out to Mr. Arno Rassmann, who moved with his large family into the lower rooms of the farmhouse. Herbert's mother received legal rights to occupy a small apartment on the upper floor of the two-story building as long as she lived. Horst stayed with her until he got drafted into the German navy. Hans secured a position as a clerk in the KdF organization[13]. Herbert was pleased with this settlement. Little did he know, his decision to rent out the farm would cause him much grief later on.

Herbert's mother visited her two older sons often. To see Herbert—who seemed to move every two years to another town in Thuringia—she needed to take the train. This is not an easy task; since St. Bernhard did not, and still does not, possess a train station. Therefore, Herbert often would come with his new car to take her to his home.

After Paula and Herbert married, his insurance company moved him first to Stettin[14], a town at the mouth of the river Oder. He was exceptionally competent and soon received a promotion. As a result, he and Paula moved back to Thuringia. This time, they lived in Gotha. In December 1932, Paula gave birth to their first son at home. Her mother, Mrs. Oemler, came to help her daughter. She was in for a shock. When Paula's water broke, the midwife assisting her during the birthing did not want to call a doctor. After hours of exhausting birth pangs this woman reiterated, "I have seen worse situations than this one. Mrs. Höfer, you must strain more to help the

---

13   "Kraft durch Freude" (Strength through Joy) was a state-controlled organization in Nazi Germany, connected to the "Deutsche Arbeitsfront" (German workers front), through which workers could take paid vacations away from home.

14   Stettin (Szczecin since 1945) in Poland just across the Polish German border, see map on pg. X.

baby through the birth canal." Finally, Mrs. Oemler called a doctor, who saved the child. The umbilical cord had been wrapped around the baby's neck. The face of the newborn had already turned a ghastly bluish color, but the doctor was able to get the baby to breathe. He saved the young mother as well, although Paula's facial nerves were damaged, so that the muscles on her right cheek were paralyzed. She could hardly speak clearly. It took months of physical therapy for her to recuperate.

In 1932, the political scene in Germany presented itself as anything other than quiet. President Paul Hindenburg's term in office expired on May 5, 1932. The attempt to have Hindenburg stay on for another year without an election was spoiled by the National Socialists as well as by the Communists. Most Germans revered Hindenburg as an accomplished Prussian soldier, who symbolized the Weimar Republic.

At "Stammtisch"[15] gatherings all over Germany, heated debates could be heard among the members. The groups consist of regulars sometimes including a pastor, one or two farmers, a pharmacist, maybe a teacher, the mayor, a shopkeeper, a butcher, and any other person of a respectable profession. In bigger towns, a banker or lawyer might replace the farmer. They would gather over a beer and play a round of cards. Often, they debated everything of interest, and in 1932 their main concern was political. Like everywhere else in the world, the media altered the news; reporters often tainted their statements, thinking they made the news more dramatic and exciting. At a Stammtisch, this news would be speculated on, considered, and talked over.

In one of the villages in the middle of Germany, a Stammtisch member, the pharmacist, turned to his group and said, "Our trouble started with the uncontrolled inflation in 1923." He paused, remembering the effect it had on everybody. "Even here in our village, a few people committed suicide because of the financial uncertainty."

---

15   To this day, the Stammtisch is a group of mainly men who reserve a table for a designated time and day of the week in an inn to drink beer, play cards, and discuss current events.

The teacher agreed. "Yes, that's when we had all of these foreigners come and buy our cultural heritage, even our old castle was bought by somebody who wanted to pretend he belonged to the venerated aristocrat class."

A farmer chimed in, "We should have kept our old castle."

"How could we?" the teacher replied, "I went with a basket full of money to buy some rolls, and when I was at the bakery, the inflation had reduced my money to half its buying power. I needed one more basketful of paper money to pay for a few rolls."

"We, at the farm, had it better when it came to food," the farmer nodded. "But we could not afford to repair our machines, or pay for seeds, let alone keep up with salaries for our workers."

The mayor sighed. "Whoever had foreign currency could buy anything. Outsiders came and wanted to purchase our Romanesque church, and when I refused to sell it, they behaved like big shots."

Members of another group at the inn entered the debate. "Foreigners and Jews are to be blamed for our plight."

Somebody suggested, "I would not do that. Just don't forget Chancellor Gustav Stresemann[16]; he got us out of the trouble."

A shopkeeper moaned, "Too bad he had to die three years ago."

Their debate continued, with one member exclaiming, "Oh well, that's quite some time ago! What about now? The election is coming up. What about President Hindenburg? Did you hear they could not extend his term for another year? Now, we must have an election."

"What do you think about that new guy, Adolf Hitler?"

"Wait a moment, he's not so new."

"Isn't he the one who was in prison?"

"Yes! He wrote a book there."

---

16   Stresemann, Gustav 1878-1929. German Chancellor 1923, Foreign Minister 1923-1929,

7

"I read *Mein Kampf* [17], as he called it," the teacher said, and he went on to voice his opinion. "Everybody needs to read it. It gives you an idea of why he is the leader of the National Socialists."

"Bah, he is not a candidate. You might quite as well say the Communist's Thälmann is a contender as well."

"I, for one, hope they vote for Colonel Düsterberg, the candidate of the German Nationals and the Stahlhelm. After all, I was a soldier in the Great War!"

"So was Hitler!"

"Yea, at that time he lost his Austrian citizenship because he had joined the Bavarian Army. Can you imagine? He even is not a German citizen."

"Not so! My sister, who lives in Brandenburg, told me that the National Socialist government of Brandenburg naturalized him."

"So this upstart is German now?!" exclaimed the pharmacist in disbelief.

A week later, our Stammtisch met at the same time and place, but something was different. They barely opened a deck of cards. They started their discussion right away about the outcome of the election that had taken place April 10. The mayor pointed out triumphantly, "Hindenburg got elected after all; he collected nineteen million votes. That is the absolute majority. Your candidate, Hitler, only received thirteen million and Thälmann three million."

"Hitler only acquired so many votes because Düsterberg from the German Nationals and the Stahlhelm withdrew his candidacy," the Pharmacist interrupted.

Still a few months later, in the beginning of June, the mayor thought he had good reason to shake his head. "I don't know what is wrong with President Hindenburg. He dismissed Chancellor Brüning at the end of May, and that aristocrat Franz von Papen will replace him."

---

17 Literally "My Struggle." Adolf Hitler's book originally published in two volumes, 1925 and 1926.

As one can tell by the rapid changes of leadership in such a short time, The Weimar Republic was particularly unstable in the year 1932.

Von Papen only "reigned" until November and was replaced by General Kurt von Schleicher, who was ousted on January 28, 1933. Two days later, in the evening, Hitler celebrated his appointment as chancellor with Hindenburg by his side. They stood in the grandstand, looking at the spectacular torchlight parade of his SA troops[18] marching through the Brandenburg Gate in Berlin. Hitler was always able to impress the masses by staging dazzling events. Later, the 1936 Olympics in Berlin gave rise to one of the many theatrical, dramatic spectacles.

In February 1933, Herbert and his wife recalled the incidents of the previous year. Paula, holding her baby in her arms, put some amber marbles in her mouth and sighed; "How things changed!" she rearranged the little pellets with her tongue and continued. "First Brüning then von Papen and then von Schleicher and now Hitler." Herbert smiled, "That was quite a difficult sentence, Paula, dear. Your speech is getting better." After a deep breath, she muttered, "How did this all come about?" and changing the subject, "I am glad you never were in the SA or SS[19]."

Herbert looked with pride at his little son, who enjoyed his mother's milk. "He is quite a little drinker; he will become strong. I'll make sure that he has a good future under the new regime." To set his wife at ease he continued, "I don't believe I ever will enter the SA or SS—my father did not like them—and I really have no time for their meetings and events, as fantastic as they may be. You are right how quickly things developed. After von Papen was elected, it only took until June to have the Reichstag dissolved. So much for the Weimar Republic. And just two weeks later, still in June, the SA was declared legal."

---

18 SA stands for Sturm Abteilung (storm Division). In 1921, Hitler initiated his own army for his protection and political advancement. They are also called brown shirts or storm troopers.

19 SS stands for Schutz Staffel (Protection Squad). It was formed in 1925 as part of the SA. It became the personal guard for Hitler. They wore black uniforms. Like the SA, they were initially illegal during the Weimar Republic.

Herbert took his son from Paula's arms and gently tapped the baby's back to burp him. It worked almost too well. "That was a good one, Ernst!" He turned back to their political discussion. "In July, von Papen had already filled all posts in the administration of Prussia with rightist officials, and he became the Reichskommissar for Prussia."[20]

Paula took the amber from her mouth and spoke slowly, deliberately, "He and his Baron's Cabinet." She used a nickname she had heard for the von Papen cabinet. "After all, as far as I know, von Papen appointed mainly aristocrats to his cabinet."

Herbert, glad that his wife's face looked more normal, pointed out, "von Papen's cabinet represented the moderate right.[21] That could have been good for my job. Except von Papen resigned in November."

"Yes, after the Stahlhelm staged the biggest parade Berlin ever saw. 150,000 war veterans marched and pledged allegiance to the black-white-red flag of old Prussia."

Herbert laughed after Ernst burped a second time. "Maybe we should have named Ernst not after my father, but after the Old Fritz, Frederick the Great."[22] He chuckled, and Paula tried to laugh with him.

He returned to their discussion on the demise of the Weimar Republic, "After von Papen we had von Schleicher, another of the aristocrats, in control as the Reichskommissar for Prussia. I think he might have been better suited to reconstruct all of Germany, not just Prussia."

Little did they know that, although von Papen resigned, he had met with Hitler and the banker von Schröder in Cologne to discuss a corporative order similar to the one outlined in Pope Pius XI's encyclical

---

20 Since Prussia was the largest state in the Weimar Republic, the person who gained the position as commissioner over Prussia had the greatest influence on the government.

21 In the Reichstag election of July 31, the National Socialists acquired 230 seats and the Communists 89, with the parties of the middle losing considerably.

22 Frederick the Great (1712–1786) reigned as King of Prussia from 1740 until his death. He was very much loved in northern Germany, but is a controversial figure in history books.

Quadragesimo Anno (1931). Von Papen and Schröder assumed that the encyclical could correspond with the corporatism of Mussolini and the demands of the National Socialists. However, this was rather naïve, since "solidarism," as foreseen by the papal encyclical, was based on the free development of human personality. It envisioned free service, voluntary association, and the acceptance of sanctions of divine, natural, and moral law, whereas the Italian Fascists' and German National Socialists' "corporatism" was centered in the absolute power of the state or the race. There was nothing voluntary or free, but instead the so-called coordination[23] of individuals and groups by means of physical and spiritual browbeating, threats, and violence. Von Papen only chose Hitler to be part of their plans because he was aware of Hitler's oratorical skills. He wanted to make Hitler chancellor as a mock figurehead—as von Papen's mouthpiece. However, Hitler took another course of action.

Chancellor Adolf Hitler called only two National Socialists into his first cabinet: Joseph Goebbels as minister of propaganda and enlightenment, and Hermann Göring as minister without portfolio. Two other commoners were appointed for agriculture and labor. Von Papen became vice-chancellor and Reichskommissar for Prussia. He and three other aristocrats filled the rest of the positions.[24]

⋙⋙⋙⋙⋙

In April 1933, the weekly Stammtisch met as always at the inn. The mayor brought up a political discussion by asking all of them, "Do you think it was really that feebleminded Dutch Communist who burned the Reichstag's building in February?"

"Maybe ..." mused the pharmacist.

"Why not? The Communists are always violent!" the shopkeeper stated.

---

23 Called *Gleichschaltung* under the Nazi regime.

24 The commoners were Alfred Franz Maria Hugenberg, minister of agriculture, and Franz Seldte, minister of labor. Hitler reached out to the aristocrats under von Papen's influence. General von Blomberg was named minister of defense, Baron von Neurath retained his position as minister of foreign affairs, and Count Schwerin of Krosgk became minister of finance.

"Well, not all of them are violent, I think," the pastor added. "They needed a scapegoat, and this Dutch man was seen near the burning building. They wanted to get rid of the Communists, and now, they can claim that the reason why they're arresting so many Communists is to protect the people from communistic vandalism."

"Who do you mean by *they*, Pastor?" asked the teacher, frowning.

The clergyman was not slow to reply. "Well, *they* are the whole Hitler cabinet, Hindenburg included. He is really getting too old to be our president. He signed the decree 'for the Protection of the People and the State.' This decree will haunt us, I tell you. *For the protection of the people and the state* can be interpreted many different ways. From now on, we have to watch what we say and who is listening. Better just keep to our card game."

"Hindenburg has become von Papen's and Hitler's puppet," the farmer grunted. "Did you know that the SA and SS are now part of the military police? I agree with you, Pastor; I predict bad times ahead—maybe even censorship again."

The pharmacist leaned back in his chair and pondered, "Many of my clients are Communists."

"You have to report them," the teacher insisted.

"And lose my clients? No, they are decent workers. Most of them are miners and farmhands," the pharmacist replied. "Anyway, I don't think they'll be arrested, even if someone reports them. The state needs them. *We* need them. Yes, they may go to jail for a short time, but who would want to replace them in the deep mines?"

"Certainly not me," said the farmer. "I need fresh air—can't stand the darkness down there." He paused, considering all the tasks waiting for him to do in the spring. "And my farmhands, who have communistic notions—I choose not to notice political affiliations. Let them arrest the Communists who staged the uprisings after the Great War, not our diligent workers."

"I don't trust the news reports on the radio. They sound biased to me," the shopkeeper noted. He looked at the teacher, who had pulled a pamphlet out of his jacket, and asked, "What do you have there, Teach?"

"It's the Treaty of Versailles, actually excerpts of it. Just the articles, which are most relevant to the German people[25]."

The pastor fell in. "I received it too. Look at the subtitle. It says: 'The reason for Germany's plight,' and in smaller letters 'with 18 drawings, maps, and a foreword by Dr-phil-h-c-Hans Draeger, in connection with German organizations published for the folk and youth.' Hmm, why do they separate folk from youth, I wonder?"

The clergyman had read the pamphlet and felt he had to tell them about it. "It is very biased, just like our newspapers. In the footnotes to various quoted articles, you read such adjectives as *vicious, vile, wicked,* and *unjust.* With these words they try to underscore the unwarranted points of the treaty. And here on page 32, they marked article 231 in red."

"Ah, yes!" the pharmacist remembered, "The infamous article 231! We supposedly started the war, and now Germany agrees to be responsible for all repairs of war damages."

The farmer listened to his friends, but he wanted to go back to their discussion about newspaper and radio reports. He interjected, "Words, words! They lose their meaning as everything and everybody seems to be watched. Soon, free press or speech is merely a dream."

The farmer predicted correctly. By the end of 1933, many political parties in Germany had been outlawed or dissolved. Only the NSDAP[26] became "insolubly tied" to the state. Many Communists were arrested. They were not the only ones. Liberals, Catholics, pacifists, and even

---

25   On June 28, 1919, the signing of the treaty by Germans took place in the same Hall of Mirrors in Versailles Palace where the German empire had been proclaimed on January 18, 1871.The German people were informed about the unfair conditions of this peace treaty by selecting articles of it and printing them in a pamphlet for "folk and youth."

26   NSDAP = Nationalsozialistische Deutsche Arbeiterpartei, (National Socialist German Workers Party).

socialists were seized, beaten, tortured, murdered, or sent to prison camps, where the inmates could "concentrate" on their attitudes and change their convictions. The Communist parties were represented in the parliament in too huge a number to be banished easily. For them to vanish from the political scene in Germany, the constitution needed to be changed. To alter the constitution, a meeting was necessary to vote on the proposal for the *Ermächtigungsgesetz* (Enabling Act). Hitler, with the support of the right-wing parties and the centrists, was able to get the necessary votes to change the constitution. Now, with the dictatorial powers obtained by Hitler, state and municipal governments were "cleansed" of all politically undesirable administrators. That meant they were ousted and replaced by National Socialists.

〽〜〽〜〽〜〽〜〽〜

When the Stammtisch met in July 1934, they were more cautious about what and with whom they might discuss their opinions.

"So, Röhm is dead," the pharmacist declared.

"What was wrong with the SA chief?" the farmer asked.

"You have no idea, do you?" smirked the teacher. "Röhm and his SA wanted to destroy our Hitler regime. He wanted to stage a coup d'état. Yes, that surprises you, doesn't it? He wanted to take over. Luckily, Hitler already had dictatorial power, so he could gain control of the situation before it became a problem. The police secretly set a date for the arrest. When the assigned policemen met and whispered the password, the arrest of Röhm was at hand. It turned out to be a deadly brawl. It was 'die Nacht der langen Messer' (The Night of the Long Knives)."

"Were you harassed too? I mean, you being in the SA and affiliated with Röhm …" the farmer asked.

The teacher answered him by pointing out that he was smart enough to change his pledge. "I handed in my dagger," he told them. "Röhm's name on it was erased. Now, our decorative SA blades will have the inscription, 'Everything for Germany.' That is more to my liking."

Before a heated debate could start between the farmer and the teacher, the minister noted, "So many of Hitler's close associates were killed too. Father Bernhard Stempfle, who did editorial work on Hitler's book and was the head of Catholic Action in Berlin, and even von Schleicher and his wife were killed. I heard von Papen has been arrested as well. But I guess he is too close to Hindenburg to be murdered."

"Hindenburg praised Hitler for his action," the teacher interjected.

"We all heard Hitler's speech over the radio. Interesting, very interesting," the farmer said, giving the teacher a short glance. "I made sure all of my workers and I heard Hitler. We left the hay wagon on the field and headed home to listen to the radio." In reality, he and his workers only heard the excerpts of that speech during the evening news. By now, the farmer wanted to be on his guard. He had started to mistrust the teacher, who could report him to the police for who knows what!

The teacher was only too happy to approve. "That is the way it should be. We have to pay attention when Hitler, our chancellor and leader, addresses the German nation. He will tell us the real reason behind sentencing the convicted."

The shopkeeper shrugged his shoulders. "You call this 'sentence'? There was no trial. They were arrested, put in jail, and killed, or even not that …"

"Shush!!!" the pharmacist stopped him. Changing the subject, he asked, "Whose turn is it to deal the cards?"

"Not mine," the shopkeeper said, and he left.

In 1934, the year of The Night of the Long Knives and Hindenburg's death, Hitler abolished the title of Reichspräsident. Instead, he assumed the title and office of Führer and Reichskanzler.[27]

That same year, Herbert and Paula moved from Gotha to Jena's outskirts. Here, their daughter arrived on August 5, 1934, three days after

27 "Reichspräsident" means president of the nation or realm "Führer" means leader or guide, and "Reichskanzler" is best translated as chancellor of the realm, the Third Reich "das dritte Reich".

Hindenburg's death. Her birth, in a hospital surrounded by competent nurses and doctors, was easy for Paula. They named her after Paula's oldest sister, Hildegard. Her father loved this beautiful little baby dearly. She was so dainty—healthy, but delicate. Paula had grown up with many servants in her parent's household. Now she decided it was time to hire at least one helper as nanny for the children.

>~~~ >~~~ >~~~ >~~~ >~~~

Later in 1934, the Stammtisch continued to meet as always. This time, the mayor's son joined them. He had just enlisted in the Reichswehr (armed forces of Germany).

The teacher's face showed clearly how pleased he was with the young man's choice to enlist in the army. He greeted him with, "So nice of you to mingle with us old folks. I am proud of you. We need young, strong men like you to protect our country. Did you recite the oath yet? I remember when I swore *obedience to the constitution and the fatherland.*"

"Yes, but with a different meaning; the wording of the oath has changed."

The teacher, surprised, asked, "To what do you commit yourself to now?"

"Not *what*, but *who!*" corrected the son. "We swear, *under God, to give unconditional obedience to the Führer of the German Reich and people, Adolf Hitler.*"

The minister remarked, "Well, at least God is part of your oath."

"You would notice that, Pastor! What I like about the Reichswehr is that from now on, we are the only ones who may have arms. The militia of the political parties is abolished, so are the municipal forces," the son informed them.

The pharmacist interjected, "Except for the police, the SS, and the Secret Police."

The son was quick to react. "But they have nothing to do with us soldiers. They are to protect the Führer, the constitution, and the homeland. So, party militias are forbidden now." Proudly, he declared, "I tell you, we will fight to get back the areas that belonged to Germany before the Great War."

The farmer, who liked to participate in kettle-hunts every January, when they shoot hares and foxes, wondered, "Do we hunters have to give up our guns now?"

The mayor shook his head. "Of course not! How can they abolish all of the hunting clubs and the competitions in target shooting throughout Germany? We will still celebrate our Schützenfest[28] just as all the other towns and villages do."

"It is too old a tradition. According to our archives, it was already mentioned in the 15th century." the pharmacist added.

In the meantime, the teacher invited the young soldier to join them for a drink. "Be my guest," he said and called the waiter. "Oskar, a beer and schnapps[29] for our young hero-to-be."

One year later, in March 1935, Germany recovered the highly industrialized Saar Basin[30] by negotiations. It was the first area to be brought back under German control after it had been lost as a result of the Treaty of Versailles. In the same year, Hitler installed the draft into the military for all able-bodied young German men. Twelve months later, he ordered his enlarged military to enter the Rhineland, which, according to the infamous treaty, should have remained permanently demilitarized. When negotiating with European governments, Hitler pointed out that the unfair terms of the Treaty of Versailles could lead to uprisings, even another war. He reiterated that he wanted peace and all Germans did not want another war.

---

28   Schützenfest is a fair where marksmen compete against each other by target shooting. The best rifleman is the "Schützenkönig" (king of all participating marksmen) His "privilege" is to pay for a round of beer for all other shooting participants.

29   A strong clear alcoholic drink made from grain or fruit. Now and then, people drink it alongside their beer.

30   The "Saar Basin" was ceded to France 1919, see the black area in the south west corner of the Germany map on pg. 3.

In 1936, Mr. Höfer received another promotion. He had covered practically the whole state of Thuringia for multiple insurance companies. One day, he came home and announced, "We are moving!"

Paula sighed, "Not again! I am pregnant, as you know, and every time we move, you are busy relocating your office, so I have to do the packing all by myself."

Herbert reassured her, "The movers will help you."

Paula refused to be consoled. She pointed out, "The last time they helped, expensive dishes we had gotten for our wedding were chipped or even broken."

"With the money I earn in my new position, we can afford new ones," Herbert said proudly, trying to cheer her up.

This time, they moved to Gera where Mr. Höfer rented a house for his family. Grete, their household help and nanny, moved with them. She slept in the servant's bedroom upstairs. It was the first time they did not live in an apartment, where the children had to be kept quiet and Grete had to take them to a park for outdoor play. Since both parents grew up on farms, they wanted their children to have the same opportunity to strengthen their little bodies in the fresh air as they had. They liked living in a house that was surrounded by a nice garden with a big cherry tree and other fruit trees. There a sandbox invited the children to play, a swing set to strengthen their bodies, and a good pathway on which they could try out their tricycles.

For Germans, physical fitness had become a virtue, ever since Turnvater Jahn (Jahn, Father of Gymnastics),[31] established the first open-air sport activities as early as 1811. Soon his students started a nationwide organization of young athletes. They frequently traveled across the country to meet other athletes in competitions, games, athletic drills, and gymnastic festivals. The members came from every class in society. As is typical for German people, who seem to love their uniforms, all wore the

---

31   Turnvater's real name was Ludwig Jahn (1778-1852). A teacher at a Berlin secondary school, he started gymnastic training for his pupils on the *Hasenheide*, a meadow near Berlin.

same outfits and had standard equipment in all clubs throughout Germany. Eventually, they extended their competitions to track and field events and added team sports.

Nowadays, soccer has become the national team sport followed by handball, water polo, field and ice hockey. All other sporting events, such as rowing competitions, are designed for individuals or small teams of two to eight athletes. These teams may compete in gymnastics, track and field, and relay races,[32] in order to be selected for the Olympics athletes practice at the Sport-und-Turnvereine.[33] They try to earn achievement badges and medals, which come in Bronze, Silver, and Gold. The Sport Bund of each state of Germany registers them. Since so many Germans participate in a variety of physical exercises, they know how hard an athlete has to work to be selected for the Olympic games. Therefore, they admire all outstanding athletes not just from Germany, but also from different nationalities and races.

By 1936, Hitler was residing in Berlin, the capital of Germany, which had been selected for the Olympic games. Hitler felt that he now had the best opportunity to show the world the superiority of the German race—the Aryan race[34]. He was confident that German athletes would reap most of the medals.

When Jesse Owens,[35] a young student from Ohio, received four gold medals, the German public adored him. He is still a legend for many. Hitler

---

32 Naturally, associations for motor sports are separate from local sport clubs, since they require much more money, and often an individual is sponsored by a car or motorbike factory. Horse races, jumping competitions, and *haute école* or *Hohe Schule* (dressage horse training) are separate as well, as are the many gun clubs. Winter sport and water sport are confined to suitable locations.

33 *Verein* is a term used for club like associations. Turnverein means a combined gymnastic and track-and-field club.

34 The concept of an Aryan race originated in the late 19th century. The term describes Indo Germanic people in Europe. In the Nazi time, Aryan race was more an idea that should become a way of life, a lifestyle.

35 Owens, an African-American, has become a legend. In every Summer Olympics since 1936, his name is mentioned in reference to the 100-meter dash, the 200-meter run, the long jump, and the 400-meter relay.

did not like it that somebody who obviously was not of the Aryan race could outdo German athletes. After the first day of the Olympics, when he extended a handshake only to some Finnish and German participants who received medals, the Olympic Committee told him that to keep the Spirit of the Olympic Games neutral, he would have to shake hands with every medalist or no one. So, claiming that congratulating everybody was too tedious for him, he chose to honor no one with his personal handshake.

CHAPTER 2

Train children in the right way, and when old, they will not stray.
Proverbs 22:6

Gera and Erfurt

Thuringia, the Green Heart of Germany

Large Thuringia Maps for Free Download and Print High-Resolution and
Detailed Maps, orangesmile.com

In 1936, the Stammtisch became adventurous. The clergyman made a proposal: "Because of the Olympic games this year, the government wants an exhibition of modern art in Munich. Who wants to join me on an art trip?" He looked at the slightly surprised faces around him, thinking *I know we will never get an opportunity like this again.* Convincingly he prompted, "this might be the only time we can see the works of our Expressionists, Impressionists, Cubists, and Dadaists."

The farmer looked at the minister with amazement. "I never knew modern art was a favorite of yours. I don't understand it; don't like it. Anyway, hay has to be brought in. The weather is just perfect for it."

The teacher, who had been promoted to headmaster of the elementary school in their village, was obviously uneasy when he spoke. "I used to teach modern art in school, but now, our Führer has declared it Degenerate Art.[36] Therefore, I have to stick to the artists of the nineteenth century and earlier, perhaps even no more Bauhaus. I must confess I am not very familiar with the painters and sculptors, let alone the architects, of the NSDAP."

"Hey, Teach!" called the pharmacist. "You and I could go with the pastor. It could be fun. We don't have to publicly approve of the art pieces. I always wanted to go to the Hofbräuhaus[37] and taste their beer."

"It is not better than the local brew!" the innkeeper chimed in. "My motto is: 'Stay at home and earn your bread with honesty.'"

The mayor sighed. "Since when are you part of our discussions, Innkeeper?" He turned to the others. "My son is in the Ruhr district. He wrote a letter, told me that they built all kinds of ..." He stopped, looking at the headmaster. After a short pause, he continued. "It looks like his letter had been opened."

---

36   Practically all of the modern art (late nineteenth to early twentieth century) was designated as Degenerate Art "Entartete Kunst" by the Nazi regime.

37   Famous beer hall in Munich. It used to be the royal court's brewery. Any shop that was a court deliverer earned the by-name "Hof," i.e. Hofbäckerei (court bakery) or Hofschneider (court tailor).

The pharmacist explained, tongue in cheek, "Nowadays, they have to know what our soldiers think and write. They have to make sure that there are no traitors among the enlisted. The military police checks on the correspondence." He bent over toward the farmer and said under his breath, "Actually, the Gestapo[38] reads those letters."

The headmaster left for a short time. That was the moment when the pastor, the pharmacist, and the farmer put their heads together, speaking softly. "We have to be on our guard with Teach," the minister whispered.

"And with the innkeeper," added the pharmacist. "I saw some suspicious strangers staying overnight here. They are snooping around, I'm sure. Better forget going to the art exhibit in Munich."

When the headmaster came back, the minister waved to him, "We discussed our trip to Munich and decided not to go. We have too much to do here."

The headmaster nodded approvingly. "It is better so."

The exhibit of so-called Degenerate Art didn't just take place in Munich, it traveled to other large cities in Germany. It did not come to Gera, a town in Thuringia. Here, my father received a phone call from the hospital.

"Mr. Höfer, your wife gave birth to a little lady, but ..."

"Thank you, nurse!"

My father put the receiver down quickly and rushed off to send telegrams to his mother, mother-in-law, friends, and all the other relatives.

Mother and third child, a son, fine. Stop. Born June 30. Name. Reinhold. Stop.

In the meantime, his wife lay in the hospital, pale and exhausted after the long, strenuous birth. Nurse Erika entered with the baby.

"How is my little girl?" my mother inquired.

---

38 Geheime Staatspolizei was the secret police of Nazi Germany. They were notorious for their use of underhanded and violent methods against persons suspected of showing disloyalty to the Hitler regime.

"She is a fine lady, madam—weighs almost eleven pounds. How did she ever fit in that small body of yours?"

She laid me close to my mother. "Try to breastfeed her now."

My mother opened her gown and hugged her third child closely. Eagerly, the little mouth searched and found the food source, drinking immediately. My mother had nursed her other two; she knew what to do, and this little one needed no coercing.

The doctor entered. Raising his eyebrows, he instructed the nurse, "Take the baby away. Mrs. Höfer needs to rest a few days before she nurses. She is highly anemic." Turning to his patient, he said, "Mrs. Höfer, you will have to get your strength back before we can let you go home, where your two toddlers and the baby will demand your attention and care. You have lost a lot of blood. I ordered finely chopped raw liver for you. You have to eat it once a day for the next six weeks. That will bring your red blood cell count back to normal."

My mother tried to smile at him. The few moments of nursing had exhausted her already. She closed her eyes and drifted off into a deep sleep. The doctor nodded at the nurse. "The medication is working; keep her sedated. Her milk is not worth much anyway. The child has to be fed by a formula."

The next day, my father came to see his baby. "Nurse Erika, where is my son, 'the little laddy,' as you called him."

She looked at him questioningly. "Excuse me, you are Mr. Höfer, right? You do not have a son; you have a daughter."

"Oh no, you must be mistaken. You told me we had a little laddy!"

"Mr. Höfer, I speak the regional dialect. 'Lady' might have sounded to you like 'laddy,' but we refer to all babies as either little ladies or little gents[39]. You have a daughter."

My father turned away abruptly, rather upset. Now he had to send new telegram messages to everyone again and tell them that they had only a daughter, not a son. How could Paula have done that to him? She should

---

39   In German "Mägdlein" (little girl) could sound like "Knäblein" (little boy).

have called him, not the nurse. He'd had it all planned in his mind. First, they had a son, the heir. Then came the second child, a beautiful dark-eyed girl, so smooth and lovely that he sometimes called her his little kitten. The third child should have been a son again. After all, Paula and he had agreed on a good Germanic name already.

He was angry when the doctor saw him. The doctor cautioned him, "You know, your wife had a very hard time with this baby. She lost a lot of blood. We have to keep her here beyond the regular seven to ten days. She needs more strength. We hope there will be no other complications." Looking at my obviously annoyed father, he added, "We are hoping she'll survive this ordeal."

The door to my mother's room was slightly open, and she heard the doctor's remarks. She thought, *My God, you know I have three children. I have to survive. I may not die; no, I will not leave them alone. As surely as I lay here, God, you have to help me!* She had been waiting for her husband to come. She wondered, *why is he so concerned about the baby's gender? It's a healthy child, right? No, Doctor, I have three children. God will not permit me to die. I'll get my strength back.* She was too weak to call for her husband.

He thought, *How can I face her, tell her what an idiot I made of myself? I have to make those phone calls, send telegrams, find another nanny for the children, if Paula needs to stay in the hospital.* To make it even more complicated for him, he knew that Nanny Grete had to leave; she was pregnant and would be due to give birth soon.

Thinking my mother was sleeping, he left the hospital without seeing her. When he arrived at home, he saw a strong, healthy, blue-eyed woman in front of the garden gate, talking with Ernst and Hildegard. All three laughed. Seeing her father, the little girl screeched happily and stretched out her arms. He picked her up gently and asked the woman, "Who are you?"

"I am answering your ad for a nanny. I am Elisabeth Braun," she replied with a slight local accent.

Herbert looked at Ernst. "Where is Grete?" Ernst pointed to the big cherry tree in the garden, where Grete sat knitting a baby outfit.

"Grete, why do you let the children speak to a stranger?"

"She ain't no stranger, I know her from the garden festivals. She is a good nanny, worked for a family. Them left fer France or so."

My father always winced when he heard her local dialect and the many grammar mistakes she made. He only hoped his children would not imitate her.

"They had three kids; you'd seen them love her," Grete answered, ready to give more information.

Elisabeth had entered the garden. She picked up the toys strewn over the path and on the lawn while approaching Grete and my father. "Mr. Höfer, I could start soon. I lost my job with the family I worked for. They had to move and could not take me with them. They left for France, I think. They had three children; I took care of them. I surely can take care of two now."

"Three," my father corrected her. "My wife just had a little girl and is very sick. She has to stay in the hospital for quite some time. Can you take care of the household as well? Do we need to hire a cleaning woman? We just moved here, rented this house from Dr. Goldstein. Well, his household staff left. They did not want to work for somebody with young children. His daughters were already in their teens. They surely did not need a nanny. I have no idea how to get a good cleaning woman. My wife usually does the hiring of our household help."

Elisabeth noticed his despair. She took her jacket off and said, "Mr. Höfer, let me give you a practical example of my work. Let me start right now, and then decide if you want to hire me." She turned to Ernst and Hildegard, who had been watching their father's attempt to interview Elisabeth with interest. "Both of you, help me find the kitchen, yes?"

The four-year-old proudly took his little sister by one hand and Elisabeth by the other and went into the house. "Here you hang your jacket, there's the umbrella stand ... this is the dining room ... here is the kitchen." Elisabeth set her bag down, pulled out an apron, put it on, and started to prepare the evening meal. Ernst brought things from the icebox and Hildegard even helped, trying to bring the tablecloth. Elisabeth set the table, put Hildegard in a highchair, cut an open sandwich into small pieces, and placed it in front of the little girl. "She won't eat it!" Ernst informed her. "She only drinks and eats spaghetti."

"She looks it—the skinniest little girl I ever saw," replied Elisabeth. "Sit down, Ernst. She might eat when you do."

"I am big. I don't need my sandwich cut."

"Now, just have the same as she has. When she sees how you eat it and what you eat, she might want to try it. Okay?"

"Okay," he sighed and started eating his food.

Hildegard played with her bread cubes. Elisabeth took one of them. "Oh, look, this little sheep says 'bah.'" All had to laugh at the funny face and sound Elisabeth made. "It wants to be in Hildegard's stomach where it is nice and warm." Hildegard opened her mouth and ate the cube. Elisabeth bleated again, and Hildegard munched the next piece. She started to feed herself, continuing what looked like a game to her, until the sandwich was gone. At the same time, Elisabeth had prepared a light evening meal for my father. She set a place in the dining room for him and sent Ernst to pick a few pansies in the garden. Ernst knew were the vases were and brought one. Water in the vase, flowers arranged, set on the table, wine bottle opened, one glass poured, and the children all the time with her.

My father had made his phone calls, saw an appetizing meal on the dining-room table, and sat down to enjoy it. Meanwhile, Elisabeth took the children for their bath and then let them show her their bedroom and beds. She played with them, always with one ear toward the dining room in case my father would need anything, but he did not call. The children were well-behaved and soon nestled in their beds. My father came upstairs to say goodnight to both of them. He finally told them about their new little sister, and that Mom would have to stay away a little longer.

During that time, Elisabeth had set the kitchen table for herself and Grete. She opened their conversation with a question. "How long, do you think, before your baby is due?"

"Six to eight weeks! I am often so worn out. The kids 're good ones. Them Höfers is nice people. I come with them from Jena when Mr. Höfer was promoted to district man'ger of his firm. Him is a very successful man. The wife has a heart good as gold. They took myself along when they visited with her mom. What a lovely place! Lots of servants, I didn't need to do nothing, just played with the kids. Then they moved here. They don't know nobody here. First, Mrs. Höfer's mom come fer some weeks t' help her and then his mom come. Those two ladies are sure different. Mrs. Oemler— Oma, as they call her—is Ernst's favrit. Mr. Höfer's mother is a li'l too harsh with the kids, more work than play. Ya know, but the li'l dress Hildegard had on, got crocheted by Grandma[40]. She does the prettiest things. Not so Oma Oemler, but she's the one who knows how t' treat the Young'uns. She takes them to festivals, carnivals, circuses, lets them touch the farm animals." Grete sighed. "I hate t' leave. I'm not married, ya know. I have to go to my grandparents. They said they'll take me with the baby in … mebbe raise it too. I can't stay here and help with three li'l ones when I have my own baby."

"Aren't you getting married to the father of your child?"

"Well, I really dunno know who the father be. There was several who took me out t' eat an' danced with me. I wanted t' be kind t' them, but what do I have t' give them, 'cept for a li'l fun in the bushes or meadow?"

Elisabeth glanced at her with pity. Poor thing did not know that she was being taken advantage of. Getting up, she said, "Well, I will do the dishes now. I think you can go upstairs and pack your things, so that I can move in. I am pretty sure Mr. Höfer will hire me. Do you need any help?"

"The stairs up t' my room under de roof are steep. Maybe you'd help me with my suitcase tomorrow? I w'da have left a week ago, but then Mrs. Höfer gone into labor early. She and me had packed all the things

---

40   Oma Oemler=my mother's mother, grandma or grandmother Höfer=my
      father's mother

for the movers, 'cause Mr. Höfer was here already. Mrs. Höfer be quite an organizer; I'll tell you, she's efficient. When I s'pected I was pregnant, I wanted t' lose the baby. I started t' carry heavy loads of wet laundry. Mrs. Höfer saw it right away and asked me why I would load up like that. I told her that I hoped to have a miscarriage, but with us simple folks, what sits, sits tight. She, of course, forb'd me t' haul big loads anymore."

Elisabeth interrupted Grete's rambling. She nodded over the sink. "I noticed this household is in good order. Even the children know already where things belong. Did you put their toys away? I mean outside?"

"Yes, I did, and thank you for helpin' right away. This mornin', I did the laundry, hung it on the line in the cellar. Well, goodnight! When d' ya come tomorrow?"

"I'll ask Mr. Höfer. You know, he hasn't hired me yet. Maybe his wife does not want me."

"Oh, don't be silly! She needs ya, so do the young'unns, and so do he." Grete's pretty face showed a smile.

"Hogwash!" said Elisabeth and rubbed her hands on the kitchen towel. "You might feel obligated to men who take you out, not me. I have my Heinz. We'll get engaged as soon as I am twenty-one, and when I have saved enough money, we'll get married, too, before we make children."

Grete bent her head; her shining blond hair fell in cascades over her face and shoulders. She cried softly.

"Now, now, Grete, sobbing is not good for your baby," Elisabeth tried to comfort her. "Be glad you have grandparents to help you. I was raised by my grandparents, too. My mother gave me to them shortly after I was born. She later married a man who never knew that I wasn't her younger sister. You see, it can work out all right, especially if you have a boy. Our government rewards us when we have strong boys. With your blue eyes and blond hair, you are the image of the Germanic race. How do they call it? Aryan or so."

"I never bother with all them fandangle words," Grete replied.

Elisabeth reassured her. "You know, the welfare agency will take care of you and your child, if your grandparents won't. Get to bed now. I'll sweep the kitchen."

My father tucked my siblings in for the night. He entered the kitchen. "Miss Braun, I think you are a godsend. Please stay with us. The pay is good. You'll get hospitalization, of course—and life insurance, paid vacation, one day a week off at our convenience, room and board, and a nanny uniform."

"All acceptable, Mr. Höfer, except for the uniform. I think Ernst and Hildegard like me as I am. And call me Elisabeth, please."

"All right, but let us supply you with a skirt, blouse, aprons, and a pair of shoes once a year."

"Fine," Elisabeth agreed. She pulled a few papers out of her handbag. "Here are my recommendations, my medical records, and my family tree. You see, I don't have any Jewish ancestry. Grete told me that, although you rent this house from a Jewish doctor, you are not Jewish, so I could apply for a job with you."

"Was your family tree approved by the authorities here in Gera?" my father inquired.

"Yes! Last year, I went right away to have my ancestry researched and my papers for hiring authorized. I did it as soon as the new laws were set up in Nürnberg."

My father looked at her approvingly and said, "So, you are aware that German families with small children may not hire any Jewish persons to help in their households anymore. You seem to be familiar with the Nürnberg Laws."[41] My father looked at the seal with the swastika and its date, and then he read her recommendation letter.

---

41   The Nurnberg Laws formalized the action taken by the Nazis against the Jews before 1935. The first law aimed to protect the "German Blood and Honor," prohibiting marriages and extramarital intercourse between "Jews" and "Germans." German (Aryan) females under 45 were forbidden to work in Jewish households. The second law stripped Jews of their German citizenship. Between 1937 and 1938, new laws were added to further segregate Jews from the German population.

Elisabeth continued, "Even if the family whose recommendation you read did not move away, I would have been forced to leave them, because they were Jewish.[42] I liked them a lot."

My father finished reading her papers and said confidently, "I am positive my wife will like you. Maybe when she feels better, you can go to the hospital and introduce yourself to her."

"Fine, I'll go tomorrow on an outing with the children. We'll take the bus to the clinic. Maybe she can see us from her window, and we can wave to her. She must be longing for her darlings."

"Good, then you'll start tomorrow morning at seven AM." "Yes! May I ask you a question? What is the name of the baby?"

"I don't know, and right now, I do not care. We expected a boy, not a girl." Elisabeth was taken aback. How could this man be so uncaring? Was something wrong with his third child? She had been told by Grete that the baby weighed over eleven pounds and was healthy as far as she knew. Didn't that child deserve a name?

Soon, my father had to register his third child with the town's authorities. He had to find a name. He went to visit my mother.

"Let's discuss a name for the girl."

"Your daughter!"

"I was thinking of your mother's or my mother's name."

"But we gave both names to Hildegard as her middle names, Minna and Frieda," she replied.

"Well, Hildegard is named after your oldest sister, what about your other sister's name then?"

---

42   In 1978, Elisabeth showed me pictures of that Jewish family. She told me that she was in loose contact with them; she even had a letter from them, but I had to promise not to tell anybody about this. She lived still in Gera, now in the Soviet zone of divided Germany. Elisabeth, like many in the Soviet occupied zone, was watched by the Stasi (secret police in the GDR) ever since she had reconnected with us in West Germany.

"You really would not want us to call her Magdalena, would you? It is a Hebrew name; that might mark our child as of Jewish ancestry.[43] It will give her problems in school later on. The Gera authorities already think we are affiliated with Jews since we rent from Dr. Goldstein. Maybe we should have bought the house from him. He begged us to do so, and we would have paid much less than it is actually worth."

"You are right, but I do not like a big mortgage. I might get promoted again, and we might have to move. In this case, we would own a property to be concerned about."

"Please, Herbert, don't even mention moving again. We are not even settled here. Right now, we need a name for our daughter."

Their discussion developed and finally led to a name that would cause the raising of eyebrows, inquiring looks, mispronunciation, and modulation throughout their daughter's life.

"Let's name her after you, Ilse-Paula," my father suggested.

My mother looked at him, smiling. "Not Paula, you know, Hebrew derivative! But Ilse, yes. You see, near my birthplace, there is a brook called Ilse. The legend has it that once there was a strong beautiful princess named Ilse who jumped over a huge crevice to escape a giant. She landed so fiercely that her foot crushed the stone beneath her, striking water. It gushed out of the rock and formed the spring named after her, Princess Ilse."

Looking at his daughter, who was drinking from a bottle, he said, "Yes, that little river might murmur and gurgle just like her when she drinks from her bottle."

"What about a middle name?" Paula asked.

"Why? You don't have one either."

"But you have two, and the last means 'Praise to God.'"

"Well, I never liked it too much."

---

43   People of Jewish background who had German names had to add a Jewish name in front of their given name. Their passports were marked with a big J extending all over the information on the passport.

"Maybe we could give her a hyphenated name; it's very fashionable nowadays."

At that moment, a gentle morning breeze swept through the open window, bringing with it a scent of blooming rosebushes, concealing the odor of the hospital. My mother took a deep breath and said, "Let's call her Ilse-Rose." And that is how I was registered under the National Socialist's regime in the books of Gera, the town of flowers … only the town clerk spelled my name Ilse-Rosa, and it took some persuasion from my father to change the *a* to an *e*.

I joined the rest of the family at home. Why keep me at the hospital, where my weak mother could not nurse me anyway? Elisabeth had made up her mind to take me to her heart. She fed me with homemade formulas and cared for me like I was her own. No matter which formula she tried, I would respond to it well. When I was six months old, I became too chubby. The pediatrician ordered malt coffee instead of full milk for me. My Uncle Martin, typical for a farmer raising livestock, noted, "Ilse-Rose is a good 'Futterverwerter'," in other words he indicated, "What this baby-girl eats is utilized well by her body."

I grew up fine and gained enough to be called "Fatty" by my brother and sister—or, jokingly, "Stinky Rose" by my Aunt Ursel. Before I received these less favorable names, my father learned to appreciate and love me, naming me "my little Rosebud" or "Roselett". I was a quiet child. I loved to stand in my playpen and stare into the big cherry tree, watching the leaves and the birds. Later, when I started to walk, I scrutinized night crawlers twisting out of their holes, the aphids clinging to the roses, the flies circling under the bedroom lamp. I loved animals and observed much, but hardly spoke at the age of two. My parents were concerned about their little daughter, so different from their two inquisitive, talkative older children. *Maybe she is slow-witted,* they feared.

One day, their anxiety about the intelligence of their third child vanished. My father was in a hurry for work. He dashed out of the door, ran to the garage, and started the car. When he looked in the rearview mirror, he noticed me dragging his briefcase over the back steps, muttering something, and pointing my chubby little finger at him. My mother appeared at the door, caught me, and called out, "Herbert, don't you ever think this child is feeble- minded! She saw that you left without your briefcase. She picked it up and now wants to bring it to you."

My father was grateful and for the first time hugged his little plump girl with fatherly love. He whispered "My Roselett," and off he went, beaming with pride and happiness about his three children.

It seemed like his embrace released my tongue. I suddenly spoke better and tried to express myself in whole sentences, although I still spoke seldom. I liked to be alone, even if my brother and sister let me be part of their games.

They often wanted me to mimic a baby who had to sit in the backseat of the sandbox car, or I had to pretend to be the servant who cleaned or the errand boy.

I could not master the tricycle. My legs were too short. I did not know how to use the scooter. I could not get on the swing without help. It sometimes was frustrating for my older siblings to let me play along. I would rather observe all the life around me, especially animals and insects.

We had moved to the capital of Thuringia when I was two years old. Ernst had remarked, "Oh, good, now we get another baby. When you move, you get kids." The knowledge of this five-year-old was great. But my mother, for once, moved with the help of competent Elisabeth and was not pregnant as she had been when they moved from Gotha, where Ernst had been born, to Jena, Hildegard's birthplace, and Gera, another town in Thuringia, where I appeared.

One day, on the back steps, my mother spotted me and said, "What is that she is holding so tenderly to her face?"

I whispered while climbing up the back steps of the apartment house in Erfurt, "Poor, poor, an'mal," holding a rather stiff grayish thing to my rosy cheek.

Elisabeth answered in horror, "My gosh! That is the dead rat I saw in the gutter the other day. I forgot to tell you about it." Both women dashed to pry the worm-eaten animal out of my fingers. Elisabeth was telling me, "Honey, dear, give it to me. This animal is dead." Reluctantly, I released my grip on the carcass. "Let's have a funeral," Elisabeth suggested while they were cleaning me with soap and water. That was the day I learned to brush my teeth and gargle with mouthwash.

A cigar box served as the casket. The rat was laid on a bed of rose petals and covered with a small rhubarb leaf. We formed a procession down the garden path to the honeysuckle bush, where Elisabeth had dug a little grave. Ernst acted as pastor and Hildegard as funeral director. I carried the casket. Elisabeth was the undertaker, and my mother prepared the funeral feast, to be enjoyed by the mourners after the burial. We sang a children's song, and then Ernst spoke solemnly as the clergyman:

Ein Huhn und ein Hahn,	A hen and a chick
die Predigt geht an.	the sermon is quick.
Eine Kuh und ein Kalb,	A cow and a calf,
die Predigt ist halb.	the sermon is half.
Eine Katz und eine Maus,	Kitty and Rover,
die Predigt ist aus.	the sermon is over.
Ich bin der Herr Pastor,	I am your pastor dear,
ich pred'ge Euch was vor,	I preach without a fear,
und wenn ich nicht mehr weiter kann	and when I am lost for words
dann fang ich wieder von vorne an	I start from the beginning,
	of course.

Then, he added, although it was not suitable for our funeral:

Ich taufe dich mit Kaffeesatz,	I baptize you with coffee ground
du bist ein alter Schweinematz.	you are an old piggy-hound.

I paid little attention, although I remembered these verses for the rest of my life. I was unfailing in learning rhymes as fast as I heard and comprehended them. That was one reason Grandma had introduced me to an additional prayer we would say every night:

Ich bin klein,	I am small,
mein Herz ist rein,	my heart is pure,
Soll niemand drin wohnen,	Nobody shall live in it
als Jesus allein.	but Jesus alone.

Grandma (Frieda Höfer neé Schadt) taught me the following verses:

Müde bin ich geh' zur Ruh,	Tired now I seek some rest
schließe beide Äuglein zu.	close my eyes that seems the best.
Vater, lass die Augen Dein	Father, keep your eyes on me
über meinem Bette sein.	looking down my bed You see.
Hab' ich Unrecht heut' getan,	If I should have sinned today,
sieh es mir nicht böse an.	don't be angry rather stay.
Deine Gnad' und Jesu Blut	It's Your grace and Jesus' blood
machen allen Schaden gut.	that will change all harm to good.

Stories of the Bible made a big impression on me, just as much as fairy tales and legends did. Early on, I started to imagine how the stories would end. I identified with princesses, but even more with the poor little girls in the tales, like Sterntaler,[3] who was so poor but still gave her last shirt away. However, God rewarded her. In my mind, my belief in God and the themes of the legends would get combined to form my own fairy tales. Later, I would tell them to my younger brother and to the many children for whom I babysat. Even grown-ups liked to listen to my stories. I had a knack for dramatizing them. I spoke with different intonations to characterize my heroes, villains, animals, insects, flowers, trees, bushes, even furniture, just everything. I loved Grimm's fairy tales, but adored Hans Christian Andersen's stories, where even a needle could have fellowship with a broken pin.

One day, my father proclaimed, "Paula, we are moving to West Prussia."

My father had opened up the whole Thuringia section of Germany for his insurance company. Now, after the Blitzkrieg in Poland in 1939 and the annexation of the western part of Poland to Germany, he followed the call to the East. Soon, he had an office established in Thorn (Toruń), the birthplace of Nicholas Copernicus.[44]

My mother took a deep breath and then exclaimed, "Oh no, not again! I just got used to Erfurt the capital of Thuringia, its shops, entertainment, theater, and Ernst is in school now. You know, he started first grade at Easter a year ago. Must we go to the east, and so far away from your mother and my mother, our friends, our relatives?" You could tell she was not happy about having to relocate, especially after she found out that Elisabeth would not move with us. She had been engaged for quite some time to Heinz, and now they wanted to marry and move back to Gera.

---

3   From "The Star Coins," a fairy tale from the collection of the Brothers Grimm.

44   The famous astronomer Nicholas Copernicus, the Latin version of Mikolaj Kopernik was born in 1473 in Toruń and died in 1543 in East Prussia. His theory on the heliocentric system revolutionized the Christian outlook of man in the cosmos.

My mother wondered about a new nanny, and new servants, but especially about how the Poles would treat her and the children. She surely was anxious about a move to the Polish Corridor newly reclaimed through Hitler's Blitzkrieg[45], but my father felt that West Prussia had belonged to Germany before, and it had been a disgrace that East Prussia was separated from the Fatherland by this strip of land.

That was one more ignominy left over from the Treaty of Versailles after the Great War. Now, in 1939, Hitler had overrun Poland and just abolished the Polish Corridor, thus uniting East Prussia with West Prussia and therefore with the rest of Germany. Poland did not exist anymore, since Hitler had made the Nazi-Soviet pact with Stalin[46]. These two dictators divided Poland between Russia and Germany. Russia—who entered the war against Poland 17 days later in September 1939—received the larger area.

⤞⤞⤞⤞⤞

An estate quickly acquired in the beginning will not be blessed in the end.
Proverbs 20:21

The Stammtisch members had their own ideas about the Blitzkrieg. The headmaster proudly wore the NSDAP button on his lapel when they met in 1939. He smiled. "Now Adolf, our Führer, has united Germany again." The former teacher was a member of the Nazi party, which the mayor also had joined, but reluctantly. He would have lost his job, might even have been arrested, if he did not belong to the NSDAP.

The pharmacist sighed. "Well, it is nice to have Posen, Thorn and Danzig back; now the *Deutschlandlied* (Germany's national anthem) has its true meaning again. 'Von der Maas bis an die Memel, von der Etch bis an den Belt.' These four waterways that presumably mark our borders."

"Yes, yes, Germany above everything else!" the farmer nodded. He changed the subject, saying, "Somehow, our Stammtisch is not anymore

---

45   A war as fast as lightning, Hitler started it September 1st, 1939.

46   Joseph Stalin (born 1878) led the Soviet Union from 1920 until his death in 1953.

what it used to be. Schumann, our shopkeeper, left soon after the Nürnberg Laws. I never knew he was Jewish."

The minister added, "You would not think so. His children were baptized in the Catholic Church."

The mayor knew from his files why the Schumann family had to move. He informed them, "His wife is a Jewish descendant; that is the reason he moved away. He could have divorced her, and then he could have stayed. But he did not want to do that to his wife and children, who might have been transported to England or France anyway."

The farmer, missing them the most, noted, "Old Schumann had a good business here, always had the best quality material for dresses and suits." He stopped and scratched his head, saying, "You know, come to think of it, what happened to all his stock? He was too thrifty to give all of his goods away. Hmm, I wonder … I never saw trucks or even wagons pulled up in front of his shop to be loaded with things from his store."

The mayor added, "I had to let the police in to check their premises after they did not come back from their so-called vacation. All the shelves in the shop were empty; no material, no yarn, no sewing thread, needles, scissors … in short, nothing was left."

"They could not have taken all of it with them when they claimed to take a vacation in France," the farmer said ponderingly. He started to shuffle the cards, ordered a beer, and invited the rest of their dwindling group to join him.

Political discussions became dangerous. Germany turned increasingly into a police state, where the "Gestapo" (Secret Police) shadowed everybody, using neighbors, teachers, even children to get information about anybody living in Germany. Of course, people could praise Hitler and his cabinet for having Germany delivered from the many uncertainties brought about by the Treaty of Versailles. Hitler had promised early on to lead Germany out of its difficulties created by that notorious treaty. By 1936, Hitler seemed to have kept his promises to the people. Germans prospered. The Rhineland was under German control again.

Social institutions were established. Mothers could have vacations in a "Mütterheim,[47]" young children were sent to retreats, and even babies were taken care of in well-run government supported "homes." Already, before the draft into the military was installed, the metal industry saw stimulation. Airplanes were developed, along with panzers and cannons. Germany's infrastructure on rivers and canals supplemented the street and railroad networks. Transport of raw goods and finished products functioned well. The draft into the military helped to keep unemployment down, as did the opportunity for jobs in social work, factories, and transportation. Politically, Germany had regained respect in the eyes of the world.

---

47   Also called Erholungsheim für Mütter They were retreats for mothers of any social level. Here they could experience relaxation, entertainment, and vacations and exchange their experiences about rearing their young children, schools, recipes, laundry, cleaning articles and the likes. The government intended to take over as far as education and training school age children was concerned.

CHAPTER 3

…a widow… has been married only once, she must be well attested for her good works, as one who has brought up children, shown hospitality…, helped the afflicted, and devoted herself to doing good in every way.
1 Timothy 5:9 &10

Klostermansfeld: Oma and Her Home

The former cloister's main building.

The front entrance of the main house is balanced between the formal dining room at the left and the "Herrenzimmer"[48] at the right separated by a tiled hallway. The tall attached building was an architectural mistake of the late 19th century.

---

48   An elegantly furnished room designated for the man of the house and his friends.

The street is paved with quarter-stones commonly used for the streets and yards in the Mansfeld district. In 1945, this surface proved to be so tough that even heavy panzers rolling over it did not leave track marks.[49]

Every night, Uncle Martin listened to the news. One evening, in October 1938, he called Oma, his visiting fiancée Ursel, and his new apprentice for agriculture. "Mother, Ursel, Fritz, come quick! Hear this …" he shouted. The announcer reported with enthusiasm how the German people living in the Sudetenland[50] greeted German soldiers with feverish excitement. He prophesied that a new era of expansion toward the east would start for Germany.

"Well," Fritz reflected, "in March Hitler annexed Austria, apparently with the same enthusiasm. Now the Sudetenland! Where will it end? The Czechs will not tolerate this. We might have a war."

Oma continued to listen to the radio. At the end, she concluded, "And to think the British are on our side. This Sudetenland thing was decided without the Czech government. Hitler only met with Chamberlain, Daladier, and of course with this Fascist dictator, Mussolini of Italy."[51]

Ursel, who had come to discuss wedding plans with Oma, mentioned, "I wonder what Günther thinks. Did I tell you that my brother has joined the panzer division?"

Oma, always ready to console, pointed out, "Chamberlain wants peace, and Hitler reiterates he does not want war. At least, if we are friends

---

49   These stones are made from *Mansfelder Schlacke* (slag). Paving and building stones made of copper slag and sulfuric acid are byproducts of mining copper. In the Mansfeld district, we find a type of shale that lends itself to be formed into tough stones to be used for paving the streets.

50   An area in former northern and western Czechoslovakia. Czechoslovakia was created by the Treaty of Versailles. It used to be Bohemia. Many ethnic Germans lived in the Sudetenland, which formerly belonged to Silesia.

51   The conference between Hitler, Neville Chamberlain of Great Britain, Édouard Daladier the Prime Minister of France, and Benito Mussolini took place in Munich on September 29, 1938. Later, this meeting was known as the Munich Conference.

with England and it should come to a war, Günther does not have to fight the British."

Fritz was concerned. He had been drafted and went through military training before being released to pursue his studies in agriculture. He voiced his opinion. "I am afraid the Czechs are not without support. France is their ally. It smacks of the Great War of 1914–18, when we Germans had to fight on two fronts. We faced France in the west and Russia in the east. Now, it will be France and Czechoslovakia."

Uncle Martin shook his head and changed the subject. "I am sorry to have called you. We can't change anything. It looks like a war has been avoided again due to this conference. Right now, it's more important for us to make preparations for Thanksgiving. We just have a few more potatoes and sugar-beets to bring in, and then we will celebrate. I reserved the big hall of my Stammtisch inn. We will have the village band for dancing later on."

Oma asked, "Who is going to cook the meal for all of our friends, our farm hands and our household workers, all of whom will bring their families?"

Uncle Martin chuckled, "You, of course!"

His mother knew better. She might bake cakes for all of them, but the meal had to be cooked by the chef of the inn.

In six years, Hitler had brought Germany back into serious negotiations with European countries. England realized the injustice done to Germany at Versailles. Chamberlain appreciated the role a conservative Germany could play as a bulwark against Communism. Therefore, the British government agreed to let Hitler annex the Sudetenland as long as Hitler promised not to further pursue any land additions beyond the established eastern borders of Germany. The German people breathed easier—another war was avoided due to the Munich Conference.

But just a little more than a month later, on November 9, 1938, a nationwide pogrom[52] was staged in Germany, to the dismay of the civilized world. During the night of the ninth to the tenth, over one thousand Jewish establishments were destroyed. The Gestapo chief, Heydrich, reported that 7,500 businesses were demolished, 250 synagogues were burned, Jewish cemeteries were desecrated, and thousands of houses or apartments were vandalized. Many Jews were beaten, killed, or thrown into concentration camps. The people in villages like Klostermansfeld experienced little of this, but they heard rumors about the pogrom. I only know of one store near us that might have belonged to Jews but the family had left Germany long before the Kristallnacht[53], as Hermann Goering termed the massacre. The pogrom happened mainly in big cities and in the south of Germany. The Nazi plan for administrative murder was a guarded secret. Freedom of information did not exist during Hitler's regime. Therefore, it is true that many Germans did not know of the atrocities committed in concentration camps, although rumors were abound. The German people were cautious not to talk about it, especially not in front of children. I knew about prisons where criminals were kept in single cells, but I had no idea about concentration camps until 1945, and then I did not believe that Germans could have committed such outrageous terror and horrible treatment of defenseless people in these camps.

Censorship of the newspaper, radio, cinema, and theater was enforced under the strict control of Joseph Goebbels, Hitler's minister of popular enlightenment and propaganda. Looking back, one might ask, "What was the Nazis' concept of *enlightenment*?" It was not light Goebbels shed on the German population, it was darkness. Two years later, the blackout followed, literally and symbolically. Literally: the German people had to make sure that all of their windows had shutters or shades that did not let any light through, so the streets would be in absolute darkness during the

---

52   Etymologically, the word *pogrom* is Yiddish from Russia and means "devastation." It was most likely coined in 1903. It refers to an organized massacre of defenseless people, especially the massacre of Jews.

53   *Kristallnacht* means "crystal night." The Nazis camouflaged their cruel actions by coining "pretty" words for them.

night. It would protect the houses and the inhabitants during bombing raids. The blackout was strictly enforced by the police. Symbolically: Germans were kept in the dark about jail sentences for high officials, administrative murder, euthanasia of mentally retarded or physically deformed people, and especially about the atrocities committed in concentration camps.

Most Germans avoided becoming informed about these actions of the government, preferring to hide behind the expression, "Was ich nicht weiß, macht mich nicht heiß." which means, "What I don't know won't make me hot (furious)."

Before we moved to West Prussia we stayed in Klostermansfeld. There, they were making preparations for Uncle Martin's wedding. He had courted Ursel from a nearby village. They had a considerably long courtship. Already in 1936, they knew each other well enough that my parents decided to ask Martin's fiancée to become my godmother.

Dressed for the Wedding.

Now I was three years old and taking part in the wedding festivities. Hildegard and I scattered flowers and petals in front of the bride. Ernst carried her veil and train.

Mother had taken a popular sailors' song with a refrain that everybody knew and wrote her own verses for Uncle Martin and Aunt Ursel. We were dressed in sailor suits. We had to march around the dinner table and salute while everybody sang the refrain. I am told that I was rather stubborn when it came to practicing for the little parade. My mother talked to Oma and sighed, "I don't know if this little skit will go over well with Ilse-Rose not cooperating at all."

"Just don't worry, Paula, Roselett is cute no matter what she does, and the older ones sing very nicely. You will lead them. Everyone will enjoy it," replied Oma, defending her favorite little granddaughter.

I only remember a few things about our performance. My sister told me that, when we presented our skit, my mother walked into the dining room where the guests were waiting for their desserts. She acted as the head sailor, followed by my brother and then my sister. All three were singing, and I was at the end. I was not singing, but when the refrain came, I repeated the lyrics solo to the delight of all the guests and pointed to myself at the line, "down to the smallest mate." Nobody suspected that my performance had not been planned. My mother reaped the compliments on having trained a three-year- old so well.

German marriage rites, especially ones in the country, are quite different from American weddings. For example, rather than having a separate diamond studded engagement ring, two simple gold bands suffice for the couple. They are commonly worn on the left hand during engagement. Then at the wedding ceremony, the minister slips them onto the right ring fingers. Also, the church service cannot take place until the couple has gone to the courthouse to receive their marriage license.

The bride and groom enter the church together. Most of the time, there is no "giving away" of the bride[54] by the father like in America.

---

54 Except for weddings of the nobility, in which the father, or a politically important man, would lead the bride to the altar.

That eliminates a lot of embarrassment when the parents of the bride are divorced, or her father is deceased.

After the ceremony, the new couple leaves the church first, but at the church door, children from the village stop them. The youngsters stand facing each other, holding ribbons or flower garlands in their hands, forming a boundary. The groom reaches into the pocket of his tuxedo or suit. He pulls out hard candy and pennies and throws them in the midst of the children. They drop their ribbons and dash for the money and sweets. Now everybody can step out of the church and continue to the place where the festivities will be held. A table is provided for the gifts. They are not wrapped, that way they serve as conversation pieces as everybody can see them, talk about them, and point them out to the couple and each other.

Usually, the wedding guests are relatives and best friends. The bride and groom sit at the head of the table, flanked by their parents. Couples do not sit with their spouses; therefore, the mother-in-law of the groom sits beside him with his father as her dinner partner. The grandparents are next in line, and then the siblings of the bride and groom, godparents, friends, and often the minister with his wife. This arrangement lets the two families get acquainted better. Children under ten years of age often eat together at an extra table, where they are taken care of by an adult. Sometimes their table is in a different room, so the children may get up early and play. They do not need to sit through the long, drawn-out meal. Between the traditional five to seven courses, speeches are made, skits are performed, wedding pamphlets[55] are handed out, and everybody sings songs or recites poems. For the many toasts, which are brought to the couple or to their parents and relatives, they serve several wines. The groom will thank the guests for their attendance and gifts.

After the noon meal, which takes hours, everybody will rest or walk around the premises to get ready for the traditional 4 o'clock coffee and cake. In the late evening a buffet is served. It will be open for helping oneself during the rest of the festivities. Meanwhile, they dance to modern

---

55   The siblings of the newlyweds create these humorous pamphlets. They often
      include poems and songs about the couple.

and old music from recordings, or a live band. Usually, the new couple leaves the wedding guests by midnight to start on their honeymoon. Both families share the cost of the feast. Relatives take photos of the event. Only lately have some Germans—predominantly in cities—started to imitate American customs such as bridesmaids, diamond rings, professional photographers, and tiered wedding cakes.

We stayed with Oma until Father found a suitable place to rent in Thorn[56]. He located a spacious flat near the garrison barracks and its church. Our new living quarters were "im zweiten Stock" (on the third floor)[57] of a big apartment building adjacent to the former high school that was now converted into a veteran's hospital. In the years to come, many wounded soldiers were treated there, healed, and sent back again to fight, mostly at the Eastern front.

Before we settled in West Prussia my father wanted to spend some quality time with his family. He took us to vacation in Hermannsbad, formerly the Polish spa Ciechocinek. We enjoyed this trip tremendously, but it was over too soon. My parents and siblings moved to Thorn and I went back to Klostermansfeld. In 1940, Hildegard entered first grade. Ernst had to leave elementary school's fourth grade and prepare to be admitted for the first high school grade called *Sexta*, which is followed by the *Quinta*. In the secondary school classes start with Latin numbers and count backward to *Prima*,[58] the last grade. To finish their education, students still have to take a difficult examination called *Abitur*. For it they need to pass many difficult exams, whereupon they receive that diploma, which opens practically all university doors in the world.

---

56 I keep the German name "Thorn" since we referred to it as such and not Toruń as the Poles call it nowadays.

57 The first floor is called "Paterre," the second floor is first "Stock," the third floor is second "Stock" etc.etc. It is different if you call the floors "Etagen," then it resembles the English system.

58 During the development of the high schools in Germany, it became necessary to add classes. They kept the Latin numbers but divided them into lower and upper Tertia, Sekunda, and Prima, thus adding three more upper classes before schooling is finished.

I visited often with Oma. She still lived with her son, Uncle Martin, and his wife, Aunt Ursel. It was understood that his mother should not move out of the house when her son married. The house was big. There was enough room for her bedroom, her living room, and her formal dining room. She used it seldom—usually for her birthday celebration. Then she invited many friends. Oma helped in the household. I enjoyed being the only child, but I was not spoiled. I was only four years old when my uncle asked me to get him a freshly drafted beer from the nearby pub. Here he met weekly with his Stammtisch to play cards and discuss the weather, the field preparations, or the harvest.

I loved my Oma. I slept in her bedroom. Our window overlooked the courtyard that was enclosed on all four sides by stables and storehouses. Only a huge gate led to the outside. It stood perpendicular to two flanking buildings. This doorway was covered by a roof. Most of the time, its two gigantic doors were closed. During thunderstorms, this roomy gateway gave shelter for a wagon loaded with crops from the fields or hay. Here was the doghouse, with a German Shepherd to guard the premises. He was chained during the day but let loose to roam the courtyard at night. People entering or leaving the place used a door alongside of the big gate. If a stranger crossed its threshold, a loud bark from the watchdog announced him.

Oma (Minna Oemler neé Töttler)

Every morning at five AM, Oma got up. She threw her shawl over her shoulders and walked downstairs to open the big oak door of the main house. She let in the faithful elderly maid Mrs. Münch, who had been with Oma for many years. Except in the warm summer days, Mrs. Münch started the fire in the tile stoves of the house. One warmed the gentlemen's room and another the "Wirtschaftsstube"[59], a room near the kitchen. We took most of our meals here. It had two windows. Both windows could be sealed off to the outside by thick oaken shutters so no light would penetrate through them. In this room stood a table that could be extended to seat twelve people comfortably. Near the street window hung a shelf stocked with books about domestic animals and a few children's books. It overlooked the big roll-top desk at which Oma did the weekly payroll for the household helpers and the farmhands.

---

59   "Wirtschaftsstube" is vernacular for a room serving multiple functions.

Oma's bedroom window, which can be seen on the light colored wall at the second floor. Attached to the left is the new building, which we called a 19th century architect's mistake.

Notice the dovecote for our pigeons above the wash-kitchen that was located in the lowest building.

View from the main house kitchen towards the dark gateway. The dung heap was kept in the center of the courtyard.

View from the gateway to the courtyard

Outside view of gateway

Later, the male workers were drafted and had to fight in the war. My uncle had no choice when it came to replacing his farm help; he had to take prisoners of war, most of whom needed training in farming and domestic animal care.

While Mrs. Münch started the fires in the various stoves, Oma came back upstairs with a can of hot water she had drawn from the water basin mounted alongside the huge kitchen stove. I would lie in my bed with my eyes closed, pretending to still be asleep. I watched Oma, who had her back to me. She faced the washstand. It was not an ordinary small one but a big dresser with a marble top. Its enormous mirror reflected the sky through the open window. A shelf on either side of the looking glass served to store combs, hairpins, and other utensils necessary for Oma's morning toilette. First, she poured some warm water into a cup for brushing her teeth. She filled a big porcelain bowl with half of the water from the can and mixed it with the cold water from the matching pitcher. She washed her face, neck, and arms and proceeded down to her feet. Then she dried herself. She still wore an old-fashioned bodice—without stays. She put on an embroidered linen shirt with lace, followed by two snow-white long cotton underskirts, covering black stockings that she had fastened onto her corset. She folded a square flannel cloth into a triangle and draped it over her shoulders, crossing its ends over her chest. Finally, she slipped her dress over her head, buttoned it in the front, added a woolen knitted jacket, and topped the outfit off by fastening a little black embroidered choker around her neck.

Now she combed her long white hair, braided it, and arranged it into a flat bun on the back of her head, tying it together with beautiful horned hair pins and fastening a very sheer net over her hairdo. Last of all, she pulled on high-buttoned black shoes. She was rather plump and had some difficulty reaching down to tie the long shoelaces. That was the moment for me to pretend to wake up, slip out from under my warm feather covers, and tie the shoes for her, being careful to get the leather tongue just right so it did not hurt the top of her foot.

Oma emptied the washbowl into a shiny enameled pail, poured the last the warm water into the washbasin, and started to wash my face, hands, arms, and the rest of my body. She dried me off with a soft cotton towel. Then she helped me to fasten the buttons on the back of my little bodice, which I had pulled over my undershirt. Two elastic bands with clasps on each end hung from this vest. The long knitted woolen stockings were fastened with these. Oma had laid out a pretty blouse and an artfully knitted jumper for me, which my father's mother had made. Grandma Höfer had an eye for beauty. She made sure my sister and I had enough of her color- coordinated, skillfully knitted or crocheted garments.

I had to wear brown high-laced shoes with uncomfortable insoles. I protested every morning. "Oma, do I have to wear those ugly insoles today?"

All my pleading was to no avail. "Well, child," the old lady encouraged me, "try it, just for a short time. If it gets too painful, you may wear your house shoes, but you have to do your foot exercises faithfully." With a sigh, I agreed, leaning forward so my head touched Oma's. I embraced her. She, in return, drew me to her chest and kissed me gently. I like to think she might have silently prayed, "My Darling, may God guard you always."

Now, it was time to get downstairs for breakfast. Mrs. Münch had set the table for Uncle Martin, Aunt Ursel, Oma, me, and visitors who frequented Uncle Martin's house. It seemed there were always guests. Among the many relatives and friends was sometimes Oma's mother—my Great- Grandmother. I was a little afraid of this stern-looking, slender, small, and energetic woman, but I loved her baked goods. She made soft sponge cakes, crisp cookies, lid-cookies[60], spiced tarts—all of them in delightful shapes and delicious.

She lived about twenty-four kilometers[61] away from Klostermansfeld, in Edersleben. When we visited her occasionally, we hitched two horses to a carriage. Oma took the reins and off we went to see Great-Grandmother. Oma seldom urged the horses to trot and never to gallop, as Uncle Martin did, but she let them go at their preferred pace. That meant some hours of travel sitting behind the horses. I looked all around me, except when it was

---

60   Lid-cookies are a German specialty. The cookies are placed on the baking sheet the night before they get baked. In the morning a white top has developed on each cookie.

61   Approximately fifteen miles.

winter and the horses were pulling the big sleigh. Then, Oma had a foot warmer for herself with two big heated stones inside of them. Both of us were wrapped up in a huge bearskin. The fur obscured my view. I never was cold on these outings, or hot when we visited Great-Grandmother in summer. The fresh breeze from the open carriage kept us cool. If we had to stop so the horses could let water, I would climb out and look for a suitable place in the woods or bushes to do the same.

Often, under a moonlit sky, we returned late from our visit with Great- Grandmother and Aunt Klärchen, my oldest godmother. She had married Oma's brother, Hugo Töttler. After he succumbed to an incurable blood decease, his wife took charge of their large estate just like her mother-in law had done. She liked to play cards. When she was alone, she amused herself with Solitaire. She taught this game to me. It is remarkable how she was accepted and welcomed at the usually male-dominated circles of various Stammtisches in the village. The men invited her to play Skat[62] with them, because she played this popular game exceptionally well. Later, when I knew the times tables, my brother taught the game to me since sometimes he and his friend needed the third "man" required for this card game.

Great-Grandmother always hired a man trained in agriculture to oversee her huge estate. She stayed in an apartment above the living quarters of the farmhand's family. Her husband had died in an accident leaving his young twenty-four-year-old widow to raise their two children, Hugo, the son and Minna, their daughter.

Great-Grandmother sent Minna, my Oma, as a young girl to the Frankische Stiftung in Halle on the Saale. This school, affiliated with the university in Halle was founded by August Hermann Franke in 1698. Its goal was to give children a well-rounded education, with special emphasis

---

62   A very popular card game in Germany. At least three players are needed. One
      player plays against the other two; his position is determined through bidding.
      Each of the four suits has a number from nine to twelve. The bidding depends
      on which Jack one has and which suit one would like to announce as trump.
      Multiplying the suit-number by the "Jack situation" determines how high one
      can bid. The one with the highest bid announces the trump and plays against
      the other two. You loose when you outbid your hand.

on instruction for orphans and half-orphans. In the nineteenth century, this tradition of caring for orphans continued. This institute enhanced Oma's education. She had learned the usual writing, reading, and arithmetic at the public school. When she entered the Frankische Stiftung, she took courses in French, some Latin, mathematics (including bookkeeping), and subjects that covered household and garden chores. In addition to that, she enjoyed music and art lessons.

Back in Klostermanfeld, it was always a special treat for me when Oma unlocked the formal dining room with the piano and played some songs for me. This dining room had a vaulted ceiling reminiscent of the cloister our farmhouse and buildings once had been. We lived in the main building of the converted monastery. Later, toward the end of World War II, when bombing raids even occurred in the countryside, I was told that those vaulted ceilings supposedly give special protection. "Bombs cannot penetrate this type of ceiling; they slip off the vaulted center," the adults said, and I thought, *Even if they get through the first vaulted ceiling, they certainly would not have enough power to get through the second vault under which we'll sit in the cellar, waiting for the "sounding of all clear."*

Every morning, Oma prepared warm rolls for me, which the baker across the street baked each weekday. She spread butter and honey on them and poured hot milk in a cup. The milk came fresh from Uncle Martin's stable, where twenty to thirty cows stood alongside one big bull with a ring through his nose. After breakfast, I went to cluck for the chickens and fed them. Usually a flock of pigeons fluttered by to get their share of grain. At the same time, Uncle Martin gave his farmhands instructions for the day. They had gathered in front of the horse stable, waiting for him. I listened, observing everything, and hoped to be allowed to go with one group of workers into the fields, preferably the crew who worked with Hans, my favorite horse. He was the gentlest old farm horse. Usually I was allowed to ride him, even when he was hitched alongside his partner, Max, to pull a wagon.

When it was plowing time, the birds and I followed the dark furrows. I watched them picking worms, larvae, or unearthed kernels. Once in a while, the plow destroyed a mouse nest, and then I watched attentively how the little pink, naked mice with slits for ears constantly opened their mouths in a sucking motion. I had mixed feelings about these babies. Should I rescue them? Should I let them starve or be eaten by a crow? I had heard how much damage these mice did to Uncle Martin's harvest.

In the evening, after work, I seldom rode sweaty old Hans, but sat on the wagon with all the women who had helped to plant potatoes. I did not like this very much. They talked with each other ignoring me. Anyway their conversations did not interest me, I had been told not to speak about things I had heard at home. I was actually a quiet little girl. That's why most of the workers really liked me. I was not in their way, and I would help if they let me. I watched them and loved to imitate their working or eating habits. Oma sometimes needed to correct the latter at our dinner table.

To me, there was nothing as wonderful as being with Oma in the country, but I was not always with Oma—only when taking care of four children became too much for my mother. In 1941, my youngest brother, Reinhold, was born. My mother had to get ration cards for food, stand in long lines for groceries, and conduct the household chores. She did have helpers, who were of Polish descent. There was a nanny named Lydia, a washerwoman, a cleaning woman, and another household helper for cooking and ironing. None of them could assist my siblings with their schoolwork, nor could they buy food for us, because they would receive lesser quality. In the evening, all returned to their homes. Then Mother was alone to take care of whatever happened to us during the night. By now, my mother had to cope with the alarms that warned us of bombing raids, although Thorn saw less destruction than Stettin or Danzig[63]. For my mother, it was a relief to have one less child to care for, and since our relatives liked me, it was easiest for her to send me away. I never felt abandoned by her. I'd rather stay at Oma's, although since 1940, I was no longer the only child. Aunt Ursel had given birth to a little boy, my dear cousin Hermjörg.

---

63   Nowadays Stettin is called Szczecin and Danzig Gdansk. Both cities are in today's Poland.

Oma also lived in the main house of the former cloister. That was much more interesting than the apartment in Thorn. The old buildings surrounding the courtyard might once have housed monks in their cells, but during the centuries they had been turned into stables downstairs and storage rooms for grains and feed upstairs. Some of these buildings had cellars underneath them. We used them for growing mushrooms and keeping potatoes, firewood, coal, and other typical things one stores in a cellar.

View outside the courtyard. The light colored wall, in the back, belongs to the main house, adjacent to it are the horse stable, chicken coupe, cow stable and the two story high barn whose corner is cut off to give travelers a clear view of the major traffic crossing in Klostermansfeld. In the rooms above the stables Uncle Martin stored grains and the shredded beet particles. The swing hung above the soft shredding.

My uncle planted sugar beets. Every part of this plant was used. He heaped the large leaves into long piles, resembling a grave for a giant, and covered them with soil. They fermented and were used to supplement the cattle feed in winter. A farmhand brought the beets to a sugar factory, where they were washed, shredded, pressed, and processed to render sugar and beet syrup. The stored dried leftover beet particles still had enough nourishment to be added to the cattle feed.

After my cousins were born in 1940 and 1942, I discovered that someone had hung a swing above the shredded-beet heaps. They lay in a long, airy, and well-lit storage room. Most of its windows faced the courtyard; only a few small ones close to the ceiling opened toward the street. I loved to swing there for hours, singing all kinds of songs I had learned. Occasionally, Oma climbed up the steep staircase. She went to the adjacent room to get flour out of huge wooden bins to bake bread. Here, too, were the rooms for some of the prisoners who chose to become civil workers[64]. They were not kept in prison cells; they slept in beds and had feather covers. Oma and the maids changed their sheets regularly. In fact, I never knew that they were prisoners.

Across from the horse stable was the wash kitchen, called so because it boasted two huge brick stoves. These stoves had no cooking surface. Instead, a large kettle could be suspended inside of each bowl-shaped opening in the center of the stoves. Here the washwomen heated water for the monthly laundry. They washed it in wooden troughs, shaped almost like wide, crude rowboats. One was for the linens and the other for the work clothing. They used detergent, but mainly soap and washboards. All of this was interesting for me, but I had the most fun in two rooms indirectly associated with the wash kitchen, namely a cellar underneath that sometimes flooded. When my cousins were older, they and I sat in the washtubs and used crudely made paddles to row around. Under the supervision of Uncle Martin, my cousins had competitions to see who could cut the corner the fastest. Usually one of them landed in the cold water.

The other room was the attic of the main house. Here, they hung the laundry on wash lines when it rained. A second staircase shaped like a

---

64   For explanations about civil workers see chapter 5.

ladder with wide rungs led to another attic above it. There, Hildegard and I found china that belonged to Oma's former household. We also discovered doll dishes in a complete set with soup- and -dinner plates, soup terrines, vegetable bowls, and platters. Little did we know that one day these would serve us at our dinner table after we had lost practically all of our belongings. On sunny days, the laundry hung above the grassy place in front of the new attached house. That building was an eyesore. My grandfather had asked an architect to build a new house adjacent to the old one. The architect had no concern for the old building, which hugged the ground with its thick walls. It spread out well balanced and generously, with vaulted ceilings and windows that could be closed by heavy wooden shutters. It also featured an inviting doorway lacking at the new building. Its rather narrow entrance was in the courtyard up a few simple stone steps. The architect had stuck a huge yellow brick house in the typical style of town buildings at the turn of the 20th century onto the majestic old building. The new dwelling featured three floors. The rooms had much higher ceilings than the ones in the old habitat. Entering through its comparably narrow doorway, you found yourself in a long corridor with a steep staircase at your left. Straight ahead, two large rooms served Grandfather as his laboratory.

Climbing the steps to the second floor, you came to another narrow hallway with two doors, one for the master bathroom and bedroom suite and the other to the nursery. Of course, it would be more convenient to reach the bedrooms via the old house and not through the courtyard. Therefore one of the former guest rooms was converted to a semi-throughway, with a few steps leading up to the second floor of the new building and directly into the master bedroom. A huge dressing room, a nursery, and a big bathroom with a tremendous copper bathtub completed the suite. You would look in vain for a toilet. For years, it did not exist in the "modern" attached house nor was there one in the old building. It was Aunt Ursel who changed this inconvenience when she told Uncle Martin before they married, "Martin, I am not using one of the two outhouses in the courtyard. If I marry you and live in that old cloister, I want a toilet inside of the house." Well, I guess Uncle Martin loved her enough to instruct a plumber to build a water closet in a corner of the old building to have his fiancée's wish fulfilled.

The second flight of steps led to two bedrooms meant for live-in maids. It started with a two-step ledge, leading to a door, from which the long roof over the grain storage above the wash kitchen could be reached. Uncle Martin kept his rain gauge in the middle of the roof. He checked it daily and often I was allowed to accompany him. We children could walk all the way over the potato-cooker room, the pig stable, the two outhouse-type toilets, and the carriage shed to an old pigeon loft that was located above the gateway. We climbed through it onto rafters that supported the huge barn roof, where hay and straw were kept.

We loved to play catch or hide-and seek on the beams above the hay and straw. We laid boards across the rafters, on which we had to balance to reach the wider beams. When I think back, I shudder at how dangerous these games were, twenty to thirty feet high above the ground. Playing there we climbed two long ladders, ran across beams, and balanced on boards, running all the time.

In the winter, we loved another form of hazardous entertainment. We tied a row of sleds together and hitched a horse in front of these. With the yell, "hü hot Grete!" the mare pulled us through the village. The most fun was sitting on the last sled. It would weave back and forth after a curve and sometimes tumble over, spilling us into the street. Luckily we did not need to fear cars. They were seldom seen during the war, with gasoline being rationed and only made available for emergency vehicles. But we could wind up in the ice-covered creek that runs through Klostermansfeld.

During the summer vacation, my mother came to visit and brought my sister and my younger brother along. I had to watch him and my cousins during the hour after lunch. This time of the day was like a siesta in Germany. Most of the stores closed from noon to 2 PM. It seemed like all grown-ups took a midday nap. You did not dare to make any noise. Somebody had to entertain the youngest children. The babies took their naps too, but the three older ones had to be kept quiet. Although I am two years younger than my sister, with my talent for reading stories or telling fairy tales, I seemed to be better able to keep the little ones occupied and was elected to babysit.

Occasionally, when Aunt Ursel and Uncle Martin and their children visited with relatives in neighboring villages, Oma interrupted her naptime, came to the pantry window, motioned to me as I was quietly playing and handed me a basket to take it to one of the special friends she supported. I had to take these trips more often after 1945. Many people were starving, even in the country. Oma paid for tailoring, shoes, and other necessities with food. It seemed we were back in the dark ages when people bartered work, clothing, and utensils for food—and in my ears rang Oma's plea, "But don't tell anybody, not Uncle Martin, Aunt Ursel, and especially not your friends."

CHAPTER 4

The nations are in an uproar, the kingdoms totter; he utters his voice, the earth melts.Psalm 46:6

Thorn War Years

Rules and Influence

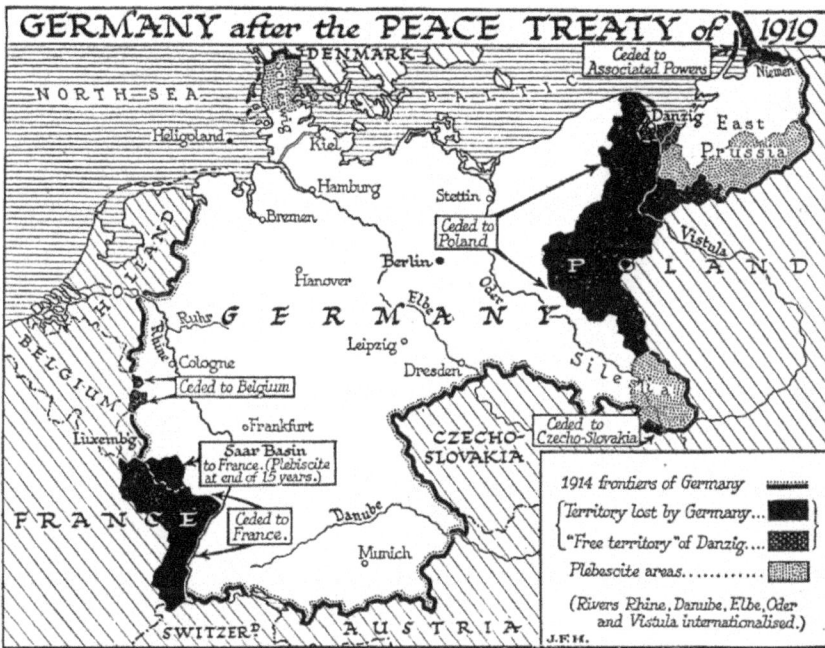

GERMANY after the PEACE TREATY of 1919

https://museumvimytojuno.ca/en/articles/end-of-the-war/artifacts/map-germany-territorial-losses

Thorn (now Toruń) located just after the sharp bend of the river Vistula in the black marking of the Polish Corridor above.[65]

---

65   See description for the map in chapter 1 page 3.

https://www.torun.pl/en/turystyka/zabytki/old_town_hall

Toruń's Town Hall, built in the typical Gothic style called Backstein Gothik[66].

***

When the Stammtisch met in midsummer of 1940, Germany had seen considerable expansion beyond the eastern borders established by the Treaty of Versailles. The headmaster praised the cunning of Adolf Hitler when he announced, "It is such a pleasure to teach Germany's geography again. Germany not only received back its Saar Basin in the southwest, but it has also grown toward the east."

The pharmacist, rather exasperated, interrupted him with, "Yes! Yes, we know."

"Wait, wait, don't turn me off so fast. Have you observed how courageously Hitler went into Denmark and Norway? They welcomed him." A triumphant smile accompanied his remark as he continued, "Some

---

66   Brick Gothic is a specific style of Gothic architecture found mainly near the Baltic Sea. Architects used brick to imitate the prevalent style of the 11th and 12th centuries, but it lacks the lace like ornaments of Gothic stone buildings, as is seen at the Cologne Cathedral.

of their best Aryans volunteered for the Waffen SS,[67] and that is not all; we have gone to the west as well. It was about time we taught the French a lesson. The British did not know what hit them when they heard of Belgium being overrun, and the French were just as surprised when they saw German panzers driving into Paris and German soldiers marching through the Arc de Triomphe."

The headmaster would have continued, but the clergyman stopped him. "Teach, you will have to play cards without me from now on."

All of them looked at him in surprise. Even the innkeeper paid attention to him and asked, "Pastor, is my beer not good enough for you anymore? Still want to try the Munich beer?"

"No, innkeeper, it's not your excellent brew. I might try Russian beer or vodka soon. I have been called to minister in the military," the pastor explained.

"Vodka in Russia?" the farmer exclaimed and then the thought crossed his mind that Hitler might want an Eastern Front, asking "Who is talking about war with the Soviets?"

The minister expounded, "Well, with France being an ally to Great Britain and Russia ... what do you think will happen?"

The headmaster was not short of an answer. He declared, "Not another Great War! I assure you, we will overrun them just as fast as we did the Danes, Norwegians, and Dutch. It is not 1914 with a Kaiser[68] in control. Now we have our Führer. He saw the war firsthand, he knows how to wage battles." The man could not be halted in his praise of Adolf Hitler.

Meanwhile, the pharmacist, keeping his eye on the rambling headmaster, whispered to the farmer, "You know, Hitler did not keep his word to Chamberlain. The Führer is deceitful. I hardly trust anybody

67   Between 1940 and 1945, non-Germans were allowed to join the Waffen SS if they met the rigorous standards for SS volunteers. Young men from Denmark, Estonia, Finland, Flanders, Netherlands, and Sweden belonged to the first foreign division of the Waffen SS.

68   "Kaiser" is the German word for emperor. Emperor William II reigned since 1888 and during World War I (1914-1918). He abdicated 1918.

anymore. When Hitler wanted Lebensraum[69] in the east, the other European nations negotiated with him for the sake of keeping peace in Europe. Czechoslovakia was sacrificed for that peace. After they realized that they could not trust Adolf, they were still unable to stop him when he attacked Poland in his Blitzkrieg last September."

The farmer nodded. "You heard Teach at that time. He was and still is so elated about Germany's military success. He wears his NSDAP button all the time …" He lowered his voice even more. "I wonder if he and the innkeeper are spies for the Gestapo?"

The pharmacist gave a quizzical look, thinking: *I should not discuss things like these with the farmer, either. Who knows if he isn't an informer too?* He listened again to the headmaster's account of the Nazi military success.

"Denmark and Norway were powerless when the German army occupied them in April," boasted the headmaster.

The mayor added, "Pretty much the same happened when my son, Erich, being in the 7th Panzer Division drove via Belgium into France in May. That boy never thought he would see Paris. Now he is stationed there."

The pharmacist pointed out, "Your son was lucky having fought under the Wüstenfuchs.[70] He is the best general we have. He spares his soldiers, but did you ever think about how many lost their lives in the battle against General Charles de Gaulle? Close to 360,000 French fighters died, and we lost 35,000 German soldiers in our divisions."

To avoid further discussion with the headmaster reiterating the propaganda they all had heard during radio reports, the farmer reminded them, "What are we here for? Let's stop discussing the military and

---

69   "Lebensraum" means living space, and was a major political campaign idea of Adolf Hitler

70   The "Desert Fox," Erwin Johannes Eugen Rommel, was a brilliant tactician. To the German public, he symbolized Germany's military strength. After the invasion of France, Hitler sent him to help Mussolini out in Italy's predicament in North Africa. Rommel's unconventional tactics in battling the British earned him the name "Desert Fox."

politics. I'll pay for the beer tonight, since it's the pastor's last game with us for quite some time. Let's play our round of cards! Eh, Innkeeper, we need a round of beer! It's on me! Teach, you shuffle, and Mayor, you sit out this time."

But the headmaster snuffed, "It's no fun with you anymore, gentlemen. I'll have my drink at the bar. Thanks, Farmer, it's appreciated." He left the group and went to talk to the innkeeper.

Prior to this meeting of the Stammtisch, my family had settled in Thorn. Ernst experienced a change in the school curriculum. The government had shifted the school year from its usual start right after Easter to the summer. There were other modifications, i.e. Hildegard learned to write in Latin script and my brother had to drop his Sütterlin[71] letters in order to use the Latin script. The government decided to cast out Sütterlin because it was reminiscent of the Weimar Republic. Looking back, it seems strange to me that handwriting was converted but printing was not. But then the old Gothic letters had a much longer history in German printing than Sütterlin. Publishers continued using the more ornate gothic characters for propaganda pamphlets, posters, and especially books under the Nazi regime. Censorship had reduced the stacks in public libraries, and pretty soon, everybody was sternly directed to put away certain magazines and books[72] they possessed. I did find volumes in the back row of the double-stacked shelves in the "Herrenzimmer" in Klostermansfeld, but none of these were in Thorn. Of course, I just looked at the pictures in them. After all, I had not learned to read yet.

When I arrived in Thorn shortly before Christmas, my sister had the whooping cough. The community nurse, Deaconess Anna, came

---

71 *Sütterlin* script is named after its creator, Ludwig Sütterlin (1865–1917). This script standardized the formerly different chancery writings mainly used by government officials in the various German states. It was taught from 1915–1941 in German schools.

72 In 1933, the SA and SS had already burned books by Jewish, Communist or anti-Nazi authors. In 1938, the Nazis staged book burnings in many Jewish communities. After annexing Austria they burned books in Salzburg.

and advised my mother, "Best you put all of your children together, then they will contract the whooping cough at the same time. Medication and treatment can be done in one room, and in a few weeks, the whole ordeal will be over with." My parents followed her directions and let us sleep in one bedroom. In those days, "sweating it out" seemed to be the cure for all sickness. The nurse and my mother wrapped us in towels and covered us with featherbeds. We laid there until the perspiration dripped down our foreheads. Then they uncovered us, washed us, and wiped us dry.

Actually, we were not so sick that we could not listen to Ernst read fairy tales to us. We also took turns telling stories to each other. I was surprised when Hildegard and Ernst laughingly said, "Hello, Fatty, tell us more about Uncle Martin and Oma!"

Were they, just for once, interested in what I had to say? I could hardly believe my good fortune and questioned them. "Do you mean it? You want to hear about Anton and Hans and the pigeons …?"

My siblings burst out laughing. I wondered why, but I continued to tell them about farm life, every so often provoking an outburst of laughter from Hildegard and Ernst. My mother came and listened. She grew very serious. "Ernst, Hildegard, shame on you! Both of you stop making fun of your sister!" Now it occurred to me that they did not care about what I said but only about how I said it. They wanted to hear me talk, because I spoke with a rich Saxon accent.[73] *P* sounds often like *B*, most *Ts* sound like *Ds*, and some *Gs* sound like *J* or *K*. They heard *bijon* instead of *pigeon*. *Tongue* sounded like *dung*, and *goose* like *juice*.

Needless to say, I became very quiet again. I listened carefully to my mother and imitated her. She pronounced words very clearly. After giving birth to my brother the right side of her face had been paralyzed for a short time. She had to put pieces of amber in her mouth and practice pronunciation. Only a person with the energy and willpower of my mother would be able to regain full control of facial muscles through that method.

My siblings were really not belligerent towards me. Ernst let me play with his farm buildings and all the wonderful animals in the barn that he

---

73   It was the vernacular of Saxony Anhalt.

had received from Uncle Reinhold and Aunt Anne. One day he asked, "Ilse- Rose, what do you think? Should we add a fence around the barn, so the cows have an enclosed pasture?"

I was eager and added, "And the sheep need a fence for their pen too."

My brother built it, as long as I would gather twigs from the trees that grew on the street leading to our apartment house. I went downstairs, and started to pick up branches, just the right size for a rustic enclosure. Upstairs again, I held the twigs so Ernst could nail them together. Now an appropriate fence surrounded the farm buildings. It looked very realistic.

When Ernst's friends came over, they played with their toy soldiers, guns, panzers, cannons, ditches, bunkers, headquarters, and Red Cross stations. They laid out battle plans over the whole everyday dining room. I was only allowed to play with them if they needed help moving soldiers into position. The boys probably thought, *what does a five-year-old know about strategic tactics?*

One day, I pulled a small sweater too hard over the head of my celluloid doll, named Hans. He lost his head. I cried, and Ernst saw me. Patting my shoulder, he said, "I fix Hans; only, you will not be able to turn his head anymore." I gave him the torso and the head, and he proceeded to our playroom, which was not too far from the toilet. You must know that in Germany, the bathroom is often separated from the toilet. My parents thought it rather practical to select the room closest to the toilet as the playroom.

It was during naptime in the early afternoon when my brother Ernst lit a candle and asked me to hold the body of my doll. He trickled melting wax on the neck to fasten the head back to where it belonged. Now, celluloid is highly flammable. It did not take long until the head started to ignite. *What to do next?* must have been running through his mind. *How to squelch the flames!? Ouch!! My hand! burning!!!* He dashed to the toilet—dripping blazing celluloid behind him—opened the door, and plunged the scorching head together with his hand into the water of the toilet bowl. I saw how the floor started to burn and screamed, "Fire, fire! Our house is burning! Help! Our house is burning!" My mother came running from her bedroom, where she had been resting. She immediately helped Ernst. In the meantime, Nanny Lydia appeared out of nowhere and stamped on the spots where the celluloid drops started to ignite the paint of the wooden floor. She managed to extinguish them all. With some water, she wiped the places clean, although the floor was marked for good. Meanwhile, I just stood with the doll's body in my hand and sobbed.

My mother turned to me. "Roselett, darling. Stop crying. We will bring Hans to a doll doctor. There, they will repair him. He will be like new." I was not to be consoled. She called Ernst into the room. "Look, Ilse-Rose, your brother is not crying. Look at his hand." I saw a blister almost as big as his fist on his wrist. He was in pain, but he also was in the Jungvolk[74]. He was German, and German men do not cry. They could withstand pain like the American Indians did when they were tortured. My brother had read Karl May's books about the Appalachian Indian Winnetou and his white friend, Old Shatterhand.[75] Almost every child in Germany knew about the adventures of these two friends who lived on the prairie in America. We admired how brave and honorable they were. We knew their values and desired a friendship like theirs.

The leaders of the HJ and BDM incorporated some of the values of these American heroes into their training of German children. Hitler approved of it. He had also been influenced by May's books. Part of their texts were revised during the Nazi era, since May spoke of nonwhite races quite favorably. A few of his books were edited to incorporate anti-Semitic passages. This was one of the many ways the regime used to indoctrinate us children. They altered well-known and cherished literature. Another means of eradicating the authorship of Jewish poems or songs that had become folk literature was to publish these anonymously. The popular

---

74   In 1922 the NSDAP founded a paramilitary organization "Die Hitlerjugend" (HJ), which was for male youth 14-18 years old. Boys between 10-14 belonged to the mandatory preliminary section of the HJ called "Deutsches Jungvolk" German Youngsters. The girls' section was called "Bund Deutscher Mädchen" (BDM), League of German girls.

75   Karl May (1842–1912) wrote a series of books on these two characters. Adolf Hitler read the books as a schoolboy in Vienna.

song *Lorelei* by Heinrich Heine had become a folk song that teachers of German in other countries used and kept alive. In American schools the "Lied" *Lorelei* evolved into a standard poem and song for German studies.

I remember one Christmas in Thorn when my father bought a tall, symmetrical, beautiful blue spruce. It smelled wonderful. He placed the tree in the formal dining room and locked the doors. Every night when he came home from his office, he disappeared behind these doors. He decorated the tree, and he built a railroad scene for Ernst on top of the fully extended dining-room table.

For us girls he set up a doll's bedroom with white and pink furniture for Hildegard and one for my repaired Hans and a yellow teddy bear. My furniture had decorative flowers against a blue background like the hope chest, which stood in our hallway. We did not see any of this until December 24, the evening when Germans receive their gifts. We never had to unwrap presents. My mother or father unpacked the packages that the aunts, uncles, grandmothers and godparents sent. My parents assembled everything so it was ready to play with when we entered the room.

My mother had given all of our helpers the day off. In the evening, we ate a simple meal in the everyday dining room. Then my father withdrew again. We heard the ringing of a little silver bell. That was the sign for us to enter the formal dining room.

What a festive display! The Christmas tree shimmered in silver and white. Silver Christmas balls in various sizes and shapes hung from the branches, covered with silver tinsel and glistening white angel hair that moved ever so gently in the slight breeze of the many burning candles on the spruce. They cast the whole room into a warm glow. I stood transfixed, looking at this beautiful tree. My brother spied the elaborate setup for his train and was ready to play—but first, we had to recite some Christmas poems and sing a few songs.

Finally, my father switched on the train set. The whole scene lit up. Several trains ran at the same time; one crossed a bridge, another went through a tunnel, and one stopped at a station. Tiny people stood and waved, while others held suitcases. A mother held her child's hand and pushed a stroller. A HJ boy held up his right arm in the Hitler salute. The conductor wore a red hat. His arm could be lifted. In his hand, he held the signaling disc. I just looked and looked. "Rosebud, this is electric. You may not touch any of it, or you might get a shock," my father explained to me.

Then I heard my sister shouting for joy, "Bärbel, my Käthe Cruse doll!"[76] She hugged the doll and then checked it out. "She has real hair. May I comb her?" she asked our mother.

Hildegard immediately started to play with Bärbel, opened the small closet, and discovered dresses, coats, shoes, skirts, and blouses. Mother pointed to a little jacket and a sweater, saying, "These, Grandma made for your doll. We have to write a thank-you note to her."

I saw my presents. Hans had a new head, and he too had new clothing, but he was a Schildkrötpuppe.[77] They do not have real hair. These dolls are more practical for younger children. I liked my teddy bear. He had an artfully crocheted vest on, another of Grandma's creations. He had considerably long fur. I went to the bathroom, found a comb, and started to comb him. I combed his fur in different directions, even gave him a part on his head. Hildegard was able to braid Bärbel's hair, but Teddy's fur was too short to be braided.

We were allowed to play as long as we liked. The candles started to burn down, and Father replenished their holders with new ones. I must have fallen asleep. I woke up the next morning in my bed with my teddy bear at my side. At noon, we ate dinner as usual—only this time, we had a roasted goose that mother had stuffed with apples. The goose was Oma's Christmas gift for all of us. To keep the tradition of Father's family, my mother had cooked red cabbage with apples, and "Thüringer Klöße,"

---

76 In 1905, Käthe Kruse dolls were made from material that did not break easily. Mrs. Kruse made them first for her own seven children. After she exhibited them in Berlin, she received two big orders from the United States that motivated her to establish her own doll company.

77 Since 1889, a German company called Rhenishe Rubber and Celluloid Works improved celluloid so it could be used in toys. Soon the company was known as "Schildkrötwerke" (tortoise factories). Their trademark is a turtle, which in German is "Schildkröte."

which are potato dumplings. For dessert, we had her delicious caramel pudding.

Our new brother, Reinhold.

In 1941, my mother had given birth to her fourth child, the son my father had wanted five years earlier when he had to settle for me instead. My younger brother had blue eyes and fair hair. Our nanny Lydia took care of him. She adored him. When she gave him a bath, she stroked the back of his head and remarked, "Handsome boy, has neck for a German officer's uniform." Did she say that to show loyalty to the German government? She had been Germanized,[78] as so many who worked for German natives. She did not care for me. To her, I was a petite awkward farm girl. She thought

---

78   The German word is "eingedeutscht". It depicted a person of non-German lands, who went through the process of belonging to Germany but did not have the same status as "Reichsdeutsche" (native Germans). The Hitler regime stressed **"Reich"** not land, nation or country to emphasize the Third Reich. Historically the First Reich was established when the Pope crowned Charlemagne also Karl der Große or Charles the Great. It lasted from 800 AD to 1806 AD. The Second Reich lasted only from 1871-1918, and the Third Reich lasted a mere 12 years: 1933- 1945.

of me as an intruder into the tightly knit family, one who suddenly showed up, lived with the family for some months, and then left again for the farm.

The other servants had less to do with us children, although I was fascinated with the work one of them did: she ironed our clothing. She even let me try to iron some handkerchiefs. She and the cleaning woman brought bed sheets and table linens to a place where they had a big roller iron.[79] A roller iron was one of the things I missed when I came to America as an immigrant.

I did not like the cleaning lady. Somehow, I was always in her way, and she let me know it. I cared for the woman who came to do the laundry. She reminded me of the workwomen at Oma's. She hardly ever was in our apartment. Once each month the tenants of our building had assigned days to use the wash kitchen in the cellar. When it was our turn to do the laundry, I went downstairs to visit with her.

I was already several months in Thorn when, at the evening meal, my mother asked, "Who wants to take care of Reinhold tomorrow afternoon?"

Hildegard right away said, "Let Lydia do it. She loves that baby."

I quietly ate, leaving the conversation to my older brother and sister.

Mother continued, "But tomorrow is Lydia's day off. You do not have to do much; just push his baby carriage back and forth in front of the church. I'll work here and can watch you from the balcony."

Ernst had an excuse. He needed to attend a meeting with the Jungvolk. He pointed out to us, "I must be at the HJ ward, and anyway, Mom, it looks ridiculous for a young man like me to push a stroller."

Hildegard chimed in, "And I am invited to play with Gertie at Sabine's house."

I nodded, "I'll do it." I took care of my infant brother that afternoon. I did it so well that pretty soon, it was understood that I would always watch

---

79   These "Mangeln" are run commercially throughout Germany. A "Mangel" is
      a rotary iron. Its cylinder drum is so long that it can accommodate the length
      of a bed sheet or a large tablecloth.

him when I was in Thorn. Reinhold rewarded me with his brotherly love and trust.

From left to right: smiling Hildegard, my proud mother with Reinhold, Grandma with still shy me, and Ernst already in military pose.

One Saturday, when Reinhold was not quite one year old, we children sat around the play table and my siblings had an idea. They had been a little jealous of all the attention their brother received from Grandma, from Father, from Nanny Lydia, and especially from Mother. They also knew how much he liked sugar. Ernst said to me, "Ilse-Rose, here is a teaspoon with salt. Give it to Reinhold. That should cure him wanting sugar all the time."

Hildegard added, "Let's watch his face. It will be hilarious."

I felt important that those two let me take part in one of their plans. We had no idea what so much salt could do to a youngster. I took the spoon, and Reinhold, completely trusting me, opened his mouth wide to receive the "sugar." His loud scream shocked us.

My mother came dashing into the room. "What happened? Why is he screaming? What does he have in his mouth?"

Instantly, we knew we had done something terribly wrong, but we did not want to explain anything. My siblings only told her, "Fatty has given him a spoonful of salt."

First, my mother took care of my little brother, making sure she retrieved as much salt as possible from his throat and mouth. He helped by spitting it out. Then she gave him a lot of milk and water to drink. By that time, milk was rationed. We had to do without it for several days. Later on in the week, when my mother took the older ones to the theater and I had to stay home, I thought of it as a punishment for me. In reality, I still was too young to participate in some of the cultural events my mother selected for my older siblings. Still, this episode haunted me. Years later, my mother told it to Reinhold when we all were reminiscing about our childhood. He shook his head in disbelief and never forgot it. He even included this incident in his speech on the occasion of our mother's eighty-fifth birthday. By then, he still thought it had been my idea to give him salt. At the first occasion, I finally told him what really happened.

From left to right: Hildegard (7½), Ernst (9), Reinhold (1½),
and Ilse-Rose (5½)

Before I entered school, my mother had been asked—actually, ordered— to send her daughters to the German "Kinderhort"[80]. No child of Polish heritage was allowed to join, and definitely no children of Jewish descent. It was a preschool and after-school program established by the Nazi government for the children of German nationals. The indoctrination of children started early, before our minds could be filled with Christian or parental values.

My wonderful play hours were forfeited in order for me to belong to the "Kinderhort". Two energetic young women ran the Hort. They kept us disciplined. Siglinde told us, "You draw pictures now! Later, we'll put puzzles together, and then we'll play picture lotto or build with blocks."

I saw a book that interested me. It had a photo of a European Finch on its cover. "Auntie, there is a book with bird pictures. May I look at it?"

"No. You just do everything according to our plan, just as everybody else does. Look how well your sister behaves and exactly fits into her group. Do you always have to have your own way?"

My eyes filled with tears. I did not mean to be difficult. I just wanted to see the picture book. At Oma's I had access to many books, especially ones about horses, cows, chickens, and their diseases. I knew a lot about their anatomy already, and especially about the different types of domestic animals all over the world.

"Now, don't be a baby," the young woman scolded. "Stop sniffling. Listen, a Spartan girl would not sniffle, and we of the Aryan race are even tougher than the Greeks had been." To become as tough as a Spartan was the rule of the day. For years, I made it a great goal to reach. I would tell myself, *Swallow your tears; don't let anybody know you have feelings or any emotions. Be tough. Be able to withstand the coldest or hottest days. Be ready to defend the country and the Führer.*

I sat at the child-sized table and played with blocks. We had to build bridges. I noticed a red half-moon-shaped block inside of a blue rectangular one. Slowly, not knowing what to do with it for the time being,

---

80 "Kinderhort" was a kind of Kindergarten where children were indoctrinated through play, books, and song.

I withdrew the red one and dropped it into my apron pocket. I turned the blue one on its base, and *voilà*! I had a bridge. I started to draw wiggle lines resembling water underneath my blue bridge. Siglinde saw it and reprimanded me. "Oh my, what are you doing now? Who told you to take a crayon? Drawing time was earlier, not now. Build a bridge!"

I pointed to the block. "But I have a bridge, and this is the water. I'll draw fishes, and frogs, and salamanders, tadpoles, ducks, and geese …"

"Stop right this minute! You are disrupting the class. Give me the crayon." Both women stared at me in disgust. I had to fight tears again; I could not speak, could not utter an apology; I knew I would start crying if I opened my mouth. I gazed at my bridge. Suddenly, Erna grabbed my arms, pulled me off the chair, and transported me to the corner of the room. "That's where you belong when you are stubborn."

In the corner, I watched a little spider crawling up and down a thin strand. Would it build a web like the ones I had seen in Oma's garden? I focused so much on the spider that I forgot I was standing there to be punished.

Finally, the "Kinderhort" ended. On our short way home, I skipped happily alongside my sister. We climbed the stairs to our apartment on the third floor. Here, Nanny Lydia took our jackets and aprons to hang them up for the next day. A little red half-moon-shaped block fell out of my pocket. Hildegard gave me a dismayed look. "Now what have you done? I did not think you stole the crayon, but you surely stole this block!"

A fight followed. My mother came to inquire about it. She listened to Hildegard's explanation, watching my reaction. Slowly she drew me to her chest and whispered into my ear while Hildegard continued to chatter about her sister's disgraceful behavior. "My little Rosebud, would you like to stay home tomorrow? Oma is coming."

My loud, happy squeal interrupted Hildegard's flow of words. She stopped her babbling, threw her head back, and left the room, the righteous judge.

The next day, I had to bring the block back to the "Kinderhort," but I did not stay. My mother was with me and explained that I would leave soon for Middle Germany, where I would enter the same type of establishment. I was looking forward to Oma's visit. Now wonderful times would come again. Oma could make Nanny Lydia understand that I was a good child and was able to accomplish more than a typical five-year-old usually does. Oma knew how responsible her grandchild already was. She had sent me on errands nobody was to know about, and I kept it as a secret between us two.

Oma stayed a few weeks and then took me back to Klostermansfeld. Already on the train, she explained to me that I needed to go back to Thorn when I had to start school. To me, that was an eternity away. I'd rather think about the farm, my friends, the old dog Karo, the cows, calves, chickens, ducks, geese, and all the people who worked for Uncle Martin. Oma noticed that I was not interested in school. She told me about the two new black horses Uncle Martin had purchased. They were not the big Belgian horses; they were meant to draw lighter wagons, and best of all, they would be hitched in front of the new elegant carriage that replaced the old two-seater buggy.

I entered first grade in 1942. My Aunt Ursel brought me back to Thorn. We took a long train ride and stayed one night in Cottbus with her mother. That night, I experienced my first bomb scare. We heard the "first warning" and left the apartment to go to the bomb shelter, which was located in the cellar. The "main warning" never came. After a half hour, the "all clear" sounded and we went upstairs again. The next day, we continued our train ride to Thorn.

Aunt Ursel took me to my first day of school. My mother had given me a "Zuckertüte" it was filled with the same things that were in Hildegard's and Ernst's "sweet-cones" when they entered first grade.

Ernst with the traditional "Zuckertüte" entering first grade in Erfurt, 1939.

In 1942 my sweet-cone contained an apple, pears, hard candy, marzipan, and a kind of play dough that did not dry out. I carried a brand new leather satchel on my back. It contained some tools I needed for school: a slate board, on which I learned to write letters, do my math, and draw pictures, a slate stylus, and a little sponge hanging from a hole in the frame of the slate board, with which we could erase our work. We did not learn to use paper until we entered second or third grade. Using a slate board eliminated the lovely custom American mothers have of putting their children's artwork on the refrigerator door. Of course, my mother could not fasten it there even if we had paper pictures and magnets, since we had a wooden icebox in our pantry. Once each week, we bought a huge ice block from the iceman, who delivered it to our kitchen. He used the steep, tight back-staircase meant for the servants.

I am not sure why my mother could not take me to my first day of school. She was very occupied with my little brother. In addition, she had to stand in long lines to get food for the family. Just once she had sent one of our maids to the market, and as a result, she had to point out, "These apples are shriveled up, and the plums are worm-eaten. At which stand did you buy them?"

The maid replied, "I went to the shortest line, so I could be back soon."

By now, Mother had to get food by herself. In the shops, she received better service than the maids. She had to personally pick up our ration cards. She also bought fresh produce from Mr. Schirkowski. He and his wife owned a big estate with a nursery and an extensive forest. In hunting season my father was invited to join them trying out his beautiful hunting guns, a drilling or his rifles. During one of my stays in Thorn I watched my father put a hare on a hook above the bathtub. My mother took its pelt off and prepared it for a roast. She was an expert in the best tasting dishes from game. Any of the activities mentioned above would be reason enough to understand why my mother was unable to take me to my first day of school, but it is also possible that this was the day when she had to attend a meeting at which the mothers who had more than three children were honored.

Das "Mutterkreuz".

My mother, Paula Höfer, received the bronze "Mutterkreuz". An insignia for mothers to be honored according to the number of her children. Paula had four children. With six offspring it was silver and with eight it was gold.

Our mother used to tell us about this event. "All of us women were sitting in a big hall, waiting to be honored by the 'Gauleiter',"[81] she said. "When he entered, everybody got up and raised their right arm in the Hitler salute. I remained seated. My neighbor whispered, 'Get up or you wind up in prison.' I retorted, 'Why? Who is being honored here? He or we?' But I did get up." Mom sighed, "I did not want to cause any trouble for Dad" and pointing to each of us with her hand she said, "or you, Ernst, Hildegard, Roselet, Reinhold."

My first teacher was Miss Sanowski, a pretty, young woman who had to handle thirty-five to forty pupils. She asked us, "What is your name? Who is your father? Where do you live? Is this your permanent address?"

Right then and there, I became confused. Did I live with Oma or with Mom? But Aunt Ursel helped out. When Miss Sanowski asked, "Who is 'reichsdeutsch'?" only five hands went up. The rest of the thirty-five pupils were either "eingedeutscht" or "volksdeutsch".[82] That is one reason why, at recess, I only talked and played with two classmates who spoke German, Anneliese and Ulla. I learned math very easily. I actually liked it, but orthography was terribly difficult for me. I liked to spell words according to the way they sounded to me. Of course, I still spoke with a slight Saxon accent, where some consonants are pronounced softer. T and D, P and B, K and G often were interchanged; even vowels would sound different.

I loved to draw, but ran into trouble with communication again. One day, Miss Sanowski ordered in her slight Polish accent, "Now all of you draw some 'Hühnchen' (little chickens)." I understood 'Hündchen' (little dog). Lovingly, I drew a dog resembling Karo, the German shepherd at my Oma's place. "My, my, don't you even know that chickens have only two legs and not four?" The teacher shook her head.

---

81 *Gauleiter* was the title for the head of a Nazi administrative district.

82 "Eingedeutschte" were of other native origins. They could belong to Germany but without the same status as "Reichsdeutsche" (native Germans). "volskdeutsch" was a person of German descent who had applied for German citizenship because he or she was born in a foreign country that now was under German occupation.

Ulla and Anneliese giggled when the teacher rebuked me. I blushed, but the rejection from my friends did not last. At recess, the girls comforted me. "We too have trouble understanding her sometimes," said Ulla, adding, "I hate school!" Her father was the janitor of the veterans' hospital adjacent to our apartment house. Anneliese's father worked for the railroad. She lived in a little house behind us. We shared the same court yard.

The family background of my friends was quite different from that of Hildegard's girlfriends. For example, Sabine's father was a medical doctor, who owned the villa next to our house. Her other friend's parents had a business in Holland. In Thorn they lived in a luxurious apartment. I only visited there once. I remember that I constantly watched my sister, thinking *did I behave correctly? Am I in their way? What are they talking about?* I was not invited to play with them. Then the mother of Hildegard's friend entered the room anxiously, "I lost the stone out of my earring. It must be in this room." She started to look for it. I wanted to make a good impression so Hildegard would not be embarrassed by me again, and I started to look for it as well. Finally, I mustered the courage to ask, "How big is this stone and what color is it?" I was informed that it was a half-carat, very clear, really expensive diamond. The lady showed me its counterpart, still hanging from her earlobe. I thought it was awfully small to make such a fuss about. My marbles were bigger than that. By now, all of us were searching for it in the thick oriental carpet. We never found it.

At home, I told my mother about this episode. "She was so upset about that tiny stone. She told us that it was very expensive. I do not believe it. The stone was not any bigger than my thumbnail, Mom."

But Hildegard gave details. "It was a diamond, Mom, a special cut of a half-carat diamond."

My mother told me, "Hildegard is right. These things are very valuable."

I was too young for Hildegard's friends, and anyway, I did not want to be with them. My sister always seemed to outshine me. I felt I never was good enough for her. I did not possess her polished manners with the guests who visited us or lived with us. I mispronounced and misspelled words, and especially names. In short, we seldom played with each other. She had her friends, and I had mine.

Ever since my mother had taken us to see the ballet *Sleeping Beauty* my sister wanted to become a ballerina. My mother would hear none of it. On the other hand, Hildegard also wanted to join the BDM. The Nazi government financially supported the two youth groups, HJ and BDM and gave their members special privileges. For boys, the "Jungvolk" and, later, the "Hitler Jugend" were compulsory. When Ernst entered high school, he had to join the Jungvolk.

The rules for the girls' groups were not as stringent until 1936, when belonging to the BDM became compulsory for girls as well. Each town or village was divided into small wards that could easily be reached on foot. In them, a BDM youth leader would meet with approximately fifteen girls twice a week. They designed the meetings so that they would appeal to children. They sang, taught folk dances and played games. At the same time, the Nazi government systematically indoctrinated the children to first and foremost pay respect and give absolute loyalty to the Führer, to be proud of their Germanic-Aryan heritage, and to conform to the Nazi ideology, which included the Gleichschaltung[83]. It forced the German people to think in line with the Nazi standards and it eliminated all opposition within the political, economic, and cultural institutions of the state. How did this work in reality?

Well, one day, when my sister was nine years old, she wanted to wear knee-socks like the BDM girls did, but my mother declared, "Honey, it's too cold today for bare knees. Here are your long stockings."

Hildegard looked at her defiantly. "You just wait until I am ten, then I join the BDM and then you have nothing to say to me anymore." She left the room in triumph.

However, concerned parents all over Germany could find ways to delay entry into the HJ, BDM or special schools. When Hildegard was close to ten years old, my mother went to our pediatrician, who certified

---

83   "Gleichschaltung" a political term meaning to bring or force into line, to conform to the Nazi ideology

that Hildegard was not advancing at the normal rate for her age and therefore should be considered unfit to join the BDM at this stage of her development. I never thought my sister was weak, but the doctor found something to justify his statement.

My father and mother went with Hildegard to the BDM leader of our ward just before March 15,[84] the official last date when girls and boys who were turning ten in the calendar year had to be registered with their respective Hitler Youth leader. They took the certificate from the doctor with them. My sister told me that the BDM leader, after scrutinizing her papers and listening to our parents, said, "All right, she does not have to enter this year." Then, looking at Hildegard, she remarked, "Well, your daughter really does not resemble the typical Aryan BDM girl anyway." Hildegard was slender, with beautiful big brown eyes and brown hair. She did have long braided hair—at least that was typical of BDM girls.

I never really got acquainted with Thorn. Hildegard had shown me which streets to take to walk to our school. She was in a higher grade. Her classes often started and ended at different times. Therefore, we very seldom went to or from school together. The women who worked for my mother did not live within walking distance and had to take the streetcar to come to work. Most of them spoke broken German. They certainly had no interest in showing me their homes.

Only once did the washwoman take me to one of the beautiful brick Gothic churches. I was amazed at its rich interior and mysterious dimness. It had a distinctive smell of dying flowers, burning candles, and incense. I entered another Catholic church in Thorn but only the foyer where they had placed a beautiful casket. One of my Polish-German classmates had died. She succumbed to an inflammation of her brain, I was told. Now she was laid out in a white lace dress with a lovely veil over her dark hair and a lily in her folded hands. To me she looked so lovely, just like a beautiful angel. We passed slowly by her casket.

---

[84] The induction into the "Jungvolk," HJ or BDM always took place on Hitler's birthday, April 20.

The garrison church across from our apartment was also a brick building. I remember having been in it only once, when a military minister baptized my younger brother. This church, used for Catholic and Protestant services for the soldiers, did not have the elaborate artwork and mysterious smell of the Catholic churches in Thorn. It was more ornate on the outside. Scenes of Christ's mission on earth were depicted on three of its outer walls. Iron fences protected the bigger-than-life sculptures from desecration by people or animals; only the ever-present pigeons had to be dealt with occasionally.

It was my brother and, after entering school, my friend Ulla who helped me to become more familiarized with the town. Ernst walked with me to the famous town hall.[85] In front of it was the old midtown square. There, we saw maps of the eastern front. For a few pennies we could buy small nails with different-colored heads. A man handed us a hammer. We went to a map on a wooden board and Ernst marked the "front" by hammering nails along a line indicated on the map. It showed how far the German army had advanced into Russia.[86]

This was one of the many fundraising events the Nazis held. BDM girls collected money for various projects. They sold little flowers or other trinkets as fundraisers for vacation homes for mothers, children's homes, the Red Cross, the Winter Help Work[87], and the wounded soldiers, among other causes and organizations.

The BDM girls had designated streets on which they offered these trinkets to pedestrians. People proudly pinned the emblem on their clothing, thus showing their support for the different institutions.

The garrison church stood on a spacious square that became my playground, except for when the soldiers of the garrison lined up for

---

85   The old town hall dates back to 1274. It is one of the most enormous town halls in central Europe. See the picture in the beginning of this chapter.

86   On June 22, 1941, the German military launched Operation Barbarossa, the invasion of the Soviet Union.

87   "Winter Hilfs Werk" abbreviated "WHW" an annual drive to help finance food and warm clothing for needy people and the military.

parades. In this case, the yard of the former high school bordering our apartment house sufficed for play. The building had been turned into a huge hospital for wounded veterans. Big sandboxes sat in the yard. They were meant for extinguishing fires created by phosphor bombs. Fortunately, Thorn did not see many bomb attacks. My friends and I used these big sandboxes to build our own little world.

I recall the times when my mother played out scenes of fairy tales with us children. She included my friends Ulla Spatkovskie and Anneliese Blomann. Anneliese, the railroad conductor's daughter, lived in the back of our apartment building. She was the youngest of several already married daughters. We played with dolls handed down to her. We had to be careful not to undress them or comb their hair. I had a hard time understanding this—after all, I liked to get to the bottom of things, and wanted to play real- life stories. Putting dolls to sleep, undressing them, washing them, combing them were all a part of life. Why were we not allowed to play like that? My sister explained to me, "These dolls are very expensive show dolls, not toys. They portray people from other countries. They wear typical clothing called *costumes*. They are collector dolls to be placed behind glass in cupboards and are not meant to be played with."

I had my own ideas telling Hildegard, "How good is a doll if you only look at it, if it just catches dust on a shelf?"

When Anneliese came to play at my place, we built a house under the big dining-room table. We hung blankets and tablecloths on either side of it, dividing this "house" into kitchen, bedroom, and whatever living quarters we needed. Sometimes Ernst and Hildegard joined in, but unfortunately, we usually ended up quarreling, and I gladly left with Anneliese for another game.

One morning, Anneliese's older sister took her to school. Ulla picked me up and said, "Let's skip school." That was all right with me. She advised, "Put your school bag in this dark corner; nobody will notice it there. We'll be back home when school is over." The staircase in our apartment building had no windows. Daylight could filter in through a glass-roof at the attic floor. It was very dark on the first steps of the staircase where their triangular shape formed a corner. There I hid my satchel. It was just big enough for it. I asked Ulla, "What shall we do now?"

Ulla had it all planned, "Let's get tadpoles at the Gristmill pond."

I shook my head. "Can't do. I don't have money for the tram, and it's too far to walk."

Ulla had thought about this. "We can use the money we were supposed to bring today as contribution for the Reich's Mothers' Homes."

Without any qualms, I agreed, "Okay. Let's run. We might catch the next tram to the pond." Off we went, happy to spend the sunny spring day in the country.

At the millpond we found an old can and collected many little tadpoles. Some of them already had legs; others had only a body and tail. We even found a cluster of frog eggs. We loved to catch the slippery creatures and gather them in the rusty old container.

Suddenly a bicycle appeared on the horizon. A heavyset man peddled up the hill. "There you are!" he yelled. "Ulla, Ilse-Rose." We were startled. It was Ulla's father. He ordered us to dump the tadpoles back into the pond. He lifted Ulla onto the bar in front of him and pointed to the carrier behind him for me to climb onto. Home we went. It was too late for school. Years later, my mother told me that she quite often had to ask Mr. Spatkovskie to find Ulla and me.

I loved to play with Ulla. She was an only child. Her parents lived in the cellar quarters of the hospital. The pipes of the heating track ran under the ceiling of their kitchen, bedroom, and living room. We often played in the long hallway. Mr. Spatkovskie gave us play dough that the wounded soldiers used for their rehabilitation therapy. We formed the neatest doll furniture, pots, pans, and dishes for our dolls. Hour after hour we spent in delightful play. The play dough had an army-green grayish color, but we managed to get some brick-red clay to "bake" layered cakes and formed little clay balls as cherries on top. There was no limit to our playful fantasies, but we also liked to roam through the hospital instead of going to school.

Ulla was smaller than I. She had a dark complexion, black hair, and black eyes, and she was quick as mercury when allowed to run loose. She always had new ideas for games. Anneliese was taller than both of us. She sported very curly blond hair and blue eyes. Her behavior reflected the strict upbringing she experienced from her parents and her older sisters. One time, we lingered around in the hospital's big yard. At its end stood a high flagpole. Every morning, wounded soldiers raised the flag and in the evening, they took it down again.

Ulla looked at the flag and said to me, "Ilse-Rose, I dare you to touch the flag when I let it down." That was not a great adventure for me. Ulla unfastened the rope and brought the flag down. It was made of strong material, bright red with a white circle and the black swastika in the middle of it. I touched the solid material. Ulla looked at Anneliese and asked her, "Would you help me pull her up with the flag?" I thought it might be fun to be lifted up high above the ground.

"Just let me get a good grip on it," I said.

The two girls had to strain to pull up the flag with me hanging on it, higher and higher, and … suddenly, two soldiers came running out of the hospital, yelling, "Desecration! What are you doing to our flag? Shame on you!" My girlfriends let go of the rope and bolted as fast as they could out of the yard. Luckily, I was not too far off the ground. With my weight on the flag, it came whirling down; one of the soldiers caught me before I could hit the cement slab. He was wounded. He had only one arm to break my fall. I tore myself loose and dashed after my friends with the soldiers running after me, but the moment I passed the gate, they stopped. Apparently the wounded were not allowed to leave the hospital grounds without permission. In the meantime, the ward appeared. He could have caused trouble for the two soldiers if they followed me outside the gate. For a few weeks Ulla and I were afraid to be seen in the hospital. We stayed in the cellar and played there.

Ulla's father was not just the janitor of the hospital; he took care of many other tasks. Whenever he had to carry out special errands for the doctors, or for military officers, he invited his daughter and me to come along. I recall that, during one Advent season, my mother went to the specialty store to buy authentic "Thorner Katharinchen," a big, aromatic cookie. When she left the store with her precious purchase, she saw a huge wagon drawn by two large horses. Overstuffed leather easy chairs, a sofa, and a giant oak desk stood on its flatbed. My mother could not believe it—took a second look—was this her daughter on top of the wagon? Snuggled in the easy chairs sat two little girls, one of them her child, acting like a queen in a parade through town.

The Nazi government employed artists, singers, comedians, and magicians—anybody who could lift the morale of the wounded soldiers. The shows took place in the auditorium of the former school. My mother, after conferring with Mr. Spatkovskie, allowed me to watch these. The first time we went, Ulla and I sat in the front row. We were fascinated by the magic, but the other performances were rather boring for Ulla and me. The jokes were over our heads. We were familiar with the songs, but were not allowed to sing along. We watched more of these events, however we never sat in the front row again. Ulla suggested, "Let's sit in the back, so we can sneak out when it gets boring." I readily agreed.

I visited with the wounded by myself when Ulla was not at home. One of them taught me how to play chess. I caught on readily, to the delight of the other patients in the room. They showed me certain moves, and once in a while, they let me win. I was too young to become an expert player, but it was fun for the soldiers. It was a change from their boring routines and actually added to their therapy. They laughed when the nurse asked me to leave the room because one of them had to get an injection. I experienced how some of the soldiers had traumas, but they tried to hide their condition out of fear to be branded as cowards.

One time, a nurse came with a big bowl of steaming water. She went to one quiet soldier, whom I had watched carve a beautiful statue out of clay. "Okay, buddy, here comes your inhaler session," she said.

He lifted up his arms, crying, "Nurse, please, not again; no, no, not again!" I anxiously turned toward him. *Why was he screaming at the nurse?* I wondered. I had seen his composure when they tore caked-on bandages off his chest; he never flinched when getting an injection. This time, he only needed to put his face over a bowl to let the nurse cover his head with a big army blanket. He was told to breathe in the aromatic steam. *What was so bad about that?* I thought. Years later, I realized that he probably suffered from shell shock or another trauma acquired in the trenches. Under the Nazi regime, psychological problems were not tolerated. They showed weakness, which an Aryan should not possess. We were taught to be tough like the Spartans.[88]

When asked by the town authorities to let people stay with us, my parents were eager to share their apartment. These were families who wanted to settle in Thorn and were looking for a suitable place to live. Sometimes they might be wives and family members of the higher military personnel stationed in Thorn. Since I often lived with my Oma, I hardly remember any of them. I only recall two men in uniform who stayed with us, except for my father. He had been drafted in late 1943.

In the fall, my Uncle Hans[89] was on a short leave and visited with us. We sat at the dining-room table. I had collected a few colorful leaves. They lay in front of me. I tried to draw a scene with trees. He took my pencil and said, "Look at a leaf of a tree. Look how the shape of one leaf resembles the whole contour of the tree it came from." To make his point, he started to draw what looked like a scribble to me, but turned out to become a pine tree, then the oak and linden tree followed. I started to guess what he would depict next.

The other officer I remember was Major Alfred Conn. His family lived with us, but I cannot picture any of them. We called him Uncle Conn. He seemed to prefer me to my siblings. When he was back at the Eastern Front, he sent me a package with a sweet cherry preserve. I was lying

---

88   Spartans inhabited a Greek city-state. Their social system and constitution focused mainly on rigorous military training and education, with the goal of excellence in both programs. They were considered undefeatable by the other Greek states.

89   Apparently, the military did not consider his epilepsy too severe for him to be drafted into the army for clerikal duties.

on the couch in the "Herrenzimmer" with a slight cold when my mother brought it to me. She had a letter in her hand from him.

"Look what Uncle Conn sent you, Ilse-Rose! These are special cherries; we cannot buy them here. I opened the jar for you. Taste them."

They were delicious and cool, the best medicine I ever had. Mother proceeded to read the letter to me[90]. I did not understand everything. Sometimes she stopped, as if to skip a line or two, but one sentence the major wrote I never forgot: "I am sending you a jar of my bloody tears I collected when I cried thinking about being unable to see you."

I looked at my mother and asked, "Did he really cry bloody tears?" I guess I would have tried hard to cry this type of tears, but at that time my mother introduced me to analogies and symbolism. I only tasted those cherries once. After a few days, when I asked for more, they were gone. My mother was very angry. She could not find out who ate them. She suspected our servants savored them. With ration cards we only could get the necessities, never delicacies. The temptation must have been just too great.

My mother also had to get theater or concert tickets for the officers. The best seats were reserved for the upper ranks of the military personnel and their hosts. Therefore, when children's plays were performed, we were fortunate to sit in the front rows. Twice I saw plays at the theater when I spent Christmas in Thorn. I especially loved *Hänsel and Gretel* by Engelbert Humperdinck.[91] The ladder leading to heaven from which the angels came down to protect the two lost children was very impressive. Hänsel and Gretel were sleeping on the ground in the dark woods near a deep cavern.

---

90 Uncle Conn, knowing that all mail was checked by the Gestapo, gave coded information to my mother, hoping that a letter to a young child would not be scrutinized as thoroughly.

91 Engelbert Humperdinck (1854–1921) wrote other operas, but this fairy-tale opera is his most famous one. He was strongly influenced by Richard Wagner, and he in turn influenced Arnold Schönberg with his "Sprechgesang", a vocal technique halfway between singing and speaking.

It is a children's opera with songs that are unforgettable. My sister and I sang the melodies and danced to them. Oh yes, when it came to music, Hildegard and I understood each other. We both loved to sing and dance. She danced with very graceful movements, and I enjoyed our rounds—even if once in a while, I stumbled over my own feet with those insole shoes. She developed a high soprano and I an alto. We could sing duets together, to the delight of the grown-ups.

Another thing Hildegard and I had in common was our perception of the hierarchy in our world. My sister asked me, "Who has the highest position in the world?"

I answered, "God."

"And who comes next?"

"That must be the Kaiser," I said. At Oma's, in Klostermansfeld, I had seen a big picture of one of the Prussian emperors hanging on the wall. In her room was a picture of Queen Luise. Oma belonged to the "Luisenbund".[92] It was clear to me that the Kaiser had to be next in line. In Thorn hung a photo of Adolf Hitler, so he held the third position in our pyramid of importance. Then came the kings, the dukes, the counts and the barons. We were still very much attuned to aristocracy, as we knew them from our fairy tales.

That year, I also saw *Thorner Katharinchen*, a play depicting the discovery of the recipe for the aromatic cookie. I never forgot the analogy between the scent of carnations and cloves, one of the major spices in the treat. The year before, I had seen *Sleeping Beauty* but was not too impressed, since the hedge of thorns was not realistic enough for me. Nevertheless, I loved the theater, and at home, I imitated all the characters in the musicals and plays. My mother helped us to dress up our dolls and my teddy bear in dwarf costumes to play *Snow White and the Seven Dwarfs*. Hildegard always was the beautiful princess. I took all the other

---

92   *Bund Königin Luise* was a monarchist nationalistic women's movement during the Weimar Republic It was founded in 1923. Although the goals of this association were the same as Hitler promoted for Germany's women, it was abolished under the umbrella of the Gleichschaltung in 1934.

roles, even if it was the prince, the bad queen, or the stepmother. I just loved to act. I seemed to be destined to become an actress.

My father was wounded twice during the war. The first time, he was hurt by friendly fire. He had to train young recruits. One of them did not follow his directions; he shot my father through his wrist. My father reflected, "I was lucky. The gun was not loaded with live ammunition." The second time, a Soviet bullet penetrated his upper left arm. "It is only a flesh wound, no damage to my bones," he used to say. He recuperated in Scandinavia. Sometimes he served in Denmark or Norway, but mostly he fought in Russia. We were relieved that he was not with the 6th Army when it collapsed after fighting for over a half year in Stalingrad.[93]

Soon, the civilians had to cope more and more with the effects of the ongoing war. Danzig, Stettin, and other East German cities were bombed. My mother, as with so many German women, had no help from her husband. She had her hands full when all four of us children were with her. My father was somewhere with the military. When she wrote letters to him, she never knew if they were opened and either forwarded to him or destroyed. Often she waited for weeks before she received an answer. By that time she'd had to make decisions—even for my father's office—by herself. She had to deal with the rising difficulties for us all. Not only was it harder to get enough food for us, but also, living in Thorn became more dangerous.

For example, one day the leader of Ernst's Jungvolk group had eleven of his boys swim in the treacherous Vistula, when a whirlpool pulled several of them under. The leader realized the danger and dove in to rescue the boys caught in the downward swirl. Ernst managed to get out of it by himself. He swam to shore, and watched the leader dive again and again—one of his young "Pimpfe"[94] was missing. It was Ernst's best friend

---

93   The battle of Stalingrad was the turning point of WWII in Europe. It lasted from the middle of July 1942 until February 1943. In the end, the German 6th Army was destroyed. About 2 million casualties among Russian and German armies and civilians have been reported.

94   *Pimpf* is a term for the ten- to fourteen-year-old members of the Jungvolk.

who drowned that day. The death of his companion was hard on Ernst, although he avoided showing his grief.

Ernst was excellent in school. He was soon chosen to transfer to a special school called "Adolf Hitler Schule" (Adolf Hitler School). My mother was not very excited about the suggestive political curriculum of this school. My father, on the other hand, was proud that his son was selected from among so many. He persuaded my mother to let Ernst go and pointed out two convincing arguments: firstly, the school emphasized a greater diversity—languages, science, and sports—and secondly, the school was in the heart of Germany near our grandmothers. Mother thought, *in his vacations, Ernst can easily visit with my brother and Oma in the country, away from bombing raids in the cities and anyway it will be good for Ernst to leave Thorn, his HJ group, the HJ leader, and the boys who constantly will remind him of losing his best friend in the Vistula.*

Mother knew that in Middle Germany her children would be safer than in the east, so close to the Soviets and exposed to the hate of some Polish people. Most of the Poles never became true naturalized Germans, especially if they had a communistic background. They influenced their children, and nasty encounters occurred. We experienced this once while we walked in front of our house. Suddenly, some older boys passed us and threw sand in our eyes, screaming profanities at us. My mother concluded, *it is time to send my children away under some pretense.* For Hildegard, who was an excellent student, Mother again relied on her daughter's delicate body structure and health to get permission to send her away from Thorn. At the school office, she claimed that it was advisable to let her daughter finish the school year, but spend the vacation with Oma on the farm, where she would toughen up and have better food.

Grandma came to Thorn to help with my younger brother. Their love for each other was mutual. After some weeks, Grandma took Reinhold with her to St. Bernhard. He was too young to be in any Kinderhort, let alone school. In my case, my mother told the principal of our elementary school that I had to visit Oma, because in Klostermansfeld, I apparently learned better than in Thorn, anyway there I had a good tutor and also an

NSDAP teacher. Soon I said good-bye to everybody again and went with Oma back to Middle Germany, to the farm, to the old dog Karo, the cows, calves, chickens, ducks, geese, and all the people who worked for Uncle Martin—and last but not least, my "country" friends.

CHAPTER 5

For you have been a refuge to the poor, a refuge to the needy in their distress, a shelter from the rainstorm and a shade from the heat; when the blast of the ruthless was like a winter rainstorm. Isaiah 25:4.

Klostermansfeld
A Safe Haven

The long stone trough with the iron pump. The water needed to be pumped by hand. Some cows are enjoying the sun on the enclosed manure heap.

Many of the young male farmhands were drafted into the military after war was inevitable in 1940. Uncle Martin had to take in Polish prisoners of war who had the status of civil workers[95]; The Nazi government forced them to choose this status over POW. If they refused, they were sent to prison camps. Some of these workers were not familiar with farming. Uncle Martin had to instruct them how to care for domestic animals and how to plow, sow, plant, and harvest. I liked Anton the most. He was in charge of my favorite old farm horse, Hans, that used to pull heavy wagonloads. Anton let me ride him when going to work in the morning. He treated Hans well. In the evening, he drew water from the big iron pump into the long stone trough for Hans to quench his thirst.

We took Hans to the blacksmith, Mr. Fleming, across the street. Anton held the horse while the smith took off the old horseshoes. I watched and asked,

"Does that hurt Hans?" The blacksmith was a little gruff.

"Does what hurt?" he grunted.

"I mean, pulling all those nails out of his hoof." He loosened up and explained to me,

"No, of course not. Does it hurt when your Oma cuts your fingernails?" I had to laugh.

"No!"

He continued cutting the hoof into the correct shape and pointed out, "See, now I am cutting his nail. His hoof is really like his thumbnail or toenail." After he had formed the hoof, he shod Hans with shiny new horseshoes.

Every so often, the blacksmith came into the courtyard to take care of the cows' feet as well. That was especially necessary since my uncle's

---

95   A civil worker forfeited his legal protection from the ICRC (International Committee of the Red Cross), and with it the rules set up in the 1929 Conventions in Geneva that Prisoners of War could not be turned into slave workers. The members of the ICRC were responsible for visiting POW camps, organizing relief programs for civilian populations, and administering the exchange of messages regarding missing persons and prisoners.

cows hardly ever left the stable and could not walk off the horn on their feet. Sometimes a few cows were put into the fenced-in square in the center of the courtyard. It was heaped full of used straw and other refuse from the stables. The liquid manure ran into big tanks covered by thick wooden planks. In March, the men loaded the manure onto wagons and carted it out in order to fertilize the fields. They also emptied the tanks for the same purpose. Every March, our courtyard stank.[96] Oma and I did not leave the bedroom window open during that time.

Once in a while, Anton made a windmill out of straw for me, or he braided Thanksgiving wreaths from wheat stalks. At Christmas, he showed me how to make straw-stars for the Christmas tree. It was easy to weave these stars. I still make them to decorate our Christmas tree.

Straw-stars among other ornaments

---

96 At that time, the whole farming country reeked. It was, and in some areas still is, customary to have dung heaps close to the house, even located near the kitchen windows.

I had no idea that the Polish workers actually had fought against German soldiers and should be considered enemies. Here they were not in prison camps. There was no barbed wire to keep them confined. They slept upstairs in some rooms above the horse stable. None of them thought of escaping. They could not have gotten far if they attempted to flee. The German police would have picked them up very soon. Anyway, where should they have gone? Their homeland, Poland, did not exist anymore; it had been divided between Russia and Germany.

When the Polish prisoners opted to become civil workers they were at the mercy of their masters. Some farmers in our area treated them like slaves; they worked them hard and used whips on them. Oma never allowed such acts. She instilled in us that God is the Creator of all people and therefore every person should be respected.

My uncle and aunt did not adhere to all of the regulations for civil workers. One of the rules stated that they should not receive meat, but on Uncle Martin's farm, their food was much the same as ours. The soups had chunks of meat in them, and at Christmas Oma roasted a turkey or goose for them as well. The civil workers had to observe a curfew and were not allowed to have friendships with Germans, especially relationships with German women. My mother observed, "Martin and Ursel always have one foot in prison themselves." If anybody reported my uncle and aunt, they could be incarcerated, or at least made to pay a hefty fine.

Uncle Martin did not treat his Polish workers like detainees. They received the same consideration as his German workers had, who had helped on the farm before the war. I never thought of Anton or his fellow workers as enemies. Some of them were my friends. I did not even realize that they spoke with an accent, did not use correct grammar, used unfamiliar words, or, if they thought nobody was listening, spoke in a foreign language to each other.

In 1943, when I came back to Klostermansfeld during my school vacation, there were more foreign workers. Two Russian women soldiers lived in a room above the wash kitchen. One of them was pregnant. Oma helped. She called for a midwife when the woman's time for delivery was near. She gave the new mother clothing and diapers for the baby. The Russian girls were quite different from the Polish workers, who had been here for such a long time that I considered them part of the farm. The *Flintenweiber* ("gun wenches," as the British soldiers called the Russian female soldiers) had no word of thanks for anybody. Oma took me upstairs to see the little baby. The room was in shambles with sheets, clothing, and foodstuffs everywhere. The baby lay in a crib, no doubt also supplied by Oma. Both women shouted something I did not understand. Oma tried to signal to them. She knew French, but not Russian or Ukrainian. These women just refused to see that neither Oma nor I would harm the newborn. Oma turned to me and whispered, "You better leave." She did not need to repeat it. I hoped never to see those two again, or even consider forming a friendship with them as I had with others.

I was all too happy to run downstairs and across the courtyard into the cow stable. Here was the dairyman, Mr. Rosenhahn. He took care of the cows like they were his own. He knew each individual animal and its need. He let me feel the rough tongue of the little calf.

"Ilse-Rose," he said, "dip your hand into this milk. It is still warm from milking the calf's mother. Now, let the calf smell it."

Sure enough, the calf recognized the milk and started sucking on my hand. It felt funny. It tickled. Mr. Rosenhahn had shown me before where the calves liked to be stroked and scratched. I stayed with him until it was time to eat the evening meal.

Since I stayed with Oma so often, I gained two close friends when I was in Klostermansfeld. My best friend was Klärchen, a heavyset, rather quiet girl my age who had older sisters just like Anneliese in Thorn. Klärchen lived in a small house, which stood to the right of our house facing its front yard. Helga lived across the street opposite Klärchen. Helga was really my sister's girlfriend. She was a year older than I. Her mother lived in Berlin. Her grandmother and grandfather raised her. The latter mined copper in the Mansfeld mines. When Helga's grandfather had to work the second shift, we were not allowed to make any noise so he could sleep during the day. At those times, we played in the front yard of Oma's house. One of our favorite games was Catch the Ball. We played it in a competition. The new yellow brick building attached to the old farmhouse—the "eyesore," as the grown-ups called it—was ideal for this game. Helga and I liked that it had tall, wide walls on which we could practice our catching skills. We could play this game for hours. Sometimes Klärchen joined us, though she was not the athletic type.

Aunt Ursel forbade me to play it during her midday rest from one to three P.M. our ball bounced against the wall of her bedroom. It was impossible for her to sleep with the constant thuds against this side of the house. Oma said, "Sleep is holy." I did not forget Oma's words. They haunted me later, when I crossed the Russian border illegally.[97] It caused me to spend an uncomfortable night at an overcrowded railroad station. I did not dare to wake up my godmother, Aunt Anne, at midnight. I could have phoned her. She lived nearby and would have let me stay with her.

The hired hands in the household also had these hours of rest. Usually, they went home to take care of their own place and children until they came back for the afternoon. Mrs. Rabehl often brought her daughter, Christa, with her to watch Aunt Ursel's children. Sometimes she had time to join us in our games. The men and women working in the fields took a shorter break of about one hour. I remember when I was with them, the woman in charge called, "Lunchtime!" The workers all laid down their tools, got their bags or lunch pails, and looked for a shady place to eat. They sat in the grass and put an empty horse's feedbag down for me to sit on. We ate and then most of them leaned back to take a short nap. During their rest, I went to see the horses, or spoke to one of the workers who did not sleep. I talked about school, but never about what was going on at home. Uncle Martin, Aunt Ursel, and Oma made that clear to me. They said, "Do not tell what we eat, what we drink, who is coming to visit, what we are discussing. If they ask you questions, say you don't know." These were my instructions, and I followed them faithfully.

---

97 After July 1945, the border went through the center of Germany, dividing it into the Soviet-controlled eastern sector and the western sectors occupied by British, American, and French forces.

When Hildegard visited, she claimed Helga for herself. Sometimes they let me join in their games. Helga did not care whose friend she was; she just loved to play with anybody from the farm. I, in turn, loved to go to her house, where I often stayed for dinner, eating the meager meal with the miner's family. I could have had much better food at Oma's, but maybe I was trying to avoid Uncle Martin's steel blue eyes seemingly looking straight through me. I wondered, *is he seeing what I did in the wheat storage room? Or does he know I brought a basket of food to Oma's friend?* I was afraid of him. I sometimes did not know if what I did created some damage, or was forbidden or dangerous. For instance, when I played with my friends in the stored wheat, we trampled it down.[98] Usually it was the boys in the neighborhood who suggested games like these. "Let's play tag on the grain," they would say. "It's harder to run there, but softer when you fall down."

Uncle Martin reached for the switch to hit me when I had done something precarious or destructive. I was not disobedient, but just living sometimes in a city and then again in the country I had to find out by myself what was "verboten" (forbidden). The grown-ups thought that my mother told me how to behave in Klostermansfeld and my parents concluded Oma or Aunt Ursel showed the taboos on their farm to me. None of them instructed me. Anyway it seemed best to stay out of Uncle Martin's way. Decades later, after my uncle had died, Aunt Ursel said to me, "I had pity on you when your Uncle Martin looked at you over the dinner table and you— out of fear—started to sob and piddle through the cane work of your chair."

What the older boys and girls suggested was sometimes downright dangerous. They said, "Let's play tag. Not here, no, but there," pointing to the boards and beams in the barn high up above the hay. Often, the only escape from being tagged was to jump into the hay, scramble through it, climb up the ladder, swing onto the beam, and start all over again. Sometimes, bales of straw were stored with the hay. These huge cubes were too hard to jump into. It was especially hazardous when we played

---

98   My uncle grew seed grain, a very expensive commodity. The damage we caused cost my uncle hundreds of Reichsmarks (German currency until 1948).

tag on these beams after winter, because then only a thin layer of hay and straw remained underneath us. If we had ever fallen down the thirty feet, we could have been killed or badly hurt. Once, when we played above the diminished hay covering the barn floor, I jumped down and fell through the thin layer, landing rather hard. I felt a dull pain in my lower back in spite of having bent my knees to lessen the impact. I never told anybody about it, fearing Uncle's switch. Years later, however, a school doctor in Mülheim on the Ruhr found an unexplainable abnormality on my spine, which prevented me from pursuing my dream vocation.

Helga's grandma, Mrs. Nebert, set the table in her kitchen. This room was small, oblong, and always dimly lit, since it had only one window high up against the ceiling. We sat very tightly together. Usually, they left the kitchen door open to allow light to filter into the kitchen from the narrow hallway leading to the courtyard. Here they kept their chickens, which scratched for food between the cobblestones. A high fence, made from thick wooden boards, separated them from the baker's yard. The fence extended into a stonewall ending in their chicken coop. Another family shared this place and its outhouse opposite the two dwellings. I remembered especially the time when their rooster pecked at me. I screamed. Helga's grandma came dashing out of the house, grabbed the barnyard fowl, and threw him into the henhouse, closing the door tightly. "Whenever you have to use the outhouse, let me know," she declared. "I'll get rid of the rooster. It's a nasty critter." I trusted her almost as much as Oma.

Mrs. Nebert's pudding soup was my favorite. But one day when I asked, as I had so often, "May I stay for dinner?"

Helga's grandma answered me. "You get better food at your house. You do not need to eat away the little we have." It never occurred to me that I was consuming the food meant for their family. I did not know that they were poor. They always had been very kind and protective of me.

I fought back my tears and went to Oma. Sniffling, I told her about the rejection I had just received. I was hurt; I did not want to go to Helga's home again. Then a few days later, Oma heard that one of the Nebert's older daughters was "in a bad way." She was pregnant and had gone into labor too early. Oma went across the street and stayed with her for hours. When I was sent to look for her, Helga was playing in the attic. Her grandma sent me up to stay there with her and told me, "Don't come down until I ask you to do so". I found a wonderful doll kitchen up there. Helga informed me, "This is where I play with Hildegard. She likes these things a lot."

I agreed. "I like them too. Let's play with the kitchen," I suggested. "I promise to be careful."

Some hours later, Helga's grandmother called us into the living room to look at a tiny, healthy baby. "I am an aunt, you know," Helga said proudly.

That evening, I had my favorite soup at the miner's house again. Oma had talked to Mrs. Nebert and asked about what they needed, and then she sent food to them whenever possible. She often helped people in the village. In the evenings, she sold milk to our clients. She generously measured liters into the milk cans that people handed her. Sometimes she deliberately would ladle whole milk into their cans but ask to be paid the lesser price of the skim milk.

Now and again, when a poor woman died, Oma gave away one of her pretty nightgowns for the deceased to be buried in. Oma's nightclothes had lace trimmings and were embroidered. In them, the departed was dressed decently for burial. I ran errands for Oma. She was wise to send me, it saved the person in need from embarrassment or looking like a beggar, as can happen when an adult hands out food. Nobody rejected Oma's help given through a young child.

When Hildegard came to visit Oma, Helga played with her. Then I sat with my playmate Klärchen in the Victorian garden house that functioned as a retreat but also as the entrance into the garden. It was covered with climbing clematises shading its south side. Inside this lovely place stood a bench in front of an oblong table. Here we sat and drew pictures.

Ilse-Rose in front of the door to the garden house.
This picture was taken by one of the Polish Civil Workers.

Paper had become scarce,[99] even in school. We had to be careful not to use up too many pages in our notebooks. The teachers handed out only a certain number of sheets per pupil. Therefore, for our drawings Klärchen and I used unfinished cigarette-card albums given to us by Klärchen's father. He owned the tobacco shop in Klostermansfeld that was filled with many of these books for collecting cigarette cards. His clients would get the picture cards when purchasing tobacco products. When they grew tired of gluing them into albums, they returned the unfinished books. So it happened that we penciled our drawings inside of empty squares,

---

99   Many German authors used blank backs of calendars or even margins of newspapers to write their poems, short stories, or novels. One of them, Berlin author Wolfdietrich Schnurre (1920- 1989), wrote a whole novel on them. It was never published and is now in the "Handschriften- Abteilung" (manuscript department) of the Schiller-Nationalmuseum, Deutsches Literaturarchiv, Postfach 1162, 71672 Marbach, Germany.

which were designated for war-scenes from Germany's history[100]. Yes, war pictures dominated the albums' themes. I especially remember the ones from the Thirty Years War[101].

Klärchen was Catholic and would draw religious symbols. She had just entered Communion classes and was looking forward to dressing like a little bride on the day of her First Communion. We sketched a dove with an olive branch—the symbol of peace—right among battle scenes. Klärchen drew the cross often, but her Jesus was never good enough for me. I was afraid to attempt a picture of Him. He was too celestial, too beautiful for me to do Him justice with my clumsy pencil. I knew Jesus through my nightly prayers. Here He was so tiny that He could fit into my heart. I also knew Him through a church song, *Fairest Lord Jesus*. In the song He was described as being fairer than meadows, woodlands, flowers, sunshine, and stars. I would opt for stars, the sun, and the moon, arguing with Klärchen that these were symbols for Jesus. We scribbled angels among pictures of fighting warriors, knights, and mercenaries of the Thirty Years War.

Klärchen drew many symbols that I did not recognize. "Let's draw a white dove," she suggested.

"Fine, but why white? All of my uncle's doves are blue, gray, and brown," I questioned her.

"You are talking about pigeons," she explained. "I mean the dove, which is the Holy Spirit."

I thought, *what or whoever is this spirit?* and carefully copied Klärchen's dove.

"It looks like a pigeon to me," I said.

100　The Dresden cigarette-card service supplied the pictures. Especially popular was the Great War album depicting WWI.

101　This devastating religious war started almost 100 years after Martin Luther nailed his famous 95 Theses on the Wittenberg Church in 1519, namely in 1618, and ended in 1648 with the founding of the Protestant Church and thus separation from the Roman Catholic Church.

She did not want to argue, so calmly she suggested, "Now it's your turn to say what we draw." I wanted to mention something I could do well.

"A flower."

Klärchen wanted to be specific. "What type of flower?"

I looked around the garden. Behind us grew several lilac trees under which my grandfather's hunting dogs had been buried. The names of the dogs were carved on gravestones. Lilacs would be too hard to draw. The lattice wall on the opposite side was covered with dark blue clematis. "Clematis," I declared. When we were finished with our flowers, I had to confess hers had the better resemblance. It was Klärchen's turn.

"Now, let's draw a heart."

"Fine." I knew how to do that, but when I looked over at Klärchen's square, she had drawn an arrow through her heart and drops of blood were oozing from the wound. Now, I wanted to know specifics.

"Why is this heart shot through the middle? Mine is just a plain red heart."

Klärchen sat up straight and looked at the ceiling of the garden house, as if she could look right through it into heaven.

"It is Jesus' heart, pierced for our sins."

Although I had started to have enough of this religious stuff, I found it fascinating. It was so different from my church. On Sundays, I went to the children's service in the Protestant church, where my grandmother had reserved seats for the whole family. There was no fear that their red velvet covers would be worn out, as it was seldom that any of the adults went to church, except for Oma. Our church had an altar, but there was only a small cross without Christ on it. Two angels were portrayed there. The organ stood opposite the altar on a balustrade above the pews. When I was older I sat up there, since I sang in the children's choir.

Klärchen and I went to school together. As a rule, most of the German schools separated boys from girls into parallel classes. The exceptions to this regulation were very small villages like St. Bernhard, where they still had a one-room schoolhouse. Klostermansfeld had enough inhabitants to afford a large school building. There were so many children that we needed several parallel classes for the girls alone, with thirty to thirty-five pupils in each of them. Klärchen and I were in the same class. Oma might have arranged that, so the principal did not place me in the parallel class. She had quite an influence in the village. Even the mayor would listen to her suggestions.

Klärchen was much better than I in Orthography, but I outshone her in Math and Sports. Our classroom teacher was Miss Karsdorf. Now and then, Oma sent me to her with a little container filled with soup, or a basket with sausage, some milk, and even a piece of cake. Times started to get tough, even in the country. All of us had ration cards. Each year, the individual provisions on them diminished. Oma paid Miss Karsdorf for my tutoring sessions with food. Although I disliked her, my mother had told the principal in Thorn that I would get help with spelling from an NSDAP teacher, so I had to put up with her.

Klärchen did not like physical games. Hopscotch was the exception. She rather played with marbles sitting down and shooting them skillfully with her fingers into the little holes we had dug into the ground. I was often too active for her. I also played with other children in the village. Their favorite games were hide-and-go-seek or catch. Uncle Martin allowed them to play in the barn if I was there too. After the incident with the seed grain we set rules: "No hiding between the horses, cows, or other animals." The stables and the grain storage rooms were off limits ever since we had trampled down the wheat. I did not fear any high places. I hid and jumped into the hay just in front of the seeker. "Free!" I screamed with delight when I had outsmarted the older boys.

When my mother visited with my siblings, Ernst took part in the games, but Hildegard rarely did. She was too refined for farm games. She was actually smart. She did not get those little burning scratches from the straw, which stung especially bad in warm water. Although that did not happen often, just once a week when we took our Saturday bath. At that time, two of the male workers went upstairs into the attic to bring down a bathtub shaped like a big cradle. You could rock back and forth in it. "Make sure the water does not splash onto the floor," my mother warned us when we attempted to rock the tub. The men put it in the ironing kitchen. Here, a servant heated water on a coal stove. In summer, this room was hot like a sauna. My mother always opened the window when it was our turn to take a bath.

The tub was not big enough for all of us children. Hildegard and I took our bath together, and then it was Ernst's turn in the same water, which had already been used before by my cousins, Hermjörg and Lutz. The house did not have a shower. I preferred Oma's sponge baths.

I celebrated some of my birthdays in Klostermansfeld. Two of them I remember especially. Oma had planned a party for my friends and me. We sat around the table in the garden house. We ate the cake, which was decorated with a prettily colored number 6 carved from wood as a little candleholder. After I blew the candle out, Oma allowed us to use a toy stove that she had stored in the attic. It was not a pretend one. She poured some kind of fluid into a little canister attached to the stove. You could turn the knobs and a row of little flames heated the baking compartment, or you could cook on the stovetop. Oma gave us an egg to fry and some dough, left over from the cake, to bake in the oven. We heated milk and drank it out of tiny cups.

From then on I often begged Oma to let us cook. Sometimes Uncle Martin shot sparrows because there were just too many. They flew into the courtyard and ate the grain I fed to the chickens. They became a nuisance. Uncle Martin gave us the dead sparrows to cook. He showed us how to pull off their feathers with their skin attached in one stroke, so only the meat and bones were left. Oma taught us how to remove the innards, and then we were allowed to cook sparrow soup. I never attempted to roast one. They were really too small.

The handcart that was converted into a birthday wagon. On the front seat, cousins Lutz Oemler and Jochen Oemler holding the reigns; back behind Lutz, cousin Hermjörg Oemler and behind Jochen my brother, Reinhold Höfer. Here the young boys—ages between 2 ½ and 6—sat more comfortably than I at my 10th birthday.

Another special birthday came in 1946. The war was over, and we had experienced a lot. Our world had crumbled. In St. Bernhard, children had called me a Nazi pig. Here in Klostermansfeld, my friends wanted to show me that they liked me after all. Helga and Klärchen, along with cousin Hermjörg, my brother Reinhold, Hildegard, and the young apprentice, Eberhard Fleisher, built a birthday wagon for me. It was a handcart that they had converted to be pulled by a goat. They put willow boughs, decorated with flowers, across the wagon and fastened a seat for me under those boughs. They carted me through the village. The goat behaved well. It refrained from eating the flowers on the wagon. I was rather uncomfortable; the seat was too high, the boughs were too low. I had to stoop forward, crouch down, and pretend to be happy doing so.

Soon I told them, "Let's go and have cake." Oma and my mother had set the table in the garden house. There we were crowded, but we did not mind. Oma even had juice for us, which was a rarity by then. The farmers had to deliver their fruit to the Soviets. They could hardly keep any for themselves. To have cake and juice was a feast for my guests and me.

Later, my mother played games with us. She preferred games through which we could learn geography, get acquainted with artists and their works, and recall the names of animals, plants, trees, and famous people. Mother avoided history, since she was not sure how much the teachers were told to distort this subject in our Soviet controlled schools.

I remember telling my teacher that dogs were developed not only from wolves but also from foxes or jackals. But this was not in her textbook. I knew it from a book I had read, called Die *Höhlenkinder*[102] by Alois Theodor Sonnleitner, 1918-1920. It was one of my favorite books.

I do not remember any birthday party for me in Thorn, although at the breakfast table my place had the traditional decorations every birthday child received. Flowers surrounded my plate, and a burning candle stood in front of it. Nobody else was allowed to blow it out; only the birthday child could extinguish the flame.

My friends were girls and boys from good hardworking families. Most of them had blue-collar jobs. I befriended former Polish soldiers in Klostermansfeld and German wounded veterans in Thorn. There was no difference between them for me. They were people who shared their skills with me. I liked them all and yet, I lost contact with every one of them. Blame forty-three years of a divided Germany for this. After 1951, it became almost impossible for me to cross the border into the Russian zone.[103] Keeping contact by letter soon became hopeless. We had to be increasingly careful about what and to whom we wrote so as not to endanger the addressee or our own families. The Cold War reared its ugly

---

102 *The Cave Children* by Alois Theodor Sonnleitner, a Pseudonym for Alois Tlučhoř (1869- 1939).

103 Germany was divided among the allies into 4 sectors. See the map on the book cover and in chapter 7.

head after 1948. It developed into a monster until 1989, when it died with the tearing down of the Berlin Wall.[104]

The bombing raids on big towns and cities increased from year to year. To protect the civilians, the German government agencies shipped people wherever they estimated it was less dangerous and where there could still be some room for them. The case of a young Berliner mother and her four children may serve as an example of how civilians repeatedly had to relocate inside of Germany.

First the young woman, Mrs. Kleefeld, and her children had to follow the mandate to leave the constant bombardment of Berlin. She was sent to East Prussia. After living there for a short time, she had to flee the Russian onslaught and try to settle in the comparatively safe middle Germany. Uncle Martin received the order to house her little family. They occupied the two rooms high up above the master bedroom in the attached yellow brick building. After WWII, she had to move back where she originated from, namely to the still bomb-marred Berlin. To transport all the evacuees, fugitives and refugees to the center of Germany caused trains to overflow with them. Often children would be separated from their mothers. The German Red Cross had their hands full to relocate the family members and bring them together again.

In the summer of 1944, the Stammtisch gathered as usual. The headmaster asked, "Where is the mayor? If he does not come, we won't have a round of three for Skat."

The farmer, who always came because of his love for Skat mentioned how their number had dwindled during the still raging war. "First Schumann left. He was Jewish."

The headmaster interrupted him. "No, not he, but his wife."

The farmer waved at him.

---

104 The concept of the Berlin Wall was put into force on August 13th 1961 by the Soviet controlled government of the Russian sector in Germany.

115

"Yes, yes. They probably are not in southern France anymore." He scratched his head and asked, "What do they call that little part of France? The new French state?"

"Vichy France since the armistice was signed on June 22, 1940," the headmaster was eager to inform him. "Hitler really shined that day," he continued. "He had the old railroad wagon pulled out of the museum and rolled onto the exact spot where the armistice had been signed in 1918. It ended the Great War with a disgraceful defeat for us, as you very well know … but our Führer did not forget the humiliation of the Treaty of Versailles. He redeemed us. He showed them who is superior." The headmaster reveled when speaking of the victories of Germany a few years before.

The farmer heard enough; he cut in with, "Now we are in World War II. We are at the end of it and will be humiliated again, I am sure. Look! Just look at how they have destroyed our cities, how even we in the country need to get into shelters because of all those air raids. American planes over us during the day, British at night!"

The headmaster resented the farmer's remarks. "Are you giving up?" he argued. "Did you not listen to Goebbels? He told us of a wonder weapon they are developing. They have tested the V-1. It is a type of rocket. And now, they are testing the V-2. They develop all kinds of secret weapons.[105] Soon, we can eliminate whole cities with just one rocket, or bomb, or rocket- bomb, or bomb-rocket."

The farmer, tired of the headmaster's enumeration, sighed,

"I know; I heard about it being tested successfully.[106] But I am more concerned about the Schumanns. Where are they?"

---

105   The rockets were developed in Penemünde at the Baltic Sea.

106   The V-1 was tested by Hanna Reitsch (1912–1979), who was a famous German test pilot under the Nazi regime. She was the first female helicopter pilot. The Nazi party used her for their propaganda. She flew many of Germany's latest designs. She became Hitler's favorite test pilot and was awarded the Iron Cross First Class. In 1943, she piloted a rocket plane (Messerschmitt Me 163). In 1944, she flew trials of a jet aircraft.

The headmaster had his own ideas about their former shopkeeper and stipulated, "As for Schumanns, they most likely went to the land of unlimited possibilities, to America, before the French could hand them over to the Gestapo." He stopped for a moment, thinking back to the friendly Stammtisch member, and then he continued. "If only Schumann did not marry this half-Jew" He paused, waiting for some opposition to his remark, but everybody in the room was quiet. He stood up and declared, "And anyway, Jews belong to a much-too-old race. Old races have to go. They lose their strength, bodily and mentally. Hitler wants to cleanse Germany of all other races like Jews and gypsies. We want healthy Aryans and no physically and mentally defective people. They have to be sterilized." He looked around the room and reiterated, "We want to keep our Aryan blood and soil free from unhealthy influences."

The farmer had heard enough. His blood started boiling. He faced the headmaster. "You are still a dreamer!" he chided. "You still believe this Aryan stuff, don't you? I ask you, what is wrong with the Jews, the Sinti, and the Roma? They belong to our culture, contributed to literature, music, sciences ..." At that moment, he saw the innkeeper reaching for the phone. "Hello, Innkeeper. Get us some beer, the local brew, please," the farmer called. The innkeeper gave him a contentious look. He put the receiver down and started to draft the beer as it is traditionally done in Germany. It takes seven minutes to draft a good glass of beer. It is never ice-cold, so it will not lose its flavor. In winter, some customers even like a hot metal stick plunged into the cool beer to warm it before consumption. The farmer's suspicions arose when the innkeeper looked for the phone. He had been successful in diverting him by calling for beer. Now, he had to deal with the headmaster. "Teach, you know how my tongue sometimes runs ahead of my brain."

"You can say that again!"

"Please don't tell the Gestapo about me. I mean, what I just said about Aryans, gypsies, and Jews. I just have a hard time with things like this. I know breeding. Give me a prize bull and a good milk cow and you get a good stock."

The headmaster nodded, "Yes. They already do this with excellent young German men and women who fit the standards for the Aryan race ..." Looking out of the window he stopped talking and whispered, "Hey, look at our mayor, something is wrong with him; he looks terrible." Both men watched as their Stammtisch brother entered the inn and went to the bar, addressing the innkeeper.

"Innkeeper, in two days I want a funeral meal served in your special events room." He choked, but caught himself and continued. "My oldest son fell in the battle at Normandy[107]." The headmaster and the farmer got up, joining him. They wanted to console him. The farmer uttered, "Now your son too ... our minister was killed in Stalingrad. We have not heard from the pharmacist since he had to leave for Yugoslavia."

The innkeeper poured schnapps for all of them saying,

"I heard that the partisans are especially bad in Yugoslavia.[108] Maybe they ambushed him." Holding up his shot-glass he exclaimed, "Let's drown our grief with this!" The farmer chugged down his drink. *Who of us will be next?* He wondered.

In the fall of 1944 my Uncle Reinhold called my mother. "Paula," he said, "I have to make it short." My mother was surprised that he was able to get through to her. The phone lines had been down in many areas of Germany. "You have to at least get the children out of Thorn. The violin teacher, Mr. Sternmann leaves tomorrow for Cottbus. He can take the girls with him. I'll wait for them in Cottbus. I'll bring them to Klostermansfeld." *Click.* He hung up before my mother could answer or have any other suggestions. She was grateful that Uncle Reinhold had made arrangements with the violinist to bring us to Oma. Only my ten-year-old sister Hildegard

---

107   Also known as D-Day (June.6, 1944). At the Battle of Normandy the Allied forces diminished the German army and the end of Nazi Germany followed. News of fallen or missing soldiers was often slow to reach their relatives.

108   On April 6, 1941, Adolf Hitler ordered German forces, backed by Axis allies, to invade Yugoslavia and Greece. Yugoslavia was defeated, but no efficient occupational forces could be employed because of Operation Barbarossa against Russia. Therefore, partisans were able to commit their notorious cruelties.

and I were still with my mother in Thorn. Ernst was already in Thuringia, where he attended the Adolf Hitler School, and Grandma had taken little Reinhold with her when she returned to St. Bernhard.

My mother could not leave right away. After we had moved to Thorn we had enough room to accommodate families who were house or apartment hunting. My parents had offered their assistance to the town authorities who placed newcomers with native German families until they could locate a suitable home for themselves. Currently, Mr. and Mrs. Reusel rented a room from us. Now my mother had to help them to make arrangements for another place to stay in Thorn. She also had to take care of Father's office. In the back of her mind lurked the fear that she never would come back to Thorn after forsaking our apartment. What about our furniture, our dishes, the 800- carat silverware, Father's hunting guns, Ernst's coin collection, her daughters' favorite toys, the bedding, the curtains, and so much more?

She contacted the violinist and said; "Reinhold Seume told me you are willing to take my two girls with you to Cottbus. Can you take a few suitcases as well?"

He replied, "No problem, Mrs. Höfer. I only have one briefcase."

The next day, we stood alongside of the teacher on the platform of the station. The train arrived. It was already overflowing with passengers. Mr. Sternmann managed to squeeze into one of the compartments somehow. The locomotive pulled out of the terminal … and we? We still stood with Mother in front of the empty tracks. There had been no chance to enter the train, let alone follow the violinist.

"That's it," Mother said. "Next time, we go together."

We went back to our apartment. Mother took care of all the pressing errands, and then she packed only one suitcase.

Two days later, we were at the station again. While Mother stood in line to exchange our tickets and obtain one for herself, I observed posters that warned against spying enemies. One showed two masons working on a wall, talking to each other. A man's shadow covered both men. Behind the back of the one worker was the warning, "Pst—Feind hört mit." ("Hush—enemy is eavesdropping.") The Nazis warned us about enemy spies who supposedly used terrible, despicable, cruel means to obtain secret information so they could defeat Germany.

The Hitler government officials were instructed to discourage us from fleeing the encroaching Soviet Union army. Actually, they wanted totality— either Germans won the war or all Germans should perish. Many Germans started to doubt Goebbels' speeches. They started to doubt the reports on the radio or in newspapers, in which they read about an orderly retreat of the German military. We lost hope in those wonder weapons we had heard about. Scientists had allegedly developed and worked on them near the Baltic Sea. Would these be ready for combat soon enough to turn the war around for Germany?

My mother informed us, "We have to be on platform four for our train." We went down the steps to the underpass that leads to all railroad tracks of the Thorn city station. We followed the tunnel like structure underneath the platform for the first and second tracks, passed the stairs leading to them and took the staircase to the platform for the third and fourth tracks. Many people stood there, waiting for the train to arrive. My mother was anxious about how she could get close enough to the incoming train so that she could reach the door before others would. After the disastrous experience of trying to enter the compartments two days before, my mother instructed us, "You have to stay close to me. Ilse-Rose, you hold on to the suitcase. Hildegard, you hold my hand. When I reach for the door handle, grab my skirt and don't let go."

Then we heard a pleasant female voice over the loudspeaker: "Attention, attention. The train to Cottbus will not leave from platform four. It will leave from platform eleven." The whole mass of people who were waiting became one huge wave of movement. We were pressed against the banister, not able to reach the steps. The people dashed like mad to get to platform eleven.

Mother sighed, "So be it." She waited until the crowd thinned out and then went with us to the Red Cross station. "Would you have some milk for my girls, please?" Mother pleaded.

The nurse inquired, "Do you have your ration cards with you?"

"Yes, here they are. This one for my daughter, Hildegard, and this one for Ilse-Rose." The woman snipped several squares off the card and gave us a small cup of milk. Mother saw the amount of milk-stamps the nurse had cut off and gave her a puzzled look.

The woman shrugged her shoulders. "That is all the milk I have."

Hildegard and I shared the little cup, while my mother inquired about the train. "Do you have any idea if the train to Cottbus will be punctual?" The nurse told her that she was not the information booth. At that moment, we heard a sonorous voice behind us. "Lady, don't even try to make this train. People have been at this station for two days already. Everybody tries to get to the center of Germany. The tracks around Berlin are bombed. No train goes there."

"But I bought tickets to Klostermansfeld via Cottbus and Halle on the Saale," my mother informed him.

The owner of the deep voice motioned her to the corner of the room. I clung to the suitcase, Hildegard to Mother's skirt. He whispered, "Take a different route. Go via Posen. That train leaves in an hour from now on platform four. In Posen, you take another train route to Cottbus. That one is scheduled to arrive at the platform right across from where the Posen train stops. In Cottbus, ask for the train to Halle with railroad cars designated for Göttingen."

My mother was not sure if she should trust this man. She saw that he did wear the typical railroad outfit. He had a little coal dust in his whiskers and eyebrows; maybe he was the stoker or boiler man of a locomotive. "Thank you!" she said.

He continued to advise her. "And lady, go to the front of the platform. There are the cars reserved for the military; they will let you enter with those lovely young girls of yours." It was true children were loved, and often the soldiers made room for them. Mother paid for the milk, thinking, *I hardly have enough ration stamps for milk left for my girls ... but at Oma's, there are cows, and where there are cows, there is milk.*

121

We had to go back to the ticket booth to exchange our boarding passes. The station hall was crowded. Long lines had formed in front of the little windows behind which the railroad clerks sold the tickets. Mother looked at the clock; the line moved ever so slowly. She had to get back to platform four in time to reach the front cars of the train to Posen. After forty-five minutes, she knew we would not make it. She left the line and went with us to platform four—but first, we had to pass the control booth again, where they punch a hole in your ticket. The railroad clerk, without looking at my mother, mentioned, matter-of-factly, "Your tickets are already punched."

"Yes, I know, but we were unable to get the train to Cottbus from platform eleven," she tried to explain, anxious about the further delay.

The people behind us pushed against us. We clung to Mother, pressed between the gate and luggage. The clerk looked up and—waved us through, yelling, "Good luck!"

Platform four looked deserted. We were able to walk to the front part of it. At that moment, the train rolled in. Would it ever stop? We saw the uniformed men in the first cars. The train slowed down and came to a screeching halt. The military cars stood beyond the platform, where it ended in grass. We stumbled off the concrete walk and through the vegetation. During this time, people streamed from all the other platforms toward our location. Apparently, everybody was hoping to enter this train, but the wagons were already filled with soldiers who were being ordered to the Western Front[109] and with many civilians who, just like us, were trying to leave East and West Prussia.

My mother is not tall, and not having a platform to stand on, she hardly could reach the handle of the compartment door. Some people had caught up to us. They pushed Mother aside. Somebody pulled me into the car. Another person grabbed Hildegard, but where was Mother? The soldiers were standing in the passageway; the compartments were filled.

---

109   Soldiers were pulled from the Eastern Front to fight on the Western Front because German intelligence hoped that Stalin would delay the Soviet offensive once the German assault in the west (Ardennes) had begun and wait for the outcome before launching his offense.

They passed us over their heads to the middle of the wagon, where they put us into one compartment. We cried,

"Mother, our mother!"

We heard her yelling outside,

"Hildegard, Ilse-Rose, where are you? Where are my children?" Her voice was filled with panic.

"Hello, Mom, here they are," a soldier called, leaning out of the window. "Give me your suitcase." He lifted it into the compartment above everybody's head into the nets above the seats, and then he reached out again. The train had started to move already.

"Fast, Mom, your hands," he shouted. My mother threw up her arms and the soldier lifted her right through the window into the car. Not until she was inside did the train roll faster. The conductor had watched the whole maneuver and made sure we were not separated. Was he the man with the deep voice we had met at the Red Cross station?

My mother breathed a silent prayer *Gott sei Dank (God be thanked!)*. She stood between two soldiers, not able to even turn around. I sat on the lap of one and Hildegard was crammed between two more. Seeing the anxious look on my mother's face, they handed us to the place where she stood, squeezed in between everyone else. During the trip to Posen we stayed in our positions, unable to move, let alone go anywhere else from there. Mother explained to the soldiers that we had to take another train in Posen. Two of them told her they also had to depart there and take the train to Cottbus. They would help her.

In Posen they and we climbed out of the window. The ones left behind handed us the suitcase. We followed the two uniformed men, who had special privileges to get through the controls. When asked about us, they just said, "They are with us." We found the platform with the train already waiting and followed the soldiers into a compartment. Soon we were on our way to Cottbus.

Again the train was overcrowded, but those soldiers even secured a place for my mother to sit. I leaned against her.

"Where is Hildegard?" my mother called out.

My sister answered, "I am behind these big boxes. Somebody put them in front of the WC while I was using it." They had placed huge artists' cases in front of the toilet door, not noticing that my sister was in there. One of the soldiers leaned against the containers, reached over, and grabbed Hildegard. He pulled her out and handed her again over the heads of all the people down the wagon to where we were. We took turns sitting on Mother's lap during the long ride before reaching Cottbus. Here, the track to Halle was still in working order. We were able to get on a train that had some cars designated for Göttingen. These would be dislodged in Halle and connected to another train, which stopped in Klostermansfeld.

By the time we departed Cottbus, the train was so overcrowded that people were standing outside on the wagon steps and hanging from the compartment doors. Fortunately, we had reached our Göttingen car early. Our luck lasted until we reached Halle. Here, everybody had to leave the train because a full alarm howled over the city. An air raid was in progress. All of us were directed to the station's waiting rooms or a bunker outside of the terminal. When we arrived at the bombing shelter, it was closed. An elderly man with an "official" band on his upper arm told us to go back to the station's waiting room since the place was full. We returned and sat on our suitcase, waiting for the high pitched alarm announcing "all clear"[110].

By now, people asked a consistent question all over Germany, "Will we get out of all this alive?"

The bunkers could be a deathtrap. Some people said, "Don't go in a cellar. There, you are cornered. There is no way out. You suffocate or burn to death." We actually might have been lucky not to sit in a bunker. My mother had seated us close to the door. A man wanted to order us farther into the room. Mother only said, "No, we have to stay here until the bombing raid is over." He did not argue. Bombs were falling, and he

---

110 The warning system for civilians was organized: First, we heard the forewarning. Usually we had a few minutes to get our emergency knapsack or suitcase and gas mask together and go to a shelter. Next, we heard the full warning. Usually now the bombs were starting to fly. After the planes left, we heard the "all clear" and then we could leave the shelters.

crawled back to the others. "Put your hands over your ears and bend your heads on your knees!" Mother said and covered her own ears. With each bomb the whole room shook, and dust mixed with smoke poured into the shattered windows. Mother yelled over the noise, "Cover your mouth and nose with your hankies."

Finally, we heard the short rhythmical blare of warning sirens announcing: "No more danger!" The station had been bombed. Tracks were torn apart. The sound system was broken. Where could we go? We had to find out if we could continue to Klostermansfeld. Which platform was still accessible? After a long clatter filled time due to the repair work and avoiding the dust clouds, we heard a train entering the station. My mother asked if it would stop in Klostermanfeld.

"Yes, it does," they said. We could not use the demolished underpass. We had to climb over twisted tracks. My mother pushed us into an already overly filled car.

Klostermansfeld is not far from Halle. When we arrived at our destination, not one of our relatives was there to give us a lift to the farm. We girls and Uncle Reinhold had been expected two or three days earlier. "We have to walk to Oma's," Mother sighed. She headed to the luggage storage room and lifted the suitcase onto a low counter.

"May we keep this suitcase here until tomorrow?" she asked. The clerk wanted to know if he should ship it ahead of us to another destination.

"No, no," Mother assured him. "We stay here. I cannot carry the suitcase any further. Somebody will pick it up tomorrow." After the clerk handed her a claim ticket, we walked the long way to Uncle Martin's farm.

We arrived overly tired. Had we traveled one day or two? I do not remember. Before the war, it took about twenty hours to go from Thorn to Oma's. When we visited her or when they came to see us, one often stayed overnight with Aunt Ursel's mother in Cottbus or at Aunt Bohne's apartment in Berlin and then continued the trip the next day. By now staying in either one of these cities was out of the question—too many bombing raids!

CHAPTER 6

The Lord helps them and rescues them; he rescues them from the wicked, and saves them, because they take refuge in him. Psalm 37:40

Towards the End of WWII
Winter 1944-45

It was in late fall of 1944 in the early evening when we entered the old familiar farmhouse. Oma had prepared my bed in her room and a bed for Hildegard in the adjacent transit room that led to the master bedroom. Mother could sleep in the guest room near the formal dining room, but first, we had to drink and eat something. There had been no nourishment for us since we drank the scanty cup of milk in Thorn.

We soon noticed that our relatives' life had changed. The household helpers periodically extended the noon dinner table. From now on many relatives, friends, and others who had lost their homes, came to hospitable Oemlers seeking room and board.

Aunt Ursel's sister, Aunt Bitta, and her husband were among the first to search for shelter. I met Uncle Nold, who had been drafted and ordered to bring his horses with him into the military. He expected to be in the cavalry, but he had been placed in the bicycle infantry fighting against the Soviets[111], although his stallions were very welcomed by the army. Now he was on leave, because he nursed a nasty wound on his leg.

Germans, especially in rural areas, had to make room for the countless relocated people: the evacuees, refugees, and fugitives. Many city people had lost their apartments and houses. The destruction of civilian housing culminated in 1945, when the British government decided to demoralize

---

111   In World War II, most of the transports near the battle scenes were still done by horses.

the German people by constantly bombarding cities, towns, and villages. Bombs had fallen on industrial cities before, but now culture centers like Dresden, called Elb-Florence[112], were destroyed in an attempt to halt Germany's war efforts by discouraging the civilians. It did not work for the Allies. German civilians only resented the enemy more.

In spite of the bleak times, German traditions continued in 1944. Grown-ups did not want us children to go without some Yuletide celebration. A few days before Christmas Eve, Oma asked the owner of the grocery store to act as Santa. We were lined up against the wall of the hallway. Santa came and—oh goodness gracious—he knew all about our blunders and bad behavior. He warned us to be good … or else! He had some sweets for us after we recited a poem and sang some songs. During the Advent season our teachers taught us Hohe Nacht der klaren Sterne[113] supposedly a Christmas song. I liked it almost as much as Stille Nacht Heilige Nacht [Silent Night]. I knew it by heart just as the longest poem, which I recited with gusto. The grown-ups were impressed, but it did not earn me anything extra.

This time the tree was in the formal dining room upstairs. It stood in the middle of the long table. Our presents were placed around it. Hildegard and I did not need much space for our gifts; we only had one each. Grandma had managed to send a sweater for Hildegard and a pair of knitted knee socks for me. My three younger cousins—baby Jochen had joined his brothers, Hermjörg, and Lutz—received the most. My mother just expressed her feelings by hugging Hildegard and me whispering, "The best for me is that you are alive and we have a good place to stay with Oma." Turning to Uncle Martin, she indicated that she needed to go back to Thorn.

"I must try to get more things from there. The girls need dresses, pullovers, blouses, skirts, and shoes. And my sons," she sighed, "I hope

---

112   Elb-Florance because Dresden, located on the river Elbe, possessed many art-treasures.

113   "High Night of clear stars". It reminds one of "Stille Nacht, heilige Nacht" (Silent Night), but has no real Christian undertones.

Ernst and Reinhold are safe." The thought of her sons brought tears to her eyes. She swallowed hard and said softly, "When they join us, they will have grown and need different clothing, too. We only could take one suitcase with us."

Oma tried to discourage her return to the approaching Eastern Front. "Paula, don't go back East. We can help you and supply what you and your children need." Mother knew they would do that, but still, there were matters in Thorn that had to be taken care of. She needed to go back in January of 1945.

My sister and I stayed with Oma. My mother had been with us for Christmas, but now she had left for Thorn hoping to get more of our belongings. She would try to make arrangements to even have our furniture shipped to Klostermansfeld. It was a hopeless dream.

On the radio, we heard about the "orderly retreat" in which the German troops were engaged.

Now the German soldiers came closer and closer. Some deserters had passed by our farm already. Usually they were hungry and nursing wounds. They brought bad news with them. Oma quietly gave away civilian clothing and food. She did this secretly, of course, or she would have been imprisoned for helping deserters and the soldiers would have been shot. She had to be especially careful since new families lived with us. Nobody knew enough about them. They might have been tempted to disclose information to the police, hoping to receive a favor in return.

Everybody wondered how close the Soviets were to West Prussia. Was Mother safe? We did not dare to ask. Oma knew how to ease our worries. She allowed us to play in the upper attic and snoop around in the stored treasures from her past.

"How many interesting pieces of china Oma has!" my sister marveled. "Look here at this vase!" She held up a light green vase that was formed in the shape of a slender hand holding a cornucopia. There was even a pearl on the ring finger. It was a perfect example of the Art Nouveau movement (also called *Jugendstil* or "Secession") around the turn of the century. A doll service for twelve that was painted with little roses intrigued us. We found pretty decorated glass and porcelain lampshades that belonged on oil lamps. They were brought downstairs to be used again, since the electricity was often turned off.

In the middle of January, we still had not heard from our mother. Refugees passing through Klostermansfeld told us that the Soviet troops had taken Danzig, a harbor city not far from Thorn. We were used to not knowing where our father was. He fought at the Eastern Front, as so many of our friends' fathers and brothers did, but what about Mother? She was supposed to be with us. She never would leave us. Was she still alive?

Many women shared the same anxiety about their loved ones. What would the future bring? That was the big question for all Germans, even us children. We wondered why young brides and wives looked at coffee grounds or tea leaves, or held their wedding ring fastened to a string over a cup to find out if their fiancée or spouse was still alive. Our mother had told us, "Don't believe in these things. It is stupid to think that coffee or tea can predict the future, and if a ring will circle to the right or left over a cup and then bang against its rim—that depends on the shakiness of the holder's hand."

Oma frowned upon superstition. "Black cats, the number 13, and all of that stuff is nonsense," she said. "Our address is Thondorfer Street 13, but nobody can call us unlucky."

Between late fall of 1944 and spring 1945, the Allies had set up a regular schedule to bomb Berlin at noon. Therefore, our school hours had changed accordingly. Hildegard and I left very early, so we could be back home by lunchtime. Our classes started at 7 AM. The bomber and fighter aircrafts often flew over our area. There was always the possibility of a damaged plane. In this case, the pilot unloaded the bombs, released the fuel tanks, and finally jumped out. German civilians converted the discarded tanks into canoes.

A disabled twin-engine had landed on the high mining refuse mound near our farm. After it burned out, people tried to salvage whatever possible. We could use everything. Civilian merchandise had been scaled down to the absolute minimum, since Germany's factory production focused on the military. The women coveted the silk from the parachutes, if they could get hold of them before the government confiscated them for the German military.

Radio announcers continued to talk about an orderly withdrawal of the German army. "That is a lie!" Oma said bluntly. She knew. She had already secretly helped some soldiers who had deserted, fleeing the Russian onslaught. But nobody had seen her do it. We just heard about it as a gossip. Between our stables and the walled-in garden of the neighbor stood two military medical cars. The medics fled on foot; their ambulances were out of gasoline. Our MD had permission to retrieve the medical supplies. After that, we children rummaged through the vehicles until the police stopped us. Mother on the way to Thorn also encountered bombing raids. She had to leave the train in Stettin and stay in a bunker. Bombs were falling in carpet fashion.[114] A few hours later running back to the station, she had to avoid the burning phosphor flowing through the streets. She never talked much about it. I do not know how she survived that bombing attack.

We in Klostermansfeld experienced how a stray plane, damaged by flak, dumped its phosphor bombs. One of them fell on the farmer's stable up the street from us. "He is the only Communist farmer in our village," I heard people gossiping. *Communist* was a word I would hear more often from then on. It was usually connected with horror.

When the bombs fell, my uncle stood on the roof above his grain storage room. He gripped an iron bar cemented into the wall. He told us that he had to hold onto it with all his might, or else the air pressure created by that bomb would have pushed him off the roof. He never came into the cellar when the alarm sounded. He would walk to his vantage point where he could watch all of his animals in their stables, ready to calm them if they became nervous.

---

114   Also known as carpet-bombing. A group of planes would fly in a "V" formation and release bombs from each aircraft simultaneously. This was another attempt to demoralize civilians.

During a British night air raid on Halle, he called me out of the cellar, which served as our bomb shelter. "Ilse-Rose, come upstairs! I want to show you the best fireworks you'll ever see." We stood in the front of the house close to the entrance. The sky was lit up with "Christmas trees" slowly gliding downward. They were actually flares that the British planes dropped to mark targets for the following fighter-bombers. The "Christmas trees," as civilians called them, hovered in the air.

"What is that?" I asked my Uncle Martin.

He explained, "They are flares. Detonators create these flares, which are hanging on a parachute. You'll see them slowly float down to our fields."

Nowadays, when we in America celebrate special days with fireworks, I always think back to the quiet display I saw that night and that unforgettable illuminated sky.

Soon after we had arrived from Thorn, my uncle was ordered to take in a mother with her seven children. They had fled since the Soviets had entered Silesia. My aunt asked her servants to clear out one of my grandfather's laboratory rooms. It was big enough for a little cook stove, a table, some chairs, and several bunk beds, although the smallest children had to share a mattress. That became almost normal. Soon, Hildegard and I also slept in a bed together when Mother returned and had to let us sleep in her room.

My mother after her exhausting trip to and from Thorn; her face shows how fatigued she was in early February 1945.

Mother had left Thorn on the last locomotive, abandoning the town before the Soviets entered. Because of her former connections in Thorn, she was able to bring the big painted hope chest that used to stand in the hallway. It was loaded into the coal tender of the last locomotive leaving Thorn. Through bombing raids, emergency repairs of destroyed railroad tracks, and many detours, she managed to get the trunk to Klostermansfeld. It contained featherbeds, Father's expensive hunting guns, some clothing for our family—especially a civilian suit for Father—Hildegard's favorite doll, my teddy, some silverware, and some dishes.

After my mother arrived, her first question was about her sons. Had anybody heard from them? Was there a message from the town where Ernst went to the Adolf Hitler School? Did he get drafted like so many others his age? Had he been killed already or imprisoned? Reinhold had been with Grandma, living in a tiny village in Thuringia. Was he alive? Bombs had fallen on a city near them. Were they affected? Where was Father? Was he in a prison camp? Was he missing in action? Was he killed—or might he have deserted, too?

Sleeping facilities became scarce in the old farmhouse. Mrs. Kleefeld, with her four children, still occupied the two rooms upstairs in the add-on yellow brick building and downstairs, the family from Silesia with their seven children made due in the former laboratory turned into living quarters for them.

Oma had given up her bedroom so it could be converted into a delivery room for Aunt Bitta. She would give birth any day now. She preferred home to a hospital. Anyway, by now, it was almost impossible to get a bed there, let alone a room. The hospitals had been bombed, despite being marked with huge Red Crosses[115] on their roofs. There was also a severe lack of doctors. They had been called away to take care of the many wounded soldiers and the worn-out, displaced, or fleeing civilians.

Mother's bedroom was located behind the formal dining room at the other end of the house. Aunt Ursel had moved us as far away as possible from Oma's room, so we girls would not witness Aunt Bitta in labor. The former guest room was too small for three beds. Therefore, Hildegard would lie with her head close to my feet, and I would rest the opposite way. In that manner, we both fit best on the narrow mattress. Sometimes when Mother got up early one of us girls would crawl into her bed to sleep a little longer.

Aunt Ursel often walked through our room. It led to a temporary pantry where she stored the preserved fruit and vegetables. By now, shortage of food had become normal for Germans. It was not wise to store our winter provisions in the readily accessible pantry near the big farm kitchen where many people worked. They brought their children with them in the afternoon hours. They could easily enter the pantry and help themselves. Therefore, the walk-in closet in our bedroom had been converted into a pantry, and the formal dining room was locked. Aunt Ursel showed us where she kept the key. "Do not tell anybody," she warned us, "and always lock the doors behind you." The bathroom near

---

115   The Nazi regime started to mark factories for military production with a Red Cross, hoping they would not be destroyed. This method worked for a short time until British intelligence got wind of it, with the result that now most buildings marked with a Red Cross were bombed.

the master bedroom was also used to store food. My aunt stocked more food than usual. She anticipated that her servants, many relatives, and friends would come and seek refuge in the always-hospitable farmhouse in the coming year.

Uncle Martin did not know if he could harvest any crops in 1945. His fields could become battlegrounds or be bombed. "So many mouths to feed," he said. "Such uncertainty where our food will come from. Better put what we have in a safe place, Ursel." She agreed with him and showed him the bundle of keys she had for the bedrooms and makeshift pantries.

Our mothers liked to take us away when Uncle Martin had to arrange certain events, like sterilization of young roosters, or a cow in heat was taken to the bull for breeding purposes. Then they took us on a long walk as far away from the farm as possible.

For our excursions they often chose the several kilometers long walk to a castle near Mansfeld. We loved this time with our mothers and cousins. Sometimes we stopped to play Tag or Hide and Seek in the woods. I always liked to gather flowers, or sprigs from early greening bushes.

February 1945: clockwise from lower left: Lutz, Aunt Ursel, Aunt Bitta Hosie, Hermjörg, Hildegard, my mother, Ilse-Rose, Michael, Aunt Bitta's son in the baby carriage.

Until April 1945, we still started our school day by honoring the flag of the Third Reich with the traditional Hitler salute. Sometimes Miss Karsdorf would ask us to hold up our right arm for a long time. "Our brave soldiers at the front are suffering a lot. You can stand holding up your arm for them for that short time!" She scrutinized every one of us little girls to see if our arm was extended high enough while singing one of the many songs meant to make us proud of our Fatherland, our heritage, and our Führer. Our right arm got so tired, but we were not allowed to support it with our left hand. She told us of the Spartans and how much we, her pupils, could become tough like them. Her slogan was, "Work hard, and fight for the Third Reich." She actually made us feel responsible for the fate of Germany.

New pupils entered our class. One was from the Balkan states. Miss Karsdorf made her stand in front of us and pointed to her brown arms. "This is a hardworking girl. She has arms like steel. Look, she is tanned from long hours harvesting in the sun, wind, and rain." We were supposed to admire her. She stood there and looked rather embarrassed.

At recess, I turned to Klärchen. "Maybe all the stuff Miss Karsdorf says about her brown, muscular arms is not true."

Klärchen informed me that her father had met the Balkan family. Their mother had told him how they came to Klostermansfeld. Klärchen said, "She might not have harvested, but rather has been toughened and tanned from the long trek she and her family had to endure before they reached central Germany."

I drew my conclusion and agreed. "Just the same thing that the Silesian family had to go through before they came to us. You know, their little girl is very sick. Oma tried to reach a doctor for her."

The plight of the Silesian family had not ended when they received shelter and food. Their little four-year-old girl succumbed to tuberculosis. Her mother told Oma that it was too late for a doctor. She had already died. Oma helped her wrap the little body in a white lace dress that was made from one of Oma's pretty nightgowns. I was allowed to look at her. With her black hair draped in locks over her chest and a wreath of flowers on her head, she looked like a little angel. I found her very pretty, just as beautiful as my classmate in Thorn had looked when we buried her in the old Polish tradition, but the little deceased four-year-old did not lie in a church. She lay on a blanket on the floor of Grandpa's second former laboratory, the only room not yet converted into shelter for evacuees or fugitives.

Before her burial, I begged Oma, "May I see her again? She is so pretty."

Oma nodded, took the key from the wall, and walked with me to the laboratory. "Wait behind me until I get that door unlocked," she said to me. She opened the door and looked into the twilit room. She stepped back and abruptly closed the door. I looked at her questioningly. "Ilse-Rose, my child," Oma sighed. "I don't want you to look at her again." There was tenderness mixed with firmness in her voice. *Do I see tears in Oma's eyes?* I thought to myself. *I will not plead with her anymore.*

That afternoon, I overheard a conversation between Uncle Martin and Oma. "You have to contact the priest today," she said.

"Dear me, woman! I have more to do than run after a priest," he told her.

"The little girl has to be buried today," Oma insisted.

"Why? She has only been dead for a day and a half. Her mother wanted to wait until she could get some relatives here for the funeral." My uncle grew impatient.

Oma disclosed, "Martin, the rats have gnawed at her." That settled it. Uncle Martin went to make funeral arrangements for the Silesian family. Now I knew why Oma did not want me to see the little dead girl again. It must have been a horrible sight, after the rats had eaten away on her face and body.

In April my brother arrived. For over a week he had walked with his best friend, Hermann, through the Thuringia Mountains to Klostermansfeld. Hermann was not allowed to go home, because his family most likely had been evacuated. They had to leave their house, which was in a battle zone where the Germans still fought the British.

Another plane had crashed on top of the high spoils from the copper mines and was pilfered by the villagers. The pilot's parachute had been caught on the steeple of the Catholic church. It took the men of the village longer than necessary to get him down. He was wounded and half dead, they said. I heard, too, that they delayed his rescue because they had a lengthy debate. Some of the men wanted to shoot him. They argued, "After all, he dropped bombs on our houses."

Two huge craters in Uncle Martin's fields bore witness to the terrible, destructive power these explosives had. They created such strong air pressure that the tiled roofs of the houses flew off the buildings, and all the windows were shattered. Chunks of red roof tiles and glass splinters lay everywhere. Now our school was cancelled. The air pressure of the bombs' impacts had blown out the windows of the building. Our old farmhouse was about half a mile away. Nevertheless, we did not see any damage to it. These old cloister walls had held up during many wars that raged over Germany in the last six hundred years. They held up again against modern, technologically advanced military forces. My grandparents, anticipating air attacks in WWI, had installed thick oaken shutters to protect the windowpanes.

I was not allowed to roam around anymore. I had to stay close to home and tell my family of every move I wanted to make. Still, during the midday rest, Oma continued to give me some errands to run. She seemed oblivious to the danger I might be in at that time. I trusted her and took the food to its destination. Often, these little errands would coincide with other jobs I had to do for Uncle Martin or Aunt Ursel. I had to bring foodstuffs to the shopkeepers, from whom they got hidden-away merchandise— "Friedensware."[116] I had to do it when their stores were closed to the public during the midday rest. By 1944–45 the food ration was calculated to a minimum for individual survival, and civilian consumer goods were of inferior quality. Everything was reduced to the mere basics— "Kriegsware."[117] Bartering became the way of payment,

---

116   *Friedensware* was excellent, solid "goods" left from Germany's peacetime.

117   "Kriegsware" consisted of shoddy products, made as cheaply as possible.

as is typical when the black market flourishes. For food, one even could get good quality merchandise that had been hidden away like a good-smelling bar of soap. Yes, even soap was considered a luxury. Certain soap was made from animal bones. It was rather brittle and had a peculiar smell. We used it for the laundry. A few years after the war, I heard some people claim that the bones did not come from animals, but rather from the humans who were killed in prisons or concentration camps. This became a persistent rumor.

American and British pilots had been ordered to strafe civilians on the assumption that this was also an effective way of demoralizing the Germans. The possibility of being strafed was remote for us until the beginning of April 1945. By then, our school was closed. We stayed around our own house or at friends who lived nearby. We discussed strafing with four of our most trusted teenaged boys: My cousin Klaus, my brother Ernst, his friend Hermann, and the neighbor boy Horst.

Klaus came to visit Uncle Martin and later went to Aunt Magda and Uncle Richard, since they had only one child, their daughter Ingrid, and therefore more room in their farmhouse. Klaus' mother, Aunt Hilde, thought that her son was safer in Middle Germany either at Oma's or her sister Magda's place. The only bomb that was ever dropped on Heidelberg[118] fell in Aunt Hilde's garden. She feared that more bombs would fall on their town. From a few miles away, they witnessed the numerous bombardments of Mannheim and Ludwigshafen. They watched the squadrons of planes flying over them, and then saw the sky above these two neighboring cities turning fiery red.

Horst Bollman, who lived close to the farm, was Uncle Martin's HJ farm helper.[119] He and Klaus, along with my brother Ernst and his friend Hermann, told us how to avoid the machine-gun fire from American planes. But they had conflicting opinions about what action to take.

---

118   The western Allies agreed to keep certain places intact, since they wanted to station their headquarters there. Heidelberg was one of them.

119   The Hitler Jugend boys, too young to fight in the war, had to help at home. In rural areas, they mostly did farm work.

"Stay close to the house walls! Duck under windowsills! Run into house entrances! Run right at the plane; they fly so fast, they'll shoot right over you! Stay under trees! Lie down flat on the ground, because they think you are already dead! Whatever you do, don't stay close together!"

⤜⤜⤜⤜⤜

In April 1945, the farmer, innkeeper, headmaster, mayor, and the evacuees from Hamburg, Leipzig, and Berlin met at the village square before they had to leave for the trenches near the village. They were called with their Volkssturm[120] unit to defend Germany. The headmaster reiterated Josef Goebbels' speech: "Every house in Germany is a castle. Each one of us has to defend it until the last drop of our blood is spent. Goebbels asked us if we wanted cannons rather than butter. All of us yelled, 'Cannons!' And he asked us, too, if we wanted *den totalen Krieg* (the total war), and we shouted, 'Yes!' I would rather perish than give the enemy the satisfaction of destroying our Aryan blood and soil."

The farmer wondered about the logic of the headmaster's last remark. *Doesn't he give the enemy satisfaction if he, belonging to the Aryan race, dies?*

In the background, everybody could hear the gunfire of a nearby battle. The mayor said, "We are in the middle of it. In the north, the British are fighting, in the west, it's the Americans, and in the east, the Russians. We will have to battle the Americans. The rumble and explosions sound like American weapons. How will they treat us when they defeat us?"

"Nobody will defeat us!" the headmaster exploded. "If we talk like this, we will defeat ourselves. We will deserve to be defeated. Don't forget, we are of the best Aryan stock." The full alarm sounded. "Now they try to demoralize us," he thundered. "Like they could do that!"[121]

---

120 The Volkssturm is a people's national militia, which Hitler activated in October 1944. The Hitler Jugend, invalids, elderly, and men formerly marked as unfit belonged to it.

121 The remark of the headmaster was correct. The bombing raids, strafing, and bombing squadrons flying over us did not demoralize us. They had the opposite effect. Instead of stealing from our neighbors or murdering each other, most

"I have to look after my animals," the farmer declared. "One of my horses always shies when it hears the sirens." He grabbed his cap and left. Suddenly, they heard a drawn out high pitched whistle and shortly after, a loud bang. A bomb had fallen onto the farmer's stable. The barn started to burn. The fire alarm whined at the same time as the "all clear" sounded. Instead of marching to their assigned trench, the men went to help the firefighters as they rescued the animals and extinguished the flames. Only the headmaster and the innkeeper went to the trenches, mumbling to each other, "All of them are deserters. They ought to be shot."

In April, when the fighting closed in on us, we did not know who would enter our village first. Would it be the Russians or the Americans? We prayed it would be the Americans. If it were the Russians, all women had to be hidden. We had heard horrible stories about how they treated civilians. My mother feared even for us girls. Fugitives told us that the Soviets took all jewelry from the women before they raped them. If a woman could not get her wedding ring off her finger fast enough, they would cut her finger off. They would rip earrings out of earlobes, and tear golden chains from necks. They said, "Russian soldiers flaunt six, eight watches on one arm." All of us children had nightmares. We prayed that our father would come home safely. Where was he? He had fought on the eastern front against those terrible Russians.

Two days before the enemy entered Klostermansfeld, we watched clouds of airplanes block out the sun. That was another method of trying to undermine the morale of the German people. Our mayor had to tell us to defend the village, but many women pulled white bed sheets out of the drawers, ready to hang them out of the windows as a sign that we would not fight. Oma asked, "How can we defend against these clouds of airplanes?"

When the first enemy soldiers entered our village, everybody breathed a sigh of relief. They wore American uniforms. At that time, my uncle disappeared. Was he with the Volkssturm? Was he hiding somewhere

---

Germans held together and helped each other, making room wherever they could and sharing the little they had.

where the Polish and Russian civil workers would not find him? What would happen to him—and us—when the Americans liberated these prisoners of war turned civil workers?

We heard a knock at the heavy oak door. My mother answered it. She was the only one who knew some English. I listened for any sound from the hallway. I heard the door open, some words—not unfriendly—and then ... quiet. What was going on out there? Oma, our aunts, and their children huddled together in the Wirtschaftsstube. We heard footsteps through the hallway, into the courtyard, and soon back again. Then we listened to the way the door was closed. My mother came to us. "It is okay," she said. "The young American soldier spoke German. He spoke with a Bavarian accent. He said to stay inside until the 'all clear' alarm sounds," she continued. "They still have to check many streets in Klostermansfeld. There is a curfew for today, and probably for weeks to come. We may feed the animals and milk the cows."

Oma said, "I am glad we have Horst, Ernst, and Hermann here to help. The Polish and Russian civil workers will be set free by the Americans. They do not need to work for us anymore." At that moment, the three teenagers entered the dining room.

My mother turned to them and said, "Mr. Rosenhahn will help you with feeding and milking the cows. Then the horses have to be fed and led to the trough to drink; the cows need their turn after them. Pump fresh water for them." The boys were eager to help. Aunt Ursel and my mother admonished them to be friendly to the Polish workers and let them roam freely throughout the premises. "We have to be prepared for the worst," my aunt said, holding her youngest son in her arms.

The walled-in courtyard—cover during so many wars—again supplied shelter for animals and humans. We could observe the curfew and still take care of the livestock, since we did not need to cross any streets to feed them.

In the next chaotic days, this courtyard was our refuge from liberated civil workers. Horst Bollmann saw the Russian civil workers from the Zirkel Mine plundering houses, beating people, and killing some. Our three Ukrainian women, the last of the civil workers we had to take in, ran outside to greet the Americans. They were ordered to stay out of their way. I never saw them again.

How would our Poles behave after the Americans liberated them? We saw them gather heavy sticks and clubs. *Good that Uncle Martin is not here,* we thought. My mother commanded us to stay in the house—better yet, to go into the cellar. Three of the Polish workers suddenly ran through our hallway and positioned themselves in front of the heavy oak door. A few of the others barricaded the big gate of the courtyard. Two of them stood at the small entrance for people. When the former Russian prisoners came to loot, our Polish civil workers defended us. They spoke with the Russians, yelled at them, and confronted them with their clubs. It did not come to a fight. None of these Russians entered our house this time.

The next day, suddenly, my uncle was back. Our civil workers demanded to go into the pantry and plunder it. Oma, grateful that they had defended us, let them enter. Actually, she had no choice, but our Polish workers were civilized, probably because we had treated them with civility. They took bread, some meats, milk, and cheese, all things they had gotten before anyway. Only now, they could gorge themselves on it. I was not there to observe this. I was at Klärchen's house. We were sitting in their kitchen when two of Uncle Martin's Poles entered without even knocking on the door or ringing the doorbell. They looked different to me.

There were so many questions left unanswered for me at that time. Why did Robert and his buddy come to Klärchen's father and demand cigarettes? Why didn't they work for Uncle Martin anymore? Why did I hear about farmers being killed by their civil workers? What right did they have to do that? Where did Russian miners come from? Why did I have to stay close to home? Why didn't our Adolf Hitler speak over the radio? Why was there a curfew? How come our teacher did not wear her NSDAP button anymore? She suddenly spoke pleasantly about the Americans. Had they not been our dreaded enemies before? Didn't she tell us that the Americans were bad people? These enemy soldiers looked just like ours; only their uniforms were different. I did not understand the change in the behavior of so many people. Fear had stricken me. At night, I mistook the shrieking meows of several cats for the crying of a baby who might be tortured by the enemy. My mind, fueled by stories, was filled with cruel images of the occupation forces.

In the following days, we had to give up all of our guns, including the wonderful double-bore hunting guns my mother had rescued in the hope chest. Their stocks had beautiful silver engravings. They were thrown in huge piles and burned. We had to hide the Nazi flag. Aunt Bitta said, "Best to cut it up and make a skirt from it for one of the girls."

Somebody said, "But the war is not over yet. What will happen if we do not have the flag anymore, when Hitler comes with his wonder weapon and defeats the enemy?" Oma shook her head. *There are still dreamers among us,* she thought.

After the Americans had established some order, especially by demanding that the liberated civil workers leave and go back to their homeland, I experienced some wonderful things for the first time. The Americans gave chocolate to my mother for us children. I was surprised she took it from the enemy. She explained to us that she was their official translator, and the chocolate was like a payment for her. That was the first time I can remember eating chocolate. They offered her chewing gum, too. Mother did not want us to have it. She explained, "It is not ladylike to chew gum with an open mouth, and it is bad for your teeth." She only allowed us to chew the ones laced with the wonder drug Penicillin. It was amazing how fast our sore throats were healed by moving this type of gum around in our mouths. The Americans also gave us oranges. These were another treat I do not recall ever having eaten before.

Something else was a first for me—African American soldiers. One day, when the panzers rolled through our street again, I saw many of them walking alongside huge tanks. I was wary of these dark-skinned soldiers. I only saw them once, when they marched on the main street in front of Uncle Martin's house. They did not stay with the military dispatch in our village. Many years later, I learned that in WWII, the African American and white soldiers were separated from each other. Therefore they did not stay with the white veterans who occupied the pub near our farm.

We watched the American soldiers behave in such a relaxed manner. They would put their feet on the desk while speaking with a German. They would sit on the broad windowsills, smoke coveted cigarettes, and listen to music I had never heard before. Its rhythm was enthralling. Germans picked up the cigarette butts from the streets where they had been flicked away by the Americans. The smokers opened the butts, gathered the little tobacco left in them, and carefully put it into a cigarette paper to form their own cigarette. When they could not find any suitable paper, the edges of newspapers would do for a few puffs.

Most of the fugitives resembled hollowed out bodies held together by rags and strings. They fled on foot, a few with horse and wagon. Sometimes a mother would only have a baby carriage for her child and their belongings. They would collapse on their trek into central Germany. They did not have enough food. They carried diseases.[122] The winter of 1945 was especially hard. Many had frostbite. The elderly and the babies had the least chance of survival. Thousands died on the way. The haunting question was, "What to do with the dead?" None of the fugitives could adhere to the normal burial rituals. There were hardly any caskets, and if you could get one, it was too cumbersome to pull it along with your meager belongings on your hand wagon. Digging a grave in the deeply frozen ground was impossible. There was no time to wait for it to thaw. They had to hurry along to get away from the battle zone. Sometimes, they just had to leave the dead person in a ditch alongside of the street. One alternative was to put the frozen body in an empty sack and haul it along, hoping for an opportunity to bury it.

One day I saw the street in front of Uncle Martin's house congested with long lines of refugees coming from the east to get ahead of the

---

122 The American Medical Department was prepared to deal with diseases of displaced civilians in Germany and other European countries. The most common ones were tuberculosis, typhoid fever, scarlet fever, dysentery, diphtheria, and typhus.

advancing Soviets. They brought stories with them of atrocities committed by the victorious enemies. "They are especially dangerous when they are drunk. Most of the time, they are drunk," the refugees told us. If Uncle Reinhold had not warned my mother in the fall of 1944, we would have been among these unfortunate people. Thanks to his foresight and my mother's swift reaction, we were spared their misery.

CHAPTER 7

He makes wars cease to the end of earth; he breaks the bow,
and shatters the spear. Psalm 46: 9 a-b

The End of WWII: Germany Divided

In the last days of defending Berlin, Hitler's orders verged on insanity. He commanded that all sewers in and around Berlin be flooded, thinking that this would stop the Russian army. He did not consider that the many refugees and wounded who stayed in the makeshift housing, infirmaries and hospitals would die if his mandate should be carried out and that insurmountable sewage problems could result. Hitler took cover in his bunker, where he met daily with generals and called on armies, which no longer existed or had already surrendered to the Americans. He demanded that the mid section of Germany, still undefeated, be scorched and all factories and bridges be wrecked. In short, he ordered that Germany's entire economy and infrastructure be destroyed.

His minister of armament, Albert Speer, did not heed this command, thinking ahead about how Germany could survive and rebuild after the war. Hitler named Kriegsmarine Admiral Karl Dönitz[123] as his successor. This was probably the only sensible act Hitler decreed before he died. Dönitz, like Speer, did not want more killings and destruction by burning or flooding the country. After Hitler committed suicide on April 30, German officers, as representatives of Dönitz, met with Eisenhower near Reims to end the war on May 7. A day later, the surrender was signed with the Russians in Berlin. Thus, on May 8, 1945, the war was officially over.

---

123 Karl Dönitz (1891-1980) was the head commander of the German navy. He was very respected, not only by the German people, but also by American and British navy personnel.

Even before WWII ended, the Big Three, Churchill (Great Britain), Roosevelt (the United States), and Stalin (Russia) met in Yalta and again in Potsdam shortly after WWII; France was not present, since it had been defeated by the German armies and was counted among the "liberated" countries. The Big Three decided not to make the same mistakes of 1918 when the Treaty of Versailles was devised. This time, Germany did not have to pay reparations. Instead, it would be divided into four sectors or zones and occupied by American, British, French, and Russian authorities.

Occupation Zones and States, 1947

IEG-Maps, Institute European History, Mainz/ ™A. Kunz, 2005 GHDI - Map Notice Berlin (in the North East section) is surrounded by the Russian (Soviet) zone.

Being stationed in southern Germany without access to the Atlantic Ocean, USA forces received a "Port of Embarkation" at Bremerhaven, which became the enclave for the USA forces inside of the British zone (lighter spot in the British Zone).

The Big Three agreed on several procedures:

- Russia was to finally join the United Nations.[124]

- Germany was to be divided into four zones, occupied by Britain in the northwest, the USA in the south, the USSR in the east, and France in the southwest.

- Nazi war-criminals were to be put on trial.[125]

- Poland should get a Polish Provisional Government of National Unity. Poland should soon have free and unrestricted elections.

- The Allies should help the liberated peoples of Europe to set up democratic and self-governing countries. They promised to help those new countries in maintaining law and order, carrying out emergency relief measures, setting up governments, and holding elections. This was called the Declaration of Liberated Europe.

- A commission would be set up for reparations.

Germany's capital, Berlin, eventually surrounded by the Soviet controlled sector, was split into four districts. Originally, the four Allies envisioned governing Germany from their central seat in Berlin.[126]

---

124 The term "United Nations" was first used by President F. D. Roosevelt in 1942. It became an organization in 1945, after numerous nations established its charter.

125 The war trial (it was the first of its kind) took place in Nuremberg between 1945 and 1947. To start with, five field marshals, twenty-six military leaders, fifty-six high-ranking SS and police officers, and fourteen officials from the SS organization were tried. Of the twenty-four men who were indicted, eleven were sentenced to death by hanging and seven received prison sentences from ten years to life. The trials continued in other locations until 1947. Many were arrested and tried, especially in the American sector. This became known as the IMT (International Military Tribunal), and led to the creation of the ICC (International Criminal Court).

126 It proved to be an illusion, because already in 1946, the western Allies realized they did not have much in common with their eastern ally, the Soviet Union. Churchill coined the term "Iron Curtain" at Westminster College in Fulton, Missouri, on March 5, 1946.

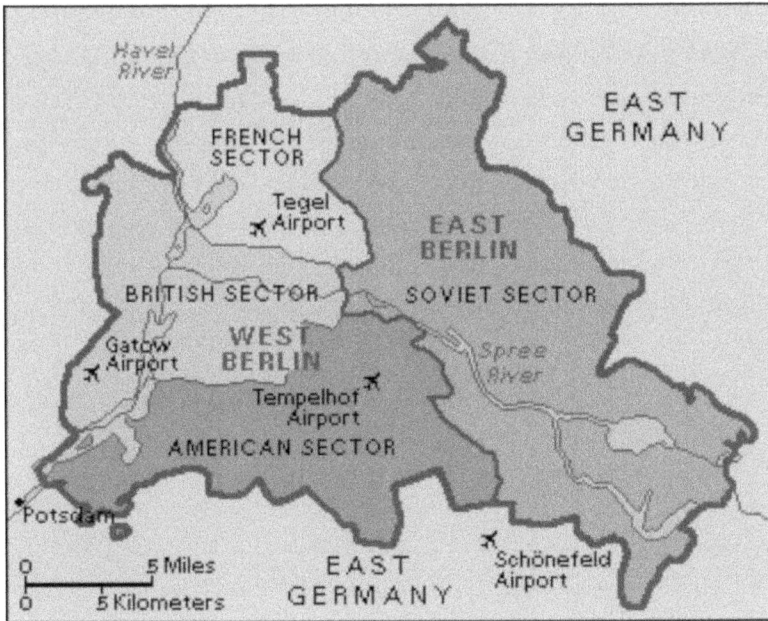

Berlin divided in four sectors/zones. Courtesy of pinterest.com

People celebrated VE (Victory in Europe) Day in the United States of America, France, and Great Britain on May 9, 1945. In the rest of the European countries, allied soldiers freed civil workers and prisoners of war. Refugees and other displaced people felt relief, but did not revel in the victory over the Hitler regime. They wanted to go home and rebuild their ruined places. Only the uprooted persons who originally came from eastern Germany hesitated to move back. They had heard about the Soviets' cruel revenge on the civilians.[127] They knew that they would not find their factories, businesses, or farms intact. The Russians dismantled anything of value in their sector of Germany and shipped it to the Soviet Union.

⟩ᴙᴙ⟩ᴙᴙ⟩ᴙᴙ⟩ᴙᴙ⟩ᴙᴙ

---

127 Many civilians were beaten to death. It is estimated that over 100,000 women were raped, some did not survive. The sick, young orphans, invalids and old people were often abandoned. They were left alone without shelter, any medical or social welfare care.

149

After the end of World War II, our Stammtisch members lived initially under American control, but on July 1, 1945, the borders between the individual sectors were adjusted and firmly established.[128] Before the Russians took control over the Stammtisch village, the farmer went to the pub ahead of the curfew at 10 P.M. He wanted to talk to the innkeeper and set up a new time and day to meet again for their card games. He was surprised to see the innkeeper's wife crying hysterically. Her daughter tried to console her, but the young woman could hardly handle her own emotions.

The farmer spotted Leipziger and turned to him. "What is going on?" he asked, pointing to the two women. "Why all this screaming?"

Leipziger cleared his throat and whispered, "She found her husband when she wanted to go to the attic. The innkeeper hanged himself on the stairs."

"You don't say! But why? He did not lose his hotel business in a bombing raid. He has a good family. We, his customers, are loyal ..."

Leipziger broke in, "Where have you been all this time? Ah, I remember ... you got clobbered by the Russian civil workers, when the Americans liberated them, right?"

"Hmm ... I did, and they thought I would not make it after they cracked my skull open. Almost bled to death. The mayor found me and made sure I got medical help. But tell me, do you have any idea why the innkeeper would commit suicide?"

"You suspected it. Yes, he was an informer for the Gestapo. He tried to hide it from the Americans, but they found out about it. For once, somebody told on *him*."

The farmer could not understand why that should be the reason for killing oneself. He uttered, "But suicide? He was not in the Gestapo. He just informed, as many others did, like the headmaster ..."

128　The American forces had advanced into Germany close to 200 kilometers into the predetermined areas for the Russian sector. They had to give up Thuringia, Saxony Anhalt, and Saxony. In return, they received parts of Berlin that the Soviet army had conquered and now occupied.

Leipziger interrupted him again. "Oh, the headmaster! He disappeared. The rumor has it that he bribed Berliner, who has medical training, to remove his tattoo ..."

"What!?" the farmer interjected. "I knew he believed in the Aryan dream, but SS?[129] He never wore a uniform. I thought he was connected with the Gestapo. But SS! Wow!"

"Actually, he never was in the SS. When he was called to the Volkssturm, he just thought it a good idea to get a tattoo of his blood type in case he would need a transfusion while wounded and unconscious and Headmaster persuaded the innkeeper to do the same."

Berliner, accompanied by a doctor, had entered and just heard part of their conversation. He continued Leipziger's report. "And now, the innkeeper was afraid the Americans would arrest him, as they do with many SS members. He feared to be put through trials, and maybe he would be tortured to death."

The farmer sighed. "What will happen next in our little village?"

"I can tell you one thing, Farmer, we evacuees have to leave." Shifting his position onto his good leg, Leipziger told him, "I may go back soon. Probably have to live in a barracks until we can find an apartment. As for Berliner and Hamburger, they do not know where they will settle, with their homes in ashes."

Berliner answered, "I'll stay here. I have permission until Berlin is divided into sectors. Luckily, Hamburg is under British control. Oh, Farmer, you might not know, they straightened out the borders. On July 1, 1945, we will be under Soviet rule. We will supposedly get a new government. They want to help us to have free elections for democratic leaders."

---

129 SS members swore unconditional loyalty to Hitler and the Nazi party. Later, the *Waffen SS* (a special military outfit) was installed. The members of the SS had their blood type (A, B, AB, or O) tattooed near their left armpit. The occupying Americans looked for those tattoos when they tried to find SS members.

"Or Communists, Socialists, a mixture of the two," Leipziger enlightened them, knowing that his great hometown will soon be under Communist rule.

The doctor had seen the body of the innkeeper and wrote the death certificate. He gave a sedative to the wife. By now, she sat sunken into herself, sobbing quietly. Her daughter stood behind the bar and served the patrons, thinking, *somebody has to run the business.*

The farmer shook his head. "So many changes, so much sadness, and still, life goes on. There is a reason why I did not succumb to my injuries. … The pastor died in Stalingrad, our pharmacist was ambushed by Yugoslavian partisans, our innkeeper was thoroughly disappointed about the outcome of the war and could not face the trials, Teach is somewhere in hiding with a new name, and our mayor has to go through the Denazification process[130], as do we all. Only for him, it will be more rigorous."

After trying to evaluate the many pages of their questionnaires, the Americans realized that this would be a prolonged task and favored a Reeducation program instead of Denazification in the hope of eradicating the Nazi ideology from Germans' heads. This took place with varying degrees of rigor in each of the four sectors of Germany.

In Klostermansfeld, the Americans had chosen the hotel right across from our courtyard gate as their base, from which they carried out some of the procedures the Big Three had agreed upon. In the beginning, my mother was the only one in the village they asked to help with translations. She interceded on behalf of many individuals and their requests. She helped to clear persons of being imprisoned because of a mistaken identity. She solved their problems with curfews when they needed to take a trip to the hospital after 10 PM, or tried finding their lost relatives, or locating a place to stay. There were so many displaced people all over Germany; the Americans had their hands full sorting out where these people should

---

130 It is estimated that about 8.5 million Germans belonged to the Nazi party. Although many government workers were not convinced of the Nazi program, they had to join the NSDAP or else lose their jobs.

be sent. Finally, they decided to order everybody back to where they originally came from, be they prisoners of war, civil workers, soldiers, evacuees, fugitives, or refugees.

Many people when arriving at "home" became shelter-seekers, since their houses or apartment buildings had been destroyed. Ernst's friend Hermann was ordered to join his family who lived near Hamelin in the British sector. He would have liked to remain with Uncle Martin, but after the harvest season in 1945, he had to join his parents and five siblings.

Since Aunt Bitta had a newborn she was allowed to stay longer with Uncle Martin, but eventually she moved to Freiburg in the French sector.

At the end of May, my father and his army comrade, Martin Bosert, arrived in Klostermansfeld. They had escaped from a makeshift American prison camp. They had surrendered to the American forces because Martin had been badly wounded. He had been shot in his back. He also hurt from a bullet in his leg and a few shrapnel wounds. Both hoped to get food at the camp and medical help for him. After a week of resting, although not comfortably, Martin felt well enough to sit on the bar of a bicycle my father had taken. They waited until an army truck would leave the prison so they could coast alongside of it through the prison gate, unnoticed by the guards. Martin could not have escaped the Russian invasion if my father had not helped him. My father never liked to talk about it, and in 1991, when I met Martin again, he—just like my father—did not want to speak about these devastating times. He was originally from Berlin, where he had dreamed of becoming an opera singer. He was unable to go back and live with his parents. Their bodies lay under the rubble of their home, which had been destroyed during one of the many bombing raids on Berlin.

By now the old farmhouse was overflowing with people. Somehow Oma, in her resourcefulness, found a place for everybody to sleep. Even for Aunt Ursel's friend who suddenly dropped in with a little baby boy and stayed with us. Oma thought, *who could turn a young mother with a baby away in these uncertain times. She needs our help.*

First, all civil workers had to go back to their homeland. Some of them followed the command reluctantly. They had liked working for

Uncle Martin, but they had no choice. With the Polish workers gone, Uncle Martin welcomed anybody who could replace them. My brother and his friend Hermann had helped already before the Americans entered Klostermansfeld. My father, along with Martin Bosert, offered their aid as soon as they arrived in May. Our young neighbor, Horst, enjoyed his former duties as an HJ- youth so much that he volunteered to continue working at the farm. Eventually some of Uncle Martin's old farm hands who had fought at the various fronts returned to their families and gladly performed all the tasks they had been used to before the war. They knew they could rely on Mr. Oemler not only to pay them on time, but also to supply them with food when their ration cards were depleted at the end of the month.

My father, with new workers arriving, and knowing that he too would be asked where he originated from, thought of leaving before he needed to fill out forms. He feared repercussions, since he had not officially been released from the American prison camp. He talked to Uncle Martin. "We will leave for my farm in St. Bernhard," he disclosed. Uncle Martin agreed, although he would have liked to keep my father and Martin Bosert as his helpers. But he knew that when we left, there would be seven people less to feed and house. He pointed out to my father, "Look here, Herbert, according to the rules of relocating—or should I say, ordering people back to where they came from—St. Bernhard is the place they will send you to. After all, you inherited this farm. That overrules going back to Thorn, where you only temporarily occupied an apartment as long as your insurance company wanted you to stay in West Prussia."

We made preparations to leave. We hoped to find Grandma and my four- year-old brother, Reinhold. Nobody had heard from them[131]. Uncle Martin understood very well why my mother was anxious to move out. He secured two Panje[132] horses and a covered wagon that had been left

---

131 It was almost impossible to make phone calls. Many lines were ruined and the occupational forces ranked first to use the connections still operable. Letters and even telegrams got lost or took much longer than before.

132 The *Panje* or *Panjeskaya* were used in East Europe. They are small horses descended from the Polish *Konik* horse.

in the courtyard by retreating German soldiers. When my mother asked the Americans for permission to trek to St. Bernhard with her children and "two workers" who would help her with the horses and the wagon, she could not reveal that one of those "workers" was her husband. He would have been put into a POW camp again. Mother told the American authorities, "We fled from Thorn, which now is Polish, I think, but Thorn was only a business post for us. We originally come from St. Bernhard, where my husband owns a farm. My mother-in-law and my youngest son are hopefully still there. I need to find out if and how they survived. Also, I am sure my husband will first search for us at our farm." She made clear to the American officials that we belonged in the Thuringia state, where Father's farm was rented to a Mr. Rassmann. The Americans did not like to lose their translator, but they accepted that she wanted to be with her youngest son and wait in St. Bernhard if her spouse ever came back from the Eastern Front. She made up names for my father and his friend Martin. After she had answered a few more questions the Americans gave her the necessary travel papers. These documents allowed Mrs. Ilse-Paula Höfer to travel through the Thuringia Mountains to St. Bernhard with her children, Ernst, Hildegard, and Ilse-Rose Höfer, and the two horse handlers. Needless to say we had to be careful how we children addressed Father in the presence of other people.

Before we could depart, we had to be vaccinated. The American medical teams wanted to make sure that all people heading home would not spread diseases throughout Germany. They set up an immunization program for all children and young adults throughout their occupied territories. They stuck the needles into our arms, chests, and behinds to prevent dysentery, typhoid fever, diphtheria, scarlet fever, and typhus. We were also tested for tuberculosis. To avoid the spreading of typhus carried by fleas and lice, the Americans dusted us and everything else with DDT.[133] Our entire bodies became sore. We were vaccinated against all of these diseases in a short time. The different serums wreaked havoc

---

133 Dichlorodiphenyltrichloroethane is a synthetic pesticide, later discovered to be very harmful for any living and breathing being.

in our bodies. Regardless of how we felt, we had to start on our trek to St. Bernhard.

We voluntarily left, not as fugitives, but as displaced people. It was heartbreaking for the fugitives from the east to follow the relocation rules. They did not want to be forced to go back to where the Soviets occupied their hometowns and estates. In the last days of the war, families had been evacuated to safer places. But when they heard that now they would be forced to go back to their Russian-controlled homeland, they despaired. Many had been deeply disappointed in their belief in a superior Germany and could not cope with the defeat of the Nazi ideology. Now, the worries about being exposed to the Russians added to their anguish. Whole families committed suicide. Many were disillusioned NSDAP members. Worst of all, they had lost all hope in Germany's recovery.

Not so my father! We loaded the painted hope chest under the canvas of the covered wagon. It was the trunk in which my mother had tried to save my father's hunting guns, only to have them taken away by the Americans. Did she really think when she left Thorn that we would be allowed to keep guns? Maybe she still believed in a German victory against all odds. Now, the old chest had room for some pots and pans, linens, clothing, and food from Uncle Martin and Oma. We sat between the hay and grain for the horses on some feather beds when we did not have to push the wagon up the high mountains of the Thuringia Woods. I must say we did not often have the luxury of sitting in the wagon.

We left Klostermansfeld in early June. Uncle Martin hitched two strong horses in front of the smaller ones to pull the wagon up the steep hill toward Bennsdorf. At its top he had to take his team back, and we dragged along the many kilometers, trusting in the strength of our little horses. We always made sure we stayed in the American-occupied part of Germany. My father knew the mountains well; he avoided towns and large villages. He led us through deep woods and over less-traveled streets.

Martin Bosert started to sing. I joined him. It was a poem by Johann Wolfgang von Goethe set to an old German folk melody, as was customarily done to popular poems in the nineteenth century.

I had my head almost buried in the crib that Father had fastened to the back of the wagon. With both hands on the trough, I marched and pushed with all my strength, still singing. My father, Ernst, and Martin grabbed the wheel spokes and hand over hand, we forced the heavy vehicle forward, helping the little Panje horses overcome the steep mountain road. Mother held the reigns.

"Hush, quiet!" my father hissed between his teeth. I stopped singing immediately. We reached the plateau. A motion with his hand indicated that we had to disappear. Hastily, my mother, Hildegard, and I climbed into the wagon. We squeezed ourselves behind the big old hope chest. Ernst covered us with a blanket and skillfully rested a sack of fodder across the chest and a suitcase behind us, thus hiding us. This was the secret shelter for us females whenever danger lurked. There were so many homeless and hungry people, who just would have loved to have our food, our wagon, and our horses. Some of them had been criminals, kept in Nazi prison camps. They were arbitrarily freed with all the other inmates, who were politically or racially unwanted people under the Nazis. On our right side we had just passed one of the notorious concentration camps, Buchenwald.[134]

Through a little hole in a board of the wagon we saw a group of men with shaved heads. We thought they looked longingly at the wagon and the horses. What would they do to us? Were we safe? My father had gone to the front, holding the horses by their halter, partially hidden by the horses' heads and chests he slowly walked on the left side of the street. Martin limped behind him. Ernst sat at the "helm," holding the reins. We held our breath. At any minute, they could pounce on us, throw us from the wagon, and drive away with our last belongings. How could we defend ourselves?

At that moment, an American patrol controlling the country road stopped us. Did we sigh with relief? Not really! Although we were sure that the liberated prisoners would not bother us as long as the Americans were there with their guns, anxious thoughts crossed our minds. *What will*

---

134   The concentration camp Buchenwald was constructed near Weimar in Thuringia.

the American GIs do? Will they let us continue to travel? Are our papers good enough?

My father showed our travel documents to the soldiers. The officer looked at him questioningly, probably wondering where the females of the group were. He counted Ernst, Martin, and my father. There were three people missing, but they allowed him to continue on the journey. My father spurred the horses on to a faster gait. Looking back, he noticed the army jeep following us. What did that mean? Would they stop us again?

Actually, the soldiers' presence kept the former "convicts" near Buchenwald at bay. "You know," Mother whispered, "that these men with shaved heads may be thieves or murderers." Was she really unaware that politically unwanted people, gypsies and Jews, had been imprisoned here? Later, we realized that the Americans had protected us, but at the time, our father feared being asked about the women of the traveling party. There was always the possibility that soldiers would take their unwritten right of the victors by raping the women. But these Americans never asked about us. They rode in their jeep, smoking cigarettes and chewing gum.

It started to get hot underneath the blanket and the fodder. Hildegard experienced leg cramps. My arms grew numb. Mother held us tightly. She was ready to protect and defend us with all the strength in her small body. She had nothing to fear. As soon as the last former prisoner of Buchenwald was out of sight, the jeep left. Now it was time for us to get out of our stuffy hiding place. I rubbed my arms. Hildegard stretched her legs. Gladly, we continued our walk behind the wagon and helped push it up the next hill.

Nightfall was near. Where would we stay tonight? Every evening, it was the same uncertainty. We had to observe the curfew. We could not simply stay at a clearing in the forest near one of the many springs in the Thuringia Woods. Before nightfall Father would leave the wagon on the side of the road, partially hidden by trees and bushes. He would walk to the next inn or farmhouse, trying to find out if we could stay in an enclosed courtyard or a barn, where the horses might get some rest and his family could sleep. We slept under all kinds of conditions—on living room floors, in haylofts, or three of us in one bed. One of the men always remained with the horses and the wagon to make sure nothing would be taken.

Once we reached a little village where my father knew people from the time when our grandfather had held the first chair of the Thüringer Landbund.[135] Here we found out from one of Father's acquaintances that Grandma and Reinhold were alive and St. Bernhard did not witness much fighting. My mother sighed deeply and wiped away a few tears. She finally would be united with her youngest son again.

Father asked one of the farmers if our horses could drink from the water pump and we could rest up in their barn.

"No, not tonight!" the old man replied. "The Americans are planning a party here. When they get drunk, nobody knows what they'll do. They might see the horses, try to ride them Wild West style...." he wanted to continue, but his wife interrupted him. "There is room in the living room. You can sleep on the carpet," she said.

"Thank you. We have blankets and pillows. We will be fine," my mother answered gratefully.

"The men sleep in the stable with the horses; we hide the wagon in the barn." The old woman organized our stay.

The farmer sighed. "You are always too trusting, Emma," he said to his wife. "But it's okay. Just as long as you know I cannot protect you and might get into trouble myself."

Ernst did not know if he was counted as a man too. He was almost thirteen years old and had done many a man's work already. Mother sensed his dilemma. "Ernst, you'll sleep with us in the living room. You sleep at the door. You are our protector if some drunken soldier should enter." The farmer's wife showed us the room where we could wash. She asked us to use the chamber pot during the night, since the way to the outhouse led across the street and therefore could not be used during curfew hours. Soon we were settled on the floor and fell asleep. Early the next morning, before we left, Emma brought some hot milk and black bread for us.

---

135   The Thuringia Farmers' Party during the Weimar Republic. See Chapter 1.

It was a beautiful summer evening when we arrived in another village. My father remembered that his former classmate owned an inn there. Sure enough, he found it and was permitted to put the wagon behind the barn and the horses in a stable nearby. We went upstairs to a large room that served as ballroom, theater or auditorium depending on what kind of function it was needed for at any given time. Martin drew back the curtains of the stage. He found a few props and started to sing a Rigoletto aria.[136] He had a beautiful baritone. My mother joined in, laughing, and soon we played along, although we did not know the opera. We were led by the text Martin sang and acted out, offering different endings to the "play." Everybody laughed and had a great time until my father asked us to find a place to sleep in this huge ballroom. Somewhere among the stage props, I found a sofa covered with dusty red velvet. I curled up on it and fell fast asleep.

"Ilse-Rose!"

"Fatty!"

"Rosebud!"

I opened my eyes. The sun shone right into my face.

"Ilse-Rose!"

"Fatty!"

"Rosebud! Where are you?"

I heard my family calling. I answered, "I am here."

"Why didn't you tell us where you wanted to lie down?" my father asked anxiously.

"I thought this was a good place to sleep."

My mother felt a disciplinary action by Father coming. "Let her be, Herbert," she intervened. "I never was alarmed about her. She is a resourceful child. She always knows how to make the best of every situation." I not only listened to her words expressing her confidence in

---

136　*Rigoletto* is an opera in three acts by Giuseppe Verdi (1813–1901) of Italy.

me, but I remembered them for the rest of my eventful life. I would always try to find something good in even the most dreadful situations.

After a few more days of travel, we arrived in Father's village. It was my first visit to this remote place. It was the tiniest settlement I ever saw. Only three streets seemed to go up the hill and two other ones crossed them, with one at the top of the hill and the other at the bottom, where my father's farmhouse stood.

We could only enjoy the wholeness of an undivided family for a few weeks under American protection. On July 1, 1945, the borders of the four occupied sectors were finalized; the result being that St. Bernhard fell under Soviet control. The Americans had to leave our district, and the Russians moved in. Since St. Bernhard was—and still is—so small, we seldom saw Russians. German policemen soon oversaw our region. They had to enforce the new Communist laws. We lived only about twenty miles away from the American sector, but it might as well have been a thousand. From then on, we were confined to the Soviet-controlled zone.

My grandma lived with my younger brother in a small two-bedroom apartment on the second floor of the farmhouse, which had two stories and an attic. Three buildings enclosed the courtyard. An iron fence at the street finished the quadrangle of the yard. The barn and the horse stable stood across from the main house and extended toward the street. The traditional dung heap lay at the gate across from a water pump, not too far from the kitchen.

When we arrived, my parents took over one bedroom. Grandma shared hers with us four children. All of us used the living room. Its couch served as sleeping quarters for Martin Bosert. The bathroom, which, as was typical, lacked a commode, was converted into a kitchen. A coal and wood stove stood alongside the water heater. A board across the tub served as a counter. A small table occupied the limited space under the window, from which we could observe activities in the courtyard. Here Hildegard and I ate our small breakfast before walking to the one-room schoolhouse.

Our father had rented the farm to Mr. Rassmann. Their contract legally should have run for nine more years. Therefore, Father could not farm, but he had the privilege of taking care of the three forests belonging to the estate. Mr. Rassmann's big family occupied the lower rooms of the house. Hildegard soon befriended his daughters. She always could associate with people easily. It really did not matter to me; we had little time for playing.

Grandma believed in the old saying, "Early to bed and early to rise makes a man healthy, wealthy, and wise." She used many of these proverbs. One was, "A girl may not rest as long as it takes for a chicken to pick a kernel off the ground." Therefore, she taught Hildegard and me how to knit and how to crochet, so we would not sit idle during a rest period. In the summer of 1945, she woke us up early so we could go with her into the woods to look for strawberries. Later we picked raspberries, then blackberries, and at last the sloes, which were best after the first frost. In St. Bernhard frost could come as early as September. After a rainy day, we looked for a variety of mushrooms in our woods. Grandma cleaned and sliced them, and then she hung them on strings close to the stove so they could dry. We gathered a good supply of them for the coming winter months. Grandma had the right to grow some vegetables in the farm garden. Her plot was not big. It was too small to grow cabbage or potatoes, but she had grown tomatoes in little containers in spring. She planted them outside in June. During the whole summer, I never saw a single ripe tomato there. Just before the frost came, she brought all the green ones into the house. We had to carefully wrap them in newspaper and store them in single layers in the small hallway located in front of her apartment. We checked the tomatoes frequently to see if they had ripened and then we used them. A few did spoil.

Grandma baked bread for all of us when we were able to get flour. She formed round loaves with her hands and placed each on a wooden slab. We helped her to bring these to the community oven. The oven, made from brick and fieldstones, stood by itself in the middle of the village. A strong wood fire heated the inner chamber. After the flames died down and the embers were covered with ashes, the villagers pushed their loaves of bread onto the hot ashes. In a few hours, the bread was baked. Fresh-baked it always tasted very good, but we were not allowed to eat as much as we liked. The bread had to last for many days. My mother marked it, dividing it into daily rations. When we told Grandma that we were hungry, she answered with one of her sayings, "Gelobt sei, was hart macht!" (Praise what makes you tough!) Sometimes a neighbor gave us one of her slices of bread. She had a few cows. She scooped the heavy cream from the milk and mixed it with our strawberries to make a delicious spread for an open-faced sandwich.

My father had sold the small horses and purchased bigger, stronger ones. We called them Lise and Hans. Hildegard had a knack for making Lise listen to her, although the mare was high-strung and nervously twitched her ears. "She is prettier than Hans; she is my horse," Hildegard declared proudly. "Don't even think of getting close to her, Fatty. Something might happen." What might happen, I didn't know.

In July and again in late August, we made hay for the horses. Father was allowed to cut the high grass and herbs in a meadow that was a long walk away from our place. Grandma, Mother, my older brother, my sister, Reinhold (he had a short wooden child's tool) and I raked the hay. Father used a scythe. He showed Martin Bosert and Ernst how to sharpen it and how to swing it so the grass would lay just right. We followed him and raked the grass into shallow rows. It needed to be turned often. Again, Grandma woke us up early and went with us to perform this task, so the evening and morning dew could not settle on the drying grass, causing the hay to spoil.

My grandfather, a forester by profession, had taught his sons how to take care of the timberland. Soon my father noticed that the beech trees needed thinning out. He decided to work as a lumberjack. With the help of Martin Bosert, he cut the trees down. He did not have a chain saw, and even if he had one, he would not have been able to get the oil or gas for it to run.

Although Hildegard was only eleven years old and I had reached nine, we had to help getting the trunks out of the deep woods and to the pathways, where they could be loaded onto a wagon. Father sold them in the nearby towns. Everybody needed wood.

My sister and I had to lead the horses through the often-narrow spaces between the standing trees. Each felled tree was fastened with chains to the horses who dragged them out of the dense underbrush. We girls had to identify the easiest path for the animals to pull the long logs toward the road. Often, the trunks would get hung up on bushes or smaller trees, and sometimes the horses, especially Hans, would have a mind of their own when it came to finding the best way to drag them out. It took all the strength we two girls could muster to direct the big horses.

Good logs were desired to repair war-damaged houses and build furniture; lesser timber was for firewood that was very much sought after. Winter would be coming soon. Many people, like us, had no oil heat; either there was no oil available, or they simply did not have the luxury of central heating.[137] Coal furnaces were of no use because all coal was sent to Russia or France and there was seldom any left for household consumption by the Germans, although each family was allotted a small amount of lignite (brown) coal for their little stoves in their kitchens. We had heard that people in big cities would burn their furniture and wooden floors to keep warm throughout the winter. My father either sold the wood or bartered with it.[138]

Coming home from a long day of work, the horses had to be fed and taken care of. One day, when I was asked to feed them, I entered Lise's stall from the wrong side, mixing up right and left as I did so often. The horse started to bolt. Luckily, Martin was standing near the stalls, but even he had a hard time calming the mare down. I pressed myself against the wooden plank that separated Hans from Lise. Hans started to get nervous as well. He turned his head toward me, showing big yellow teeth. I held my breath.

---

137 The first time I experienced central heating was in Mülheim on the Ruhr in the early 1950s. In villages, it was common to heat every room separately as needed. Usually the bedrooms did not have stoves.

138 The black market flourished in all four zones. It stopped rather suddenly in 1948 in the three western sectors. In the Russian sector, it never stopped completely, but bartering had to be done secretly. When caught, the barterers were sentenced to either fines or prison and at times were severely punished.

I heard Martin. "Ho, ho Lise, ho, ho!" To me, he whispered, "Slip out when I come from the other side of Lise." He had brought a shovel with oats, but the horse continued to stamp her hooves. Any minute now she could start kicking. Our neighbor, Mr. Schreyer, the blacksmith, heard the commotion. He came running. With a secure grip, he caught one of Lise's back hooves. "Now, now, Lise, old girl," he said in his deep, calming voice. She responded to him. Martin started to pour the oats for Lise. "Out, out" he hissed to me. I stumbled out of the stall.

"Stupidity of stupidity! Don't you even know how to approach a horse? Can't you think? Can't you understand that the poor animal does not know what is going on behind her back? You scared her half to death. She could have trampled you!" My older brother was yelling at me, and of course, Hildegard had to chime in.

"You scared my horse. You ruined her. She'll never overcome this. She'll never be the same again."

Martin thanked the blacksmith for his help, who waved it off with his hand and said, "Don't mention it. I saw what was going on. I naturally would help, as long as our Father in Heaven gives me the strength to do so," he muttered as he crossed the street and resumed splitting wood in front of his house. Everybody in the village knew that he was a God-fearing man. It was a blessing that he was always there when we needed help. Soon enough we would have to rely on him again.

Deeply shaken, I slipped into the house. Grandma noticed me. "Finished feeding the horses already?" she asked and then ordered me, "Go downstairs and help peel potatoes."

Mrs. Rassmann handed me a dull knife so I would not cut myself, and I started peeling. "How slow you do this!" she remarked. "Look how many potatoes my daughter, Lenchen, peeled already, and you haven't even finished one!"

Grandma wanted me to be as accomplished as others in the village. She really did not mean to embarrass me in front of the Rassmann children, who were my schoolmates. She just wanted to spur me on. I was not competitive when it came to showing that I could be better than others. I could be very ardent when playing games, but even there once in a while, I let the younger children win.

What was the use in peeling potatoes, if I cannot satisfy anybody? I thought. I put the knife down, thinking all the potatoes we needed this day were stripped of their skin already.

I went upstairs to play with my little brother. I lay on the daybed in the living room. I bent my knees and let Reinhold ride on my lower legs. He was sitting just above my ankles. I would toss him up and down lightly. He laughed and relished every moment. He loved his sister, who always had time for him and could tell such interesting stories, read fairy tales and even made going to bed fun. He just wanted to be tossed higher and higher. He threw his head back in delight … and then it happened. As he threw his head back, I hoisted him up again. Reinhold squealed with glee, flying up, when our hands slipped apart. He was thrown backward, and his head came down hard on the stone windowsill.

A scream, and then dead silence.

"Mom, Mom!" I wailed loudly. "Mom, I killed Reinhold, oh I killed him. I killed him, oh, oh."

Grandma was first on the scene. She opened the window and shouted for the blacksmith across the street. "George, fast, come fast, the child … the child, he fell, his head, he is bleeding." Reinhold opened his eyes and started crying. My mother had heard the commotion. She ran upstairs and lifted my brother up carrying him to the blacksmith's place. Mr. Schreyer calmly shaved off some of Reinhold's light blond hair and put a butterfly bandage on his head.

My mother could hardly hold back her tears. "Thank you, thank you so much. I would not know what to do without you. There isn't a nurse within five miles of here, and no doctor for at least ten miles. We could not pay them anyway."

He interrupted her. "It's all right, Mrs. Höfer." He looked at her again and felt compelled to speak. "May I say something? Just among us, I really do not like to interfere in other people's business." He took a deep breath, hesitated a moment but then continued, "I have seen how brave you are, how you face the people here. How you keep your children clean and neat and teach them good manners. Your hands are not made for this farm work, hitching horses, and milking cows. You do not belong here. I mean my wife and I will always help you and your family. There are a few others who will help you, too." He stopped, making sure nobody was around to hear him and in a lower voice said, "But the Russians have now taken over this part of Germany. Who knows how they will treat us? Soviets, Communists! Sooner or later, we all have to become Communists working in communes, doing even the toughest chores together."

Observing my mother as she reached for my brother, he sighed. "And the harsh winter in our mountains is approaching. I say go back to your family, to your home. This village is not the place for such a refined, sophisticated lady like you." The blacksmith seldom spoke as many words as he did this time.

My mother looked into his good-natured eyes. "As long as God gives me people like you, I can stand it anywhere," she said, and she took my brother from the blacksmith's lap, carrying him tenderly upstairs to Grandma's apartment.

At our dinner of potatoes with sour milk and a few strawberries that Grandma and Hildegard had picked, my father frowned. "Whose turn was it to feed the horses? When I went to give them water tonight, Hans looked like he did not get anything to eat. There was not a morsel in his hayrack. He had even pulled up some straw from his bedding to munch on. You know we need the horses in good condition to survive. We made hay last week. You could have given him a forkful. Can't I expect at least so much from you? Well, whose turn was it? Mother, Ernst, Martin?"

I whispered, "I tried to feed them."

Father wanted to know, "Who has asked her to help?"

My mother answered, "Herbert, I told her to help me. Tenant Rassmann said we could have as many potatoes as we could peel in an hour. I went to work as fast as I could. Hildegard and Grandma had just come back from the woods, picking strawberries that Hildegard cleaned. I know Ilse-Rose is resourceful, so I asked her to help with the horses."

"Yes, and she was so dumb as to approach Lise from the wrong side, and the blacksmith had to come, and ..." Hildegard was ready to tell of all the events that happened on this day. I could not eat anymore. I tried to swallow hard. I did not dare cry. I just waited silently for my punishment, knowing Dad had not even seen Reinhold. He was in bed before Dad arrived. My father just nodded. He understood that his little Rosebud, his third child, was overtaxed. There would not be any disciplinary action.

That evening, he took the whole family to the barn. He wore riding boots, had a small whip in his hand, and was leading Lise out of the stable. She wore a beautiful saddle. To this day I have no idea where he was able to get this luxurious riding gear. My father mounted the horse, rode two circles, asked Tenant Rassmann to open the barn gates, and rode towards the fading rosy-red light. The horse followed every slight command. Lise was a classic riding horse, definitely not a farm animal. I never forgot this picture: my father high on the beautiful mare, rider and horse in perfect harmony, encircled by the glow of the sunset, which intensified Lise's red-brown coat and reflected on Dad's shining boots.

In September 1945, all schools in the Russian zone opened again, although the teaching often took place only in cellars or other dilapidated buildings. My older brother could not attend a nearby high school. Usually, students in senior high living in a village take the train or public bus in the morning, attend their classes, and come home the same day. Since St. Bernhard had neither a bus nor a train station, Ernst needed to live in a town. My parents searched among their former acquaintances in Thuringia and found a widow who was willing to offer room and board for him in return for his monthly ration card. Father supplied money for his stay, and Mother sent food packages so the lady could cook meals for him. My brother never saw what my mother sent. When the mailman came to deliver Mother's packages, Ernst was in school. The woman took the parcels and did not give anything to him. She used the food for herself and for the black market. My brother had to survive on what she allotted to him from his ration card.

Hildegard and I were still in elementary school. We went up the hill through the old orchard and then the churchyard to the house that hosted one room for grades one through eight. I liked this school more than Miss Karsdorf in Klostermansfeld, because the teacher left me alone most of the time. I seemed to learn everything without her tutoring, except now we had to learn Russian.[139] I did not understand why we had to speak the language of soldiers against whom my father had fought a few months ago. I just refused to learn it.

On October 19, 1945, when Hildegard and I walked home from school, we felt a leery atmosphere around us. The village seemed desolate, and still there was a sense of hustling and bustling behind the closed window curtains and doors.

"Look, Fatty, there, see the cars?" My always-alert sister pointed to two jeeps. They were parked in front of the farmhouse. We had not seen a car for weeks. We ran, passing the vehicles and scampered up the stairs. We did not notice the spiteful grin on Mrs. Rassmann's face and the curious looks her children sent our way.

Our living room was a mess. Every drawer had been opened; their contents were strewn all over the room. Three policemen searched the beds, lifted mattresses. We looked at our mother, who stood against the warm tiles of the living room stove. She motioned us to come to her side. She whispered, "Quiet, don't say anything." Hildegard gave her an agreeing glance out of her big brown eyes. I nodded silently. Reinhold, four years old, leaned against Mother, sucking his thumb. My father stood at the desk, his hands in handcuffs.

"Aha, here it is. Here is a swastika!"

My mother tried to explain politely, "Officer, this is the typical mother's cross every woman would receive after bearing four children. See, this one is bronze for my four children. Others received silver or even gold ones if they had six or eight children."

"Well, why do you still have it? There are no honors in swastikas, don't you know that?" My mother did not know why she still had it. She had lost most of her jewelry with all of the other belongings in Thorn. Why

---

139 Depending on which sector German pupils lived in; they had to learn the language of the occupying forces (French, English, or Russian).

did she keep this one? She never wore it. It just so happened that when she packed the trunk in Thorn, it slid in amongst the dishes or silverware. She did not remember. Maybe she kept it because she was grateful to have given birth to four healthy, intelligent children. The policeman bent the cross, opened the stove door and threw it into the fire.

"What do we have here? A letter addressed to Sergeant H. Höfer! Tsk, tsk, tsk! Let's see what's in it!" He showed it to his companions and began to read aloud what my mother had written to Father when he was fighting at the eastern front. It was one of her love letters to him, filled with tenderness and encouraging words for him. She told him that their fourth child developed just as well as the other three. My father had never received this letter. It had been sent back to my mother. Now, the envelope revealed that he had been a minor officer in Hitler's army and that he had fought at the eastern front. The newly established German police arrested my father because he had fought the Soviet Union army and because our grandfather had been the leader of the conservative Thuringia Farmers' Party, formerly Thüringer Landbund, which was against Communism.

The policeman pushed my father down the stairs. My father turned once and looked at us as if to say, "Don't worry, I'll be back." They shoved him into the jeep and then sped away. My mother sank into a chair, tears streaming down her cheeks.

Grandma came into the room and tried to console her. "At least Martin is safe. He came from the stable when the police arrived. I pointed him toward your bedroom, and when all of the policemen were searching the living room, he climbed out of the window to hide in the woods behind the pasture."

"I hope the tenants downstairs did not see him and squeal on him," my mother moaned.

"No, I am sure they were much too excited about what was going on up here to do anything else. They would rather watch what would happen to Herbert."

My mother collected herself and put on a courageous front. She would not let the family downstairs triumph over her misery. She prepared the evening meal as best as she could with the little provisions we had. She made sure we washed our hands and sat at the table. "It is important to keep good manners. There are things nobody can snatch away from you. Always learn. Always behave well. Knowledge and civilized behavior are things nobody can take away from you."

"May I have another potato, please?" I asked.

Grandma let me know, "No, we have to keep some for tomorrow."

Late at night Martin sneaked into the stable. My mother checked on the horses. She gave the potatoes to him. They quietly talked about different times and spots in the woods, where she or Grandma could leave food and warmer clothing for Martin. We did not know if the police or the Russians were also looking for him. He had to hide. We did not trust anybody in the village. Martin could not ask someone for food. Any person could tell the police where he was just to feel important or to ask for some kind of favor in return.

The next morning, Tenant Rassmann confronted my mother asking her, "What did you do in the stable last night? I have not seen Martin Bosert. Did he disappear?" My mother knew she had to have a good excuse. "Remember when my daughter spooked Lise? Ever since, the horse seems to get restless, and sometimes she gets loose. I had to check on her. You know my husband could not do it." Mr. Rassmann grinned, "So you had to check Lise, your son or Bosert could not do it? Ha!" My mother shrugged her shoulders, pitched the fork into the hay and fed the horses.

Later, she told Grandma, "Rassmann spied on us. He knew I was in the stable. Thank God Rosebud spooked the horses! I had a good excuse for being there at night. He asked about Martin but I did not answer and just fed the animals."

It took fourteen days before Martin Bosert was able to cross the border into the American zone. On his way, he stopped at Oma's place to tell her about my father's imprisonment and in what a predicament her daughter, Paula, and her grandchildren were.

The police had arrested my father, but when they reached the outskirts of St. Bernhard there was a truck and he was told to climb into it. The driver and the guards were Soviet soldiers. The Russians had sent the German police to trap Father in the hope, by knowing the German language better, they would find any evidence in our living quarters that gave them the right to incarcerate him. Now the Russians took over. When the truck stopped, my father was led into a makeshift prison cell.

With the first light of morning, he looked out of the barred window and recognized the town. Here he had graduated from high school. He knew it was Hildburghausen. He thought about escaping, watched the guards and soon knew which ones were inattentive.

My mother still wondered what criminal act or political affiliation sent our father to prison. The question haunted her. Was it because he had fought against the Soviets? Was it because his father had been a leader of an anti- Communist party of the Weimar Republic? Soon, she received an answer.

Mr. Rassmann had denounced my father. He told incriminating lies to the Soviets about the owner of the farm. He, as leaseholder, had worked the fields under the mutually agreed and legal contract between him and Herbert Höfer. Rassmann deliberated about their settlement that had been signed before the war and would run out in 1954. He was afraid that, with nowhere else to live, Mr. Höfer would be unable to renew their arrangement under the same terms. Hoping that with my father arrested and likely sent to Siberia, it was his chance to seize the farm. It not only held workable fields but also included well designed woods now ready for harvest. These trees would supply excellent material for buildings, furniture, and heating, so much in demand right now. Rassmann showed his true colors. They had been brown with the National Socialists when he rented the farm from Father, now they turned red like the Communist Socialists' flag.[140] For him, it was time to switch to the new regime and get the most out of it, regardless what happened to us.

---

140 The color brown is associated with the early Nazi movement, since the SA had brown uniforms. Red stands for Communism. Most flags representing Communist nations are red.

After the rumor about my father's arrest as a war criminal and Nazi spread through the village, our stay in St. Bernhard became unbearable. Now we experienced a time of increased hunger, and even worse, a bitter disappointment in people. Tenant Rassmann's unfriendliness turned into hate. The schoolchildren in the village started to call Hildegard and me "Nazi pigs." Once in a while, they threw stones at us on our way home from school. But there was at least one good fact in our unfortunate situation: the wound on Reinhold's head healed well. The blacksmith had done a good job with his butterfly bandage.

My mother had to bring food for Father to the prison in Hildburghausen about twelve miles away from St. Bernhard. She arrived there in the afternoon. She had to give the sandwiches to the police. They searched them looking for files or knives, and then told her they would give them to her husband.

"Can't I speak with him, or at least see him?" she asked.

"No!"

She left, uncertain if he would receive the last slices of our smoked sausage between two pieces of dark bread. Grandma and Ernst tried to help out as much as possible. Mother knew we had to leave soon. She wanted to sell the logs, or barter with them for food. Nobody wanted our wood. Everybody was afraid of being questioned why they dared to help us. So Ernst thought about offering the wagonload to a sawmill. He left early in the morning.

About three days after my father had been taken away, Russian soldiers stormed into our rooms and demanded to know where our father was.

"He is in Hildburghausen in prison," Mother answered.

"No, he's not, and you know it. He ran 'way. Where is he?" One of them asked in broken German. My mother turned pale. She did not know where he was. Our emotions ran high. On the one hand, we were relieved he escaped, but on the other hand, where was he now? Why didn't he come to tell us?

As much as they tried to prompt my mother, she had no idea where Father might be. One soldier pointed a pistol at her chest. She held her breath and looked at us. She shook her head. Finally, she stammered, "I did not know he broke out. He never told us. He did not come here." What else could she say? She did not want to be killed in front of her children. My little brother started to cry. Maybe the Russian soldiers had children of their own. They saw us two girls staring at them and Reinhold whimpering. They must have realized that this woman really had no idea where her husband was. They probably thought that their escaped prisoner was too smart to go home after sneaking out, knowing that the police would first search the area where his family lived. He most likely hid somewhere far away by now. They knew they better leave and not waste more time on us.

After they left, my mother and Grandma sobbed. We tried to comfort her. Hildegard smoothed her hair out of her face, I dabbed at her tears and rubbed her back, Reinhold handed her his handkerchief. Mother took a deep breath, hugged us and thought to herself, *I may not give in. My children need me. I will be there for them.*

It was true. My father was only in prison for three days. He had scraped at the door hinges with a spoon until they gave way. He waited for rain and the right moment to sneak out. He knew the surrounding area well and could hide until he found his friend and hunting companion from Thorn, Mr. Schirkowski. They too had fled to middle Germany and found shelter on a farm. He knocked on their door. Mrs. Schirkowski opened it and exclaimed,

"Herbert. Höfer, you are alive. How is your family…" He smiled at her husband who had appeared behind her.

"Hi, meet your son," he said and explained that he needed to change his name, because he had escaped from prison, and now had no papers to identify himself when the police stopped him, as they did frequently expecting to find more former Nazis. Father had told the officer at the courthouse that he found his parents and wanted to get his birth certificate from them, so he could get his passport. The Schirkowskis welcomed him as their son, understanding that he had to assume their name and helped him to get "legal" papers. For one year, Father kept hiding under his incognito and constantly changed his whereabouts.

In the meantime, the Russians confiscated our farm, although it was not large enough to fall under the Bodenreform[141]. Large estates over 100 hectares were taken from their owners. The fields and animals were distributed among farm workers, small farmers, and refugees who wanted to own land and were willing to farm. The original owners had to leave their homestead and the district. In the Soviet-controlled zone, smaller farms were often taken for political reasons as well. Usually some envious or disgruntled person denounced the owner by claiming that the estate holder was a war criminal, or belonged to the Nazi party, or worked against the Communist ideology.

For a short time, Mr. Rassmann had control over the farm, but soon it became a kolkhoz (collective farm) or VEB.[142] That meant he had to give it up. He received the order to work with the rest of the farm hands and do all farm activities collectively—as the blacksmith had predicted—in a commune. Most of what they produced had to be delivered to a collection station from which it supposedly went to feed city folks, but actually it was channeled to Russia or privileged Communists. Our family had to leave the district; only Grandma was allowed to stay.

After Martin Bosert told Oma about our situation, she took the overly crowded train to Themar, a town about five kilometers away from St. Bernhard and then walked the long path through the woods to us. She carried food for us. She certainly was not used to walking with a heavy load. My mother never forgot how Oma came to our rescue. She arrived

---

141 "Bodenreform" is the German word for the land reform, which started late 1945. It was only partially heeded in the French sector and hardly at all in the British and American sectors. But under the Bodenreform the Soviets not only confiscated farms, they also claimed the right to take over whole factories, dismantle them, and ship them to Russia.

142 VEB stands for "Volkseigener Betrieb," literally translated (folk-owned business.) It had become nationally owned property, to be worked by the people, for all the people.

in the beginning of November. She did not stay long and suggested to my mother, "Paula, I have to leave soon and take Ilse-Rose with me to Klostermansfeld. Of course, all of you are welcome to come, too."

"I know, Mother. That keeps me going."

"Only, you cannot come with me right away. There is no room in our house."

"Why? You always managed to find a place for us."

Oma groaned, "Herbert's farm wasn't the only one confiscated." Before she could continue to explain why we could not join Oma now, my mother suddenly realized that most of our relatives had large estates. She wailed, "Magda, Lisbeth, Richard, Wilhelm, Tante Klärchen?"

"Yes," Oma nodded sadly, "all of them lost their farms and have to abandon them soon. So they would not be ordered to live in barracks, they requested our farm as their refuge. First your sister Magda and her daughter claimed they could live with us. Then Lisbeth, with her three little children, and Aunt Klärchen declared our address as the place where they could stay. We still have Aunt Bitta's family living with us. There is Mrs. Kleefeld with her four children from Berlin and we had to take in a new family from the Baltic states who have two children."

Mother slowly sat down and put her hands in front of her face. She moaned, "Mother, we have orders to leave here in a few days. Where can I go? Should I try Hilde in Heidelberg?" Oma shock her head, "Her place is overcrowded as well, and they do not have food." My mother swallowed hard to suppress her tears. Oma always ready to console assured her, "Paula, I will find a place for you and Hildegard."

"Mother, you say Hildegard and me, but I will not be separated from Reinhold again. He already speaks in the St. Bernhard dialect. I need to take him with me, too. Grandma hardly has enough food for herself. Winter is coming. We had the first snow already."

"Paula, there will be a place for you, I promise. I only do not know …" Suddenly, her face lit up. She exclaimed, "Wait! I have it. Great-grandmother! She has two bedrooms! Yes, that will work. You can stay with her in Ersleben[143] until Mrs. Kleefeld moves out." As always, Oma would find the best solution for our terrible situation of becoming homeless.

Oma left and took me along. I had pretty much outgrown my clothing, but in those times, nobody cared. What counted was having something warm to wear, no matter if it fit.

My mother had to sell the last logs Father and Martin had cut, the horses, and the wagon, and she had to let the police know that she was leaving for Edersleben. These errands had to be done in the town where my father had been in prison and we were registered. In the morning, she and Ernst drove the horses and wagon to the town. Ernst had to take the train from there to his high school. He had to stay with the woman who had promised my parents to give him room and board. My mother did not know how to get back to us after she completed the errands. She had to face the long twelve- mile walk. Nobody dared to offer her a ride. The police had treated her rather harshly. They had taken away the horses. I do not know how much money she got for the wagon and logs. Somehow, the people who purchased these things gave her a bottle of rum as well. She could use the strong alcohol more than the money. She would keep it as barter for food or clothing.

It snowed when she walked back to St. Bernhard. Utterly discouraged and exhausted, she cowered down against a snow bank, closed her eyes, and envisioned how it would be if she drank the rum, fell asleep, and froze to death. All the pain, all the harassment, all the anxiousness about her children would be over. Startled, she thought, *my children! No ... my children need me. I must be there for them.* She stood up and dragged herself to St. Bernhard.

Soon she left with Reinhold and Hildegard for Edersleben. There, she stayed with our great-grandmother, who still waxed her floors to a mirror's shine. One day, Hildegard slipped and sailed along the balustrade, almost

---

143   Edersleben was the village where Great grandmother and Aunt Klärchen lived; the latter had to leave her estate. Great grandmother being over 80 was allowed to stay.

all the way down the staircase. My mother had to ask the old lady not to polish the floors, especially since she insisted that everybody entering her apartment had to take his or her shoes off and walk around the place with socks on.

It was not easy for Great-grandmother to live with kids again. She had been a stern mother with her own children. My mother needed to explain to her that Reinhold was only four years old and had been away from her for a long time. He had just bonded with my mother again after living with Grandma in St. Bernhard. My mother promised he would lose his dialect and learn to speak High German.

In Edersleben it was so different from St. Bernhard, where the people avoided Grandma, because her husband voted against the Communist party and her son had been arrested. Great-grandmother had good connections in Edersleben. Soon they would celebrate Christmas. She was able to get the necessary ingredients for her famous delicious Christmas cookies. She helped my mother to prepare as well as she could at least some things for Christmas, so Hildegard, Ernst and Reinhold would get a few presents.

During his Christmas vacation, my older brother came to Edersleben. He looked terribly undernourished. My mother was shocked and asked him, "Ernst didn't you have enough to eat? You look so skinny. I tried to send packages to you. The last one had bread and some smoked ham from Great- grandmother."

"What bread and ham?" he asked back.

"The package I sent a week ago, just like all the other packages with food I mailed."

"I never got any of that food, Mother," Ernst said.

My mother was appalled. She had bartered away the rum for bread, some cheese, and preserved meats, so Ernst would get extra food. She wondered how she could get him away from that woman. She thought, *Best would be if we all could live with Oma again and Ernst could enter the High School in Eisleben.*

"I have to find a way to get you away from Gotha's senior high, Ernst."

"I'ld like that, Mom, but how?"

"I wish Father would be able to come and bring you to Uncle Martin."

And then shortly before Christmas Eve, my father appeared. He could only visit for a short time. He never dared to linger in one place. He had to stay ahead of the Russian and German police. Nevertheless, he risked celebrating Christmas with his family. Before he had to leave again my mother turned to him.

"Herbert, look how skinny Ernst has become. We have to take him away from that woman. She never shared the parcels I had sent. He will starve at her place. Despite his hunger he has good grades and…" My father broke into her train of thoughts and suggestions.

"Paula, I promise to bring Ernst to another place nearer to your mother. Halle or Eisleben have senior high schools. He could stay with Oma and take the train or bus to school."

"Yes, that would be best." Mother agreed, "I know that Mrs. Kleefeld has to go back to Berlin in the next two weeks, then we can move into her two rooms. In Klostermansfeld Ernst can attend the confirmation class and get confirmed next year on Palm Sunday."

Father left right after the holidays. Ernst still had to go back to Gotha, but he knew Father would quickly rescue him.

At Christmas 1945 I was with the many relatives in Klostermansfeld while the rest of my family enjoyed each other at my great-grandmother's. I did not know that my father was alive and in Edersleben. They did not dare to contact me or my relatives knowing that the police or the Soviets were constantly closing in on Father. He had sent word to Aunt Ida in St. Bernhard that she should urge her husband, Hans Höfer, to leave right away whenever he would show up. When Uncle Hans finally was released from the French prison camp and came to St. Bernhard, he either did not heed my father's warning or never received it. In a matter of two hours the police arrested him. He was never seen by any of us again. We heard they had brought him to Buchenwald, the notorious concentration camp, which the Russians now used for their purposes to punish war criminals, SS members, other Nazis, political opponents, and many innocent, but denounced people.

In 1990 Uncle Hans' daughter Marlis researched the Stasi[144] documents and discovered her father had died at the concentration camp in 1946. They never informed my aunt about her husband's death. For many years Aunt Ida hesitated to declare her husband as deceased, and thus she forfeited the pension[145] for soldier widows. She had hoped and waited for his return for close to 45 years.

---

144 *Stasi* is an abbreviation that the East Germans used for "Ministerium für Staatssicherheit," (Ministry of State Security).

145 After the western sectors formed a new government called the Federal Republic of Germany (FRG) between 1948–49, all widows and orphans of soldiers who fought in WWII continued to receive a portion of their husband's pension, even if they had moved to other countries. After Germany was united again in 1990, my aunt declared my uncle as deceased, applied for this pension and promptly received the payment.

CHAPTER 8

Long ago you laid the foundation of the earth, and the heavens are the work of your hands. They will perish, but you endure; they will all wear out like a garment. You change them like clothing, and they pass away; but you are the same, and your years have no end. Psalm 102:25-27

1946-47 Under Soviet Control
Traditions Survive

When Oma took me with her from St. Bernhard to Klostermansfeld, I had to face another round of vaccinations. Did the Russians think the American injections from last June were not good enough? Now I received a second dose of serums, but no DDT powder. Not long after, my head began to itch something fierce. The hairdresser, who washed our hair once a month, notified Aunt Ursel that I had lice. Oma ran a fine-tooth comb dipped in oil through my hair. She squashed the nits between her thumbnails. It did not help. Finally, we were able to get Kuprex.[146] After they had applied it to my head and hair—I had long braids—they wrapped my hair in a huge towel. Hours later, it was washed. The stench of this cure lasted for days, no matter how often we washed my hair. I stayed home from school during that procedure, which had to be repeated after a week. It worked.

"Rosebud, do not get close to anybody's head," Oma advised. "You might get lice again. I'll fasten your braids around your head so your hair won't fly all over the place and touch others." I must have followed her instructions to a T. I never had lice again.

---

146 A substance used to wash lice invested hair without rinsing right away. We covered our hair with a towel wrapped like a turban. It had to stay on the head for hours, thus killing the lice. The procedure had to be repeated to get rid of the newly hatched lice from the nits left clinging to the hair.

As before, Klärchen and I attended the same class. Miss Karsdorf was gone. We had a new, much younger teacher. When I had been in St. Bernhard, the Russian language had already become required teaching in all schools. I reluctantly learned some of the vocabulary and the "funny" letters of the Russian (Cyrillic) alphabet. Soon, the street signs at the town and village entrances were written in Russian and German letters.

I dressed for school; I did not have long stockings to wear in the frigid temperature. I just put on a pair of old boots, a skirt a little too short, a jacket over a blouse, and knee socks Grandma had knitted for me. While my knees were freezing, I still thought in indoctrinated terms, Spartans were tough and so am I.

One morning when my girlfriend Klärchen did not accompany me to school, I heard laughter behind me. "Look! The Oemler! She is wearing knee socks in this weather."

Another voice: "Oemler does not need long stockings. Her fat keeps her warm. She gets all the food she wants."

I thought, *Okay, I have been here so often, that they think my last name is Oemler and not Höfer. Should I tell them?*

Some of my schoolmates were influenced by their parents. They had been Communists before Hitler became a dictator. They never belonged to the Nazi party and wanted to show that now the tables had turned and they were in charge. My mother had called Helga's grandparents "noble Communists."[147] What she meant by this expression, I was not sure. But anyway, "noble" sounded dignified. I found that we had new classmates. They were children of displaced people who still looked for their missing relatives, always hoping to find them soon.

Uncle Große was asked to be the rector of our school again. He had been the headmaster before the Nazi regime. He disagreed with the National Socialists and never joined the Nazi party; therefore, they had replaced him. Now, in his seventies, the Soviets reinstated him. He

---

147 In my mother's eyes, they were Communists out of conviction. They envisioned sharing all the riches of the earth with each other. They definitely were not Bolshevists, or members of the Soviet's Communist party.

became my tutor, since I still could not spell correctly. He combined his dictation with anecdotes about Martin Luther and usually stopped at the most interesting places. "What happened then?" I would ask.

"You will find out when you come back on Tuesday," he would answer with a friendly smile. By keeping me guessing about the conclusions of the stories, he made sure I did not skip my spelling lessons.

I brought vegetables, meat, and sometimes a piece of cake for him and his wife. Usually when I arrived with my treasures, they would eat some of it before he started the tutor session. In his garden, he kept beehives. I admired him when he went to check on his bees without any protection except for the pipe he smoked. He reached into the hive with his bare hand, pulled out one of the frames, and gently tapped the bees off the honeycomb. If the frame was filled enough, he cut off a piece from the comb for Oma.

Late in November, Uncle Martin sent me to the butcher. "Ilse-Rose, tell Mr. Probst we need him to slaughter two pigs and a calf next week. And tell him he can keep most of the calf as payment for his service."

"Don't go into the store if you see people in there," Aunt Ursel added. "Ring the bell at the gate to their courtyard. Somebody will open it. Tell them you come from Martin Oemler and you need to talk to Mr. Probst personally."

I walked to the butcher shop a short mile away. Since people were in the store, I went to the courtyard door. Where was the bell I was supposed to ring? I could not see it in the normal place for doorbells. There was no button, only an old string hung from the upper part of the doorframe. I tried knocking … nobody came. I watched as people stepped out of the shop. Finally a moment when all the clients had left! I entered the store. The saleslady was nowhere to be seen. I stood there and waited. A new customer entered, and promptly the clerk came back. She addressed the lady, "May I help you?"

The shopper said politely, pointing to me, "This child was here before me."

I stammered, "Oh, I can wait; I only have a message to deliver."

"Well, tell it to me," the salesperson tried to encourage me. I shook my head. Losing patience with me, she served the lady and then more customers entered the store to buy the meat or sausages hanging against the tiled wall. The saleslady snipped their meat stamps from their ration cards. I went home.

Aunt Ursel asked me right away, "When is the butcher coming? What did he say?"

"There were people in the shop and I could not find a doorbell button on the courtyard door. I knocked, but nobody came. I waited until the shop was empty, but …"

"Well, did you speak to Mr. Probst?" she interrupted me. I shook my head. "You did not give the message to the clerk, did you?" Aunt Ursel was definitely anxious and displeased. "Stinky Rose," she said mockingly, "there is no bell button. They have a string you need to pull. It is connected to a little bell in their house. You have to understand that we cannot rely on electricity in these times. An electric buzzer would not work, but a bell on a string works without electricity. So go back and deliver the message." I went back, pulled on the old string, and a dog started to bark loudly.

"Quiet! Bad, naughty dog!" I heard. Then the door was opened a crack.

"I need to talk to Mr. Probst personally; Mr. Oemler sent me." Uncle Martin's name was magic. The door opened wide, the dog was calmed, and I was led into the house via a back door. I faithfully delivered my message, wondering why the grown-ups made all that fuss. I could have talked to him in the store. I was not aware of the stringent rules the Soviet government had set up. Most of the meat had to be sent to the common market. Uncle Martin did not get much pay for it. If he did not slaughter in secret, he would not have enough left for his workers, his family and his relatives who most likely would fall under the Bodenreform.[148] .

---

148   Originally, the four Allies concluded that all the big estates and factories had to be confiscated. It mostly only affected estates and businesses in the Russian sector.

A week later, Mr. Probst came early in the morning. They had prepared a roaring fire underneath both kettles in the wash kitchen. The first squealing pig was brought out by its hind legs. The new farm apprentice held the animal between his legs and by its ears. The butcher plunged an instrument against its forehead and pressed a button; a short bang, and the pig was numbed. Mr. Probst opened up the main artery in its neck with a big, sharp knife. He called to me, "Bring the pail!" Aunt Ursel had given me a large bowl. I had to hold it under the spurting stream of blood and stir with a big wooden spoon, so the blood would not curdle. When the red flow subsided, I carried the bowl into the wash kitchen, put it on the table, and stood in line with the rest of the children. The butcher jokingly said, "I have to measure your mouths so I know how big I have to make your very own blood sausage." He used a funnel and dipped it into the cooling blood. We had to part our lips wide so he could literally mark a blood red circle around our mouths. Later in the day, we did get our own sausage. It was stuffed with a mixture made from the blood, tiny bits of bacon, and the brain of the pig. Mr. Probst had even marked each with our own name. They had been boiled in the kettle, where other sausages were swimming in the hot broth. It was a delicacy not many Germans could enjoy at the end of 1945.

I also helped scour the bristles off the pig's skin after it had been doused with boiling water and was plunged into the big washtub. The water was poured through a fine sieve to catch the bristles. I had to deliver these to the brush maker in our village, who was glad to receive them, but I was not to tell that we slaughtered two hogs. The old man might have wondered what type of pigs Uncle Martin raised since one swine could render so many fine bristles, but he never asked.

The second slaughter—one sow and one calf—had to be done secretly after the farm workers and household helpers had left for the day. We had to work through the night and put some of the meat away in the pantry upstairs, which really used to be a bathroom. Pork was turned into ham, bacon, and sausage. Lesser cuts were laid in brine. Its salt preserved the meat in the unheated room during the cool winter months.

Mr. Probst took most of the boiled sausages home to cure them in his smokehouse. Intermittently, Aunt Ursel sent me to his shop to get some of them. Again, no one was to know that we had butchered another pig and a calf. By not storing all of the smoked goods in our pantry, Uncle Martin hoped that the helpers in the house did not harbor suspicions of our secret slaughter. We could not trust anybody. It was even worse than when we lived under the Nazis. At that time, we at least were not suspected of being against the Hitler regime. Now, with the political affiliation of my grandfather Höfer and my father's escape from prison, we knew we were being spied on. The informants of the Soviets used the same methods as the Gestapo did. Now it was the Stasi who targeted children for information that could be used against the grown-ups. Uncle Martin told me, "If somebody asks you a question, don't answer right away, just play dumb for five minutes. They usually give up on you."

The Russians, governing all farm production, ordered each farmer to deliver a certain amount of eggs, chickens, geese, ducks, goats, pigs, calves, sheep, and rabbits. Not only did livestock have to be handed over, but also milk, grain, fruit, and other farm products. My uncle could grow carrots, cabbage, and onions in the same field because its soil was very fertile. He brought vegetables all the way to Leipzig for the common market. The pay for these was very little. He was expected to share his produce and animals with everyone. If the delivery of the assigned foodstuffs fell short, the farmer had to find some other commodities or face a prison sentence.

We soon needed all the food we could secretly put aside. When I arrived in early November 1945, I met Aunt Bitta and her family again and her mother, Aunt Mertens, who had come from Cottbus. Aunt Hilde's mother-in- law Mrs. Bohne left Berlin-Charlottenburg not wanting to starve to death there. She could not join her daughter-in-law in Heidelberg because at that time in West Germany, food was just as hard to come by as in Berlin. Aunt Hilde's house overflowed with people too, for whom she and Uncle Willi had to supply room and board. The two elderly ladies had joined Aunt Ursel's friend and her baby.

Every one of us needed a place to sleep. My three cousins—Hermjörg, Lutz, and Jochen—slept in the small nursery off the master bedroom. For Eberhard Fleisher, the new apprentice, Aunt Ursel had prepared the room where the Russian women soldiers as civil workers had formerly stayed. The mother from Silesia with her six children had orders to move out. Her room was given to a family of four from the Baltic area. The Soviet Union had started the largest exodus in history. The Baltic family was one out of the millions who were forced from their homes because the Soviet Union had acquired parts of former German, Hungarian, Polish, and Austrian areas. The Russian Communists wanted to make sure that no Germans remained in these newly added lands under their control.

<hr/>

The Stammtisch met as usual at their pub and talked about the frustrations they and many others had to face. There was the multitude of people who still looked for their lost relatives. Many needed jobs. The farmer, wiping the foam of a beer from his mouth, opened their conversation. "Margret, the innkeeper's daughter, runs this place rather well, don't you think?"

The former mayor, now released from interrogation, agreed. "She knows how to draw a good glass of beer. She and her mother recovered rather fast. I guess in these times, you are forced not to mourn for too long." He knew it only too well. He did not have enough time to grieve when his son was killed during the battle of Normandy.

They had met with Leipziger and Berliner. Hamburger had already left for his hometown, now occupied by the British forces. As soon as the relocation of displaced people had started under the control of the Allied forces, he had applied to go back to Hamburg trying to find a place where his family could live. Leipziger and Berliner were not so keen on going back to their cities. The main reason was that they did not want to live under Soviet control. Berliner also hesitated because he first wanted to find out which one of the four sectors[149] in his hometown would be assigned to

---

149 Berlin was divided among the four Allies. The Russian sector was the biggest part of Berlin. See the map on the following page.

him. Therefore he waited, especially since not all of his family had come with him to the village. He was still searching for his wife and youngest son.

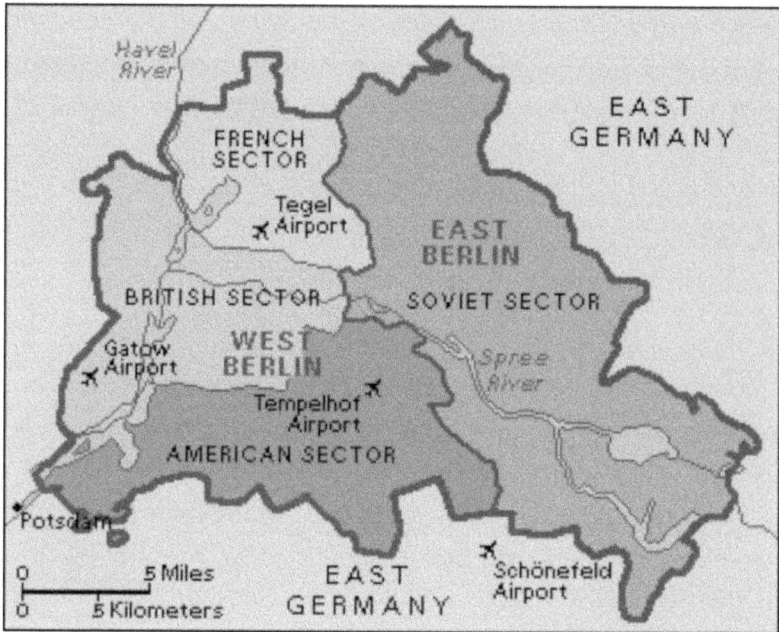

Courtesy of Pinterest History | Berlin, Berlin wall, German history

One-eyed Berliner wondered what jobs would be available for him and his Stammtisch members, although Leipziger had been offered a position as a teacher at the elementary school. Of course, it was clear to him that the farmer continued to work his fields. He asked the former mayor, "What are you doing now, since you lost your job?"

"I am helping the Red Cross to relocate people, but more importantly, I help families to find each other. You know how crowded our trains were when the people fled from the east. Many children were separated from their mothers and siblings. The Red Cross and other missions have taken care of these children, but their families are anxious to find them." He sighed and continued, "They asked me to help since I know how to keep records of people, how to file and ..."

Suddenly it dawned on Berliner where he had heard his voice, he yelled interrupting the former mayor. "Oh my gosh, Mayor—I hope you do not mind that I still call you that—it is your voice I hear every night after the news on the radio, enumerating the many people who are looking for their relatives, and later on, describing the children who need to find their parents!"

The former mayor nodded and said, "To make it simple for all of you, just call me 'Mayor'. I do not know how else you could address me now, my volunteer job in the evening does not lend itself to a title anyway."

"It could be 'Radio announcer'!" Berliner suggested.

"Or 'Family-Reuniting-Clerk For the Red Cross'." Leipziger would come up with a lengthy title like that. After all, he had been a librarian before.

"Or 'Red Cross Helper'," the farmer chuckled. He grinned since Red Cross Helpers usually were young female nurses but then he added, "Good! 'Mayor' is fine with me."

Mayor told them that the Red Cross was getting good responses to its search efforts. People who were looking for their relatives would call the radio station, and many of the missing ones answered within hours. He remarked, "After the war was over the first attempts to locate lost relatives were done by just little notes pinned on makeshift bulletin boards at train and- police stations."

"Yes, I have seen them," Leipziger cut in, and added, "They would read: 'Anja Meyer is here; inquire at the school.' Or they gave an address or phone number where they could be reached."

Mayor responded. "But that left it up to chance if their relative would ever scan the note, and young children could not read them. Yes, when it comes to lost children, we have an especially hard time. Ask a toddler his or her name, where he used to live, his or her age. It is impossible to get accurate information ... and then, there are the soldiers who came home to find bombed houses. Their families had been evacuated, or died in bombing raids or were injured or pushed by enemy forces from their homes."

"Yes, these are awful times for displaced people," the farmer agreed. Wanting to play cards instead of discussing all the problems they faced, he suggested, "Well, we will not solve all of these problems tonight. Let's have a good round of Skat. Berliner, it's your turn to deal." He shuffled the cards, and Berliner dealt.

They were playing with concentration, looking into their cards, when a fist appeared on the table, tapping the traditional "Good evening."[150] All of them looked up. Mayor and the farmer stared at the somewhat familiar face. They recognized it, only it had changed so much. Finally, the farmer remembered. He pushed back his chair, jumped up, and exclaimed, "Man, Pharmacist, I don't believe it. It's you!!"

The pharmacist nodded and answered in a hoarse voice, "It's me."

"But we heard you were ambushed by the partisans."

"There is truth to that. My whole company was, but I was not with them. I had dysentery. They let me lie in a horse stable, unable to take care of me, thinking I might die. But being a pharmacist, I knew it would help to pack myself into the horse manure, which is filled with ammonia. It created the heat I needed. And the ammonia disinfected the area around me. When I felt better, I could not find my company. Found out that all of them had been killed. So I tried to avoid the partisans and the German military. I spoke little, gave myself another name, and finally worked with a doctor in a remote village in the former Polish area."

"Polish area?" the farmer wondered. "You were in Yugoslavia, right? Why go north?"

The pharmacist continued, "I know a little Polish, and before the war ended, many Germans still lived up there who did not want to flee and leave their businesses, factories, or farms when the Russians came. There were German troops. I tried to report to the German military, but just like in Yugoslavia when I was on my way, hellish fighting started, and I, without a gun—what could I do? Before I knew it, the Russians had

---

150 In Germany, when you arrive a little late and join your familiar group of students or Stammtisch members, you knock on the table for "good evening" instead of shaking everybody's hand.

control of that area again. It went back and forth several times between the Russian and German armies. The doctor had his hands full with so many injured people, and not all of them were hurting because of the fighting, but because of the Russians, who took their revenge on the civilians." He stopped a moment and then mumbled, "I do not like to talk about it."

"We understand," the farmer said.

Leipziger was curious; he wanted to know how the pharmacist came back to his village, "But how were you able to come back here?"

"When the war was over and the borders between the Allies in Germany were established, the Russian authorities forced all Germans to leave the now reestablished Poland under Soviet control. The Russian soldiers pushed the doctor and me, along with all the other ethnic Germans, to the station. They crammed us into an open wagon. Mind you, it had no roof. Animals are transported better than we were." The pharmacist sighed, "And we were even the lucky ones. We did not need to walk. It was cold; we stood so close to each other that no one could sit down. We could not even help the sick, who would faint and lean on others with buckled knees. We had no food, nothing to drink. They brought us to Berlin first. When we exited the train, many a person's body collapsed … dead." All of them were quiet. What can one say when faced with this type of war aftermath?

The pharmacist continued after a short pause, "In Berlin, we were ordered into tents or barracks until they commanded us in which part of Germany to relocate. We were shipped to various Allied occupied zones. The ones from Poland either stayed in the Russian sector or went to the British sector. I could claim that I originated from our village, so they sent me here." The farmer knew about it. He had to give shelter to people who had been thrown from their homes in the former Polish/German area. He noted, "I heard that the Soviets ousted over 3.5 million people who had any German affiliation. Ethnic cleansing, I call it."

"I can tell you many stories about it," the pharmacist replied. "Farmer, you said 3.5 million had to be absorbed from the Baltic and

Polish areas in the four zones of Germany, but what about the people from Czechoslovakia, from Austria, and Hungary?"

"I know about these," Mayor interrupted. "They were sent to the French and American sectors. I heard there were about 3 million as well. We at the Red Cross Search Station have the grim job of telling surviving relatives that their loved ones might have been among the estimated 2,111,000 people who died during these Soviet ordered transports."[151]

"I don't know where these displaced people will find room," Leipziger wondered.

"Well, look here. My farmhouse is overflowing with people, and Berliner had to give up one of his two rooms to another family of five, whereas he himself has two children."

"And he is waiting to find his wife and his youngest son," Mayor added.

Berliner sighed, "I am afraid they died. We had been ordered to leave Berlin and go to East Prussia, then when the Russian army came closer they ordered us to come here, but we got separated. My wife could squeeze into the train with my youngest. But I and my daughters had to jump on the next train. It stopped, because American pilots strafed it. We had to leave the train and hide in the woods. —Please spare me from reliving the terror of telling you how—in the end, we landed here hoping to find my wife and son."

Mayor tried to comfort him. "You will find them. They might still be in Berlin waiting for you. Just give your information to the Red Cross. We do our best to locate family members and to find out what happened to them."

They did not continue their card game that night. They listened to the pharmacist's grim story and told him what had taken place at home—the innkeeper's suicide, the teacher's disappearance, the farmer's crushed head and Hamburger returning home.

---

151 Many people did not survive the transport in open train wagons, in trucks, or on foot.

In January 1946, my uncle's house saw a second influx of relatives. After Uncle Martin helped Mrs. Kleefeld with her four children to get to the station so they could go back to Berlin, my mother came from Edersleben with Hildegard and Reinhold. We moved to the two rooms that Mrs. Kleefeld had occupied. Somehow, Oma had arranged for a huge double bed. It was big enough for Hildegard, my mother, little Reinhold, and me to sleep in. The other room had a sofa, some chairs, and a table. At the beginning of our stay in Klostermansfeld, we did not use it as a dining room. We ate with all the other relatives downstairs in the Wirtschaftsstube. There were sixteen people for the noontime dinner. A small table was set for the five younger children. Soon after, we had to eat in shifts.

By January 16, 1946, Aunt Magda, her husband Uncle Richard, and their daughter Ingrid, arrived at Oemlers. Their farm had fallen under the Bodenreform. They had to leave their district. Uncle Richard bred beautiful horses. The Russians who had taken over his mansion tried to ride his purebreds. His heart almost broke when he saw how these beautiful stallions and mares were treated. The Russians used neither saddles nor the most basic riding gear. A halter and a whip were all they needed.

Uncle Richard only stayed a few hours until Uncle Martin could help him reach the border. He crossed into the British sector successfully. Some time later he entered the American zone to stay in Heidelberg with his brother, Uncle Willi, who helped him to secure a new position on a farm owned by Austrian nobility.

Shortly after Aunt Magda and Ingrid arrived, Aunt Lisbeth and her three young sons (about the same age as Aunt Ursel's children) needed shelter. Her husband was not with her. He left immediately for the western sectors to look for work after his farm was confiscated. Aunt Lisbeth could not go to her mother's place, since Aunt Klärchen's huge estate, located in the most fertile area of Germany, also fell under the Bodenreform. She too sought refuge in Klostermansfeld. They all ate in shifts, but now my mother decided to bring the food upstairs to our two rooms.

Despite of the danger of being ratted on by the woman who had taken Ernst's packages, my father went to Gotha to get my brother and bring him to Klostermansfeld. Cousin Ingrid lent Ernst her bicycle so he could ride it to school. His Senior High was located in Eisleben, about twelve kilometers (seven and a half miles) away. He returned late every afternoon. Once a week, he attended confirmation classes at our Protestant church.

Hildegard and I went to pre-confirmation class on Wednesday afternoons. The Russians allowed these meetings because they were called youth gatherings, a name that is without any indication of Christianity. They, like the Nazis before, wanted to indoctrinate us children against the grown-ups, and this time win us over to the Communist ideology. They celebrated certain days of the year. One of the most elaborate events was the first of May, Labor Day. Workers had to erect a huge pole near the sport field. It served as "Maibaum".[152] We watched the strongest boys as they tried to climb the slippery post. Not many could reach the top to pick one of the treasures hanging from the wagon wheel. The smaller children just looked on and clapped if one succeeded. We received hot dogs and gray underbaked chewy rolls with hot coca made from water and fat-free milk. For many of us, it was a treat we had not tasted for a long time. They ordered us to form rows of four to eight children and to march through the streets. Then we had to form a large human square around a podium. Here, a party leader addressed us. I thought his speech would never end. Afterward, we were allowed to go home. Every celebration was the same, except for the Maibaum. Sometimes we had to wait hours before we could march, especially during the cold winter days, but we always would get some kind of food. The Communist leaders tried to drill, imbue, and implant their ideology into us children. Slowly, they tried to undermine affiliations with any church. After a few years of their rule, the Soviets saw to it that preparations for Christian confirmation became a deterrent. Children attending them lost permission to enter

---

152 A telephone-pole-like mast serves as a Maypole, on its top is a small wagon wheel from which sausages, hams, bacons, and the like are hanging. Children were encouraged to climb the waxed pole. At the top, they could pick one of the food items and take it home.

higher education, such as high school or university. In 1954, the Russian occupation authorities instituted an alternative for confirmations, i.e. the fourteen-to sixteen-year-old girls and boys could have a special induction ceremony instead of being confirmed. If the family chose dedication to the Communist party over confirmation, they received favors. Many East German parents, growing up forty years under Soviet control, came to prefer the Jugendweihe[153] for their children to a confirmation in the Christian tradition, much to the chagrin of the West Germans.

In March 1946, Father visited again. He only wanted to stay long enough to bring Cousin Ingrid across the border into the British zone. Her father would meet them at the crossing point. The Russians started to be more protective of their border with the western zones. My father was familiar with several border-crossing points where you could find cover when the Russians started to shoot. My cousin told me that they were a party of four when they left for the dangerous border crossing. When the shooting started, my father threw himself on the ground and pulled Ingrid down with him. Then they crept through the furrows of a field, but the two naval officers who were with them did not survive the Soviet bullets. My father and cousin could not help them; they would have been the next victims. They had to lie absolutely still in their furrow. During the night, they finally could move again and crawl into the British zone.

---

153   To this day, in May, Germans in the former Soviet controlled states of Germany celebrate it instead of a confirmation. Now it is no longer a dedication to the Communist party, but an acknowledgment that the teens have reached adulthood.

Pentecost 1946

Hermjörg at the head of the goat, Lutz behind the goat, Hildegard behind Lutz, Uncle Nold Hosie (Aunt Bitta's husband) behind Hildegard. My mother in front of the Wirtschaftsstube window between Hildegard and me, Aunt Ursel behind me. Oma between Aunt Ursel and Uncle Martin in front of the horse stable. On the cart: in front Aunt Bitta beside her left Birgit, her daughter, behind Birgit, Reinhold in front of Uncle Martin, Jochen pretending to push the cart. Missing are my brother Ernst and my father, who had left for Gotha to bring Ernst back to Klostermansfeld.

After my father brought Ernst to Klostermansfeld as he had promised, he decided that his mother, our grandma, should leave St. Bernhard and join us. We divided the living room into a combined bed and dining room. One of Aunt Magda's tall wardrobes served as a separation wall, behind it stood Ernst's bed. Reinhold's cot and my bunk were on one side of the closet and Grandma's and Hildegard's were on the other side. My mother stayed in her room, keeping it ready for whenever Father showed up to hide him in their bedroom.

Grandma was a great help to my mother, who often was not at home. All of my relatives said, "Paula knows how to deal with the police, with legalities, the Russians, and all the ever-changing regulations for us." Therefore, she ran errands for everyone. My mother was instrumental in helping Aunt Magda to get permission to join her husband in the American zone. She even arranged for her sister to be allowed to store some of her belongings[154] with friends and us until these could be transported to the little village in which her husband had found employment as farmer by an Austrian count who owned land near Heidelberg.

Aunt Bohne was instructed to go back to Berlin. My mother made sure the old lady would receive permission to visit us often. I am positive that when my mother secured documents for my relatives, the authorities gave her the runaround. This did not dissuade her. She just wore them out.

She told us how she was able to get our old hope chest back, which we could not take along when we were ordered to leave St. Bernhard. She applied for permission to bring it to Klostermansfeld. As soon as her request was accepted, our old friend Mr. Schreyer, the blacksmith, helped her to transport it. But then police in Eisleben confiscated it a second time. With a smile Mother said, "I sat stoically on the police station's steps until they got tired of me and allowed me to take possession of the trunk if I could move it in a few hours. One call! And Uncle Martin supplied the wagon and horses to bring it to Klostermansfeld."

Aunt Lisbeth's husband and my father had the hardest time finding a place for their families in the western zones. None of us "ousted" people were looking for a place in the Russian zone. All of us hoped for employment in the western sectors.

In early summer, Uncle Martin was diagnosed with jaundice. Soon his three sons had it too, and after they were almost through with six weeks on the strictest diet, I came down with it. I laid in our living/bedroom. I was only allowed to eat toasted white bread. Any fat was out of the question, along with fruits and vegetables. I had to survive on only water and bread. We had not seen white bread for ages. Oma must have used her

---

154   My mother was able to secure one transport of furniture from Uncle Richard's farm.

persuasive skills (combined with a "present" of vegetables or meat) to have the baker make some refined wheat loaves for our sick family members.

Grandma did not think that this diet was a good way to get healthy and she had pity on me. She knew how much I liked the lentil soup Oma had cooked for everybody. Bringing a small bowl of it to my bed she instructed me, "Rosebud, you may taste some, just chew on it and then spit it out. You may not swallow it." I took a spoonful. Now, you try to chew soup without getting any of it in your stomach! "Rosebud, you are not spitting everything out that you had in your mouth."

"Grandma, I try, but it just runs down my throat."

"Well, I have to take it away from you." She gathered my spoon and dish, but she still wanted to comfort me. "I'll fry some bread in a little butter for you; you have to spit it out, but it will be easier for you to get rid of." She used the last butter she had left on her ration card for this delicacy. I nibbled very slowly and spewed it on the plate. I did not want any more; it had made me instantly, horribly sick. After six weeks, I was healthy, but rather weak. Nevertheless, I had learned how to knit the most durable heels for socks, because Grandma sat at my bedside and knitted while telling stories to me. During my illness, she patiently taught me more of the art of knitting and crocheting complicated garments. Where did she get yarn for it? She unraveled worn-out socks or sweaters, wetted the yarn, and wound it around a board. After it dried, it could be reused.

On New Year's Eve 1946, my Uncle Martin and Aunt Ursel left for a party at a friend's place. They hitched the horses to a sled, and took warm blankets, heated foot warmers, covers for the horses, and lanterns for the nightly drive back home. Oma always smiled. She liked for all of us to have fun. She would say, "Now, Martin, don't you drink too much! You know you have to drive home!" Uncle Martin laughed. "You know, Mother, even if I get tipsy, the horses know their way home. I do not need to do anything."

"Yes, I know. Just get into the carriage, well, tonight the sled, and let the reins hang loose, say *hü*, and fall asleep until the horses stop in front of our gate, and I open it for you." Silently she hoped that a Russian patrol would not stop them or even molest them.

With Uncle Martin and Aunt Ursel absent, Aunt Klärchen and Oma wanted us to have a nice New Year's Eve festival too. We were allowed to stay up late. The younger children were asleep by nine o'clock. Intermittently, one of us checked on them. We played games that supposedly foretold the future, but we had to understand that they were entertainment and it had nothing to do with reality, let alone the truth. Aunt Klärchen showed us how to melt lead and pour it into cold water. She told us, "The clump that you find on the bottom of the pan tells the future." I took my spoon with melted lead and poured a big blob. Could that be a baby in a cradle? Hildegard, more careful than I, gingerly let the lead flow into the water, and a delicate filigree shape emerged. "You can read anything out of this or nothing at all," Aunt Klärchen decided. Then we would peel apples. "You have to start at its blossom," instructed Aunt Klärchen, "and pare down to its stem without breaking the peel. Then take the peel into your right hand and walk to the door; facing the room, throw it over your shoulder to the floor. See, when it lands it forms a letter. This is the first letter of your future husband's name." I peeled very thinly and threw the rind; it formed a *J*. Hildegard's landed in an *H*. To make sure—and actually, because the apples tasted so good—we peeled another one and threw the peel anew. Mine formed a *J* again and Hildegard's a *D* this time.

"This really does not tell anything," my sister concluded. She had two different letters, but I thought that mine resembled a *J* twice. It is a funny coincidence that my husband's name is **J**amison and Hildegard's was **H**ans **D**ieter, but apple peels hardly ever form letters of the alphabet. It takes quite some imagination to read letters out of them.

The electricity had been turned off long ago. We sat around an oil lamp with one of those pretty lampshades that Oma kept in the upper attic. Aunt Klärchen played all kinds of games with us. I never grew tired. At midnight, we were allowed to drink a little of the Glühwein[155] Oma had prepared on the coal stove in the kitchen. She showed us how to toast by gently clinking the Jenaer glasses[156] together. She said, "When you are older, you can drink real wine out of glasses with a stem. Then, hold the glass by its stem. The clinking sounds so much more melodious when you toast that way." She demonstrated it with two wine glasses filled with water. She was right. Then she showed us how differently a glass "sings" when half full, filled to the brim, or just a little. She wet her finger and circled around the glass rim with it until it started to hum. Now we tried it. *We are creating a real concert,* I thought. Then, it was time to go to bed. This was a much better evening than Christmas Eve, when I had been without my siblings and parents and had to watch the toddlers who had been rather cranky.

I had so much in common with Aunt Klärchen. Both of us liked to play cards, we relished in story telling, and we were good at bookkeeping. We loved puzzle games, crosswords, or jigsaw puzzles. We enjoyed all kinds of social entertainment. We gladly worked in the garden and delighted in cooking. She was my favorite godmother. Soon she left to stay with her friends in the Harz Mountains. Since she always lived in the Russian zone and I went to the western zones in 1947, I never had the opportunity to see her and missed out on the pleasure of her company.

One time, when my father came, he was covered with sores and boils because of malnutrition. He needed good food and medical care. How my mother managed to provide it, I never found out. This time, hiding Father was worse than before. I had to watch what I said even more. Again, my best friend was not allowed to visit us.

Father was cooped up in his room and bored. When he saw me drawing a picture of spring flowers for my schoolwork, he took the paper

---

155   "Glühwein" (glowing wine) is a mulled wine made from red wine mixed with water, cinnamon sticks, some cloves, and sugar. You consume it when hot or at least very warm. Sometimes they add a little rum to it.

156   In Jena, Thuringia they produced a glass that can withstand very high temperatures. Germans like to drink hot tea out of these glasses.

and drew a beautiful picture of snowdrops. His action created a dilemma for me. Since paper was very scarce, I only had that one piece for my homework. I turned the paper over and penciled my spring flowers on it, hoping nobody would see my father's sketch on the back of it and the teacher would not collect our homework. I kept thinking, *how can I take his drawing to school? Won't they question me about it, if I show this in class? Everybody can see that I did not draw that picture. Should I lie?* I had just learned the Ten Commandments (and the meaning of each one of them according to Martin Luther's Little Catechism) in our pre-confirmation class, and wanted to obey them

I had made a commitment to Jesus Christ, the only person I knew who never had changed according to the various governments. He was the same two thousand years ago. He was not like the many grown-ups and children (influenced at home) who saluted, by now, the third flag. Miss Karsdorf had made us sing and pledge to the red, white, and black swastika flag. After the Americans entered, she had us pledge to the red, white, and blue stars-and- stripes one. After the Russians discharged her, we had to greet the red flag with the hammer and sickle, holding our right fists up. I did not anymore want to follow any authoritarian person and call him a lord. From now on Jesus was my LORD. Because *Jesus Christ is the same yesterday and today and forever.* Hebrews 13:8

When Germans received new flags in all four occupied zones these were red, black, and yellow. Later, after 1948, the DDR added the hammer and sickle, but that one, I never needed to respect. By then I was in the British zone and greeted the red, black, and yellow one with the eagle of the BRD.[157]

I believed that according to the Bible lying was a sin, but so was betraying my father—and not obeying my parents was another sin.

When we had to show our homework in school, I carefully laid my paper down. I tried to hide the side on which Father drew the flowers, but

---

157 DDR stands for "Deutsche Demokratische Republik" or in English GDR (German Democratic Republic). BRD stands for "Bundesrepublik Deutschland" or in English FRG. (Federal Republic of Germany). From 1948-1991, history has to deal with two German governments and/or countries.

my friend alongside of me saw the back page. She whispered, "You did not draw this, did you?" What was I to say? The whole morning, I had dreaded this moment and had prayed that no one would see his drawing, and now, she even asked me about it. But promptly the teacher looked at us. "Who spoke?" she asked disapprovingly. We raised our hands. "Don't talk when I teach!" she scolded. I breathed relief *Good, now I am not allowed to speak, I do not need to answer Klärchen's question. Thank You Jesus.*

However, I dreaded the walk home with her. Would she repeat her question about who drew the picture? Should I lie? Should I betray my father? As I tried to pull on a knitted hood, which was too small for me, the line from the Lord's Prayer entered my mind, *but deliver us from evil.* Would He deliver me out of my dilemma? Now Klärchen looked at me and shook her head saying, "You know, you do embarrass me when you wear this thing. It does not fit on your head. If you wear this cap, I am not walking with you. You look ridiculous." As painful as it was to hear my best friend talk to me in such a way, I was relieved that I did not need to go home with her and face the predicament, either to lie to her or betray my father.

On the next school day, when I met Klärchen, she asked me again. "Who drew the Snowdrops on your homework paper?" and I could answer truthfully, "My father." Did I betray him? No, because during the night, he had left and crossed the Russian border into the British zone successfully.

My sister and I hardly had any clothing left, since we were outgrowing the few things we owned. One day, the Russian police discovered hidden materials, yarns, and all kinds of sewing goods under the floorboards of a closed shop that formerly belonged to a Jewish family who had left in the early 1930's. These things were hauled onto an open truck. The German driver, employed by the Soviets, drove very slowly through the village. Helga's grandma yelled, "Eh, what are we waiting for? This stuff belongs to us and is not for the Russians." She climbed on the truck and began to throw things down.

My mother stood on the curb in amazement. This noble Communist deprives her Russian comrades of that good material, she thought. In the next moment, she heard Mrs. Nebert call, "Mrs. Höfer, here, take this for your girls!" with that she threw several yards of first-class Scottish woolen plaid and some skeins of yarn into my mother's arms. Oma knew a good seamstress who sewed skirts for my sister and me from this "Friedensware" and paid her with one of her food baskets. Grandma used the yarn to knit jackets for us. For years, we had worn clothing made out of unraveled yarn that scratched our skin rather badly. My sister could hardly stand it, but I clung to the old cliché, "the Spartans are tough, so am I." What did I know about the Spartans and their warmer climate, or their clothing? I pushed myself through anything that seemed unbearable with the thought of the brave Spartans. But for once a few more children and I had outfits made from brand new materials. It felt good.

After my great-grandmother died in the summer of 1946, Oma had inherited the household goods and gave all of them to us. We were allowed to transport some of her furniture to Klostermansfeld. Now we owned pots and pans again and even had bed-frames, chairs and a stable table.

Early in 1947 the Stammtisch met and as usual, the farmer opened the conversation.

"Does anybody know how Berliner is making out back in his hometown?"

Mayor answered him. "Well, he did find his wife and youngest son. They lived in Berlin in a camp for persons who needed to be relocated." The pharmacist, who had regained his job in the local drugstore, asked, "In which sector of Berlin does he reside?"

"He was lucky. He and his family were moved to the French sector," Mayor informed him. He would have liked to add aloud, "At least he is not under Communist control," but fearing somebody might denounce him, he only uttered it under his breath. "Hush!" the farmer whispered. "You know, ever since the KPD merged with the SPD and formed the "Sozialistische Einheitspartei Deutschlands,"[158] we have to continually watch out. Now

---

158   SED translated stands for Social Unity Party of Germany. It was formed under the Russian- controlled merger of the Communist Party of Germany (KPD) and

again, we have only one party to choose from when voting, namely the SED. It is just like under the Nazis and their NSDAP. Then we had to be on guard of the Gestapo, now it is the Stasi. Who can you trust?"

At that moment, a young man wearing a clergyman's outfit joined the Stammtisch members.

"What's new?" he asked. "Discussing the different controls of the four Allies? Eh!"

"Good evening, Pastor." They knocked with their fists on the table as reply to the clergy, who had disregarded the customary way of greeting.

"Sorry! I did not know you still hold to this old tradition. I heard you need a few more members for your Skat round. I thought you would not mind if I join you as long as I visit with my brother, the new mayor." The Stammtisch members looked at each other … and then the Farmer pulled a chair up for him. "You are in. Tell us where you come from."

Not answering his question, the clergyman remained standing eager to continue his train of thought, "Yes, the four Allies, they surely differ. I am positive that at many a Stammtisch they talk just like you about the Bodenreform (Land reform) for instance. It is irrational, almost funny; here in the Russian Zone, you had the confiscation of many estates, even the ones that were no bigger than 100 hectares. We in the American zone saw hardly any of this."

The farmer asked, "Well, where in the American zone, that is Bavaria, Hessen, and Baden Württemberg, do you find such huge farms as we had?" In his mind, he wondered about the motives that led the clergy to visit the Soviet sector. *Could it be just to see his brother's family? Was he a spy?*

The minister replied quickly, "Wait a minute! Baden Württemberg is split. The north for the Americans, but South Baden Württemberg, the Saar Basin even part of Tirol are under French control. Here they did experience the Bodenreform, although to a limited degree! Usually the

---

the Social Democratic Party of Germany (SPD) in April 1946. They adopted a programmatic document of goals and principles of the party.

owners of the estates could keep the hunting rights to their forest and only the lumber became communal property and none of the owners needed to leave their homes."

The farmer thought *this minister seems to know a lot about the four occupied zones in Germany.* Finally the pastor sat down and started to shuffle the cards, but now the pharmacist wanted to assess more about the clergyman. He stipulated, *one never knows for sure what type of guests are in our village,* and asked, "Ahem! You seem to be informed, so tell us how did the British handle the Bodenreform since there were larger farms in their zone? What happened to them?" The pastor surprised the Stammtisch members again with his detailed knowledge, saying.

"Reduced, but not all confiscated. Parceled out to poor farm workers, cottagers, and expellees from Poland and Lithuania, just like here."

"As far as I know, none of the western allies dismantled and transported all of the still-functioning factories as part of the war reparations," Mayor remarked. The farmer agreed. "Yes, I heard something to that effect too. The Brits and Americans only stripped or demolished the factories that supplied the arsenals of the German military." But then he continued, "Okay, let's not discuss more problems, especially the Bodenreform. It hits too close to home. I came here to play cards." Leipziger agreed and smiled at the farmer, "You deal the cards, please!"

The last time my father visited us was on Ernst's confirmation on Palm Sunday in 1947. Uncle Martin, Aunt Ursel, and Oma did not spare their provisions. They prepared a feast for all of us. On Monday, my father walked downstairs, through the courtyard, and into the gentlemen's room to thank Uncle Martin for the festive dinner. Several people who knew Father had seen him.

A few hours went by, and then a woman climbed upstairs to talk to my mother. "I have to speak with you, Mrs. Höfer," she whispered shyly. "I was at the mayor's office, and while I stood there waiting, I saw a letter on his desk. I could read that they are still asking for the whereabouts of your husband."

"Thank you for telling me," my mother said and added, knowing it was a lie, "I myself have no idea where he is. Yes, sometimes he comes, but he never stays long."

The woman left, and my mother went downstairs to catch Father before he would leave the gentlemen's room. "You must hide here until nightfall and then leave. They are looking for you and suspect you are here."

He nodded. "I'll take Ernst with me. We will stay with Uncle Reinhold in Goslar. I will try to get permission for you and the children to join me, as soon as I find a place to live." That night, my father and my brother successfully crossed the border. Now both were out of the Russian zone and in the British sector. Here, Father could be Herbert Höfer again. He was glad to shed his false name. Now he did not need to stay under cover anymore. The days of hiding him were over for us.

⟩⋯⟩⋯⟩⋯⟩⋯⟩⋯

The visiting pastor became a regular at the Stammtisch. The local members hoped he would soon leave for wherever he came from. He talked too much, and did not concentrate on the game. But they did not want to be disrespectful by asking him to rather not play Skat with them anymore. Actually, they were tired of constantly being on guard of what they said and how it could be interpreted.

At this Thursday evening, the clergyman was absent. After taking a deep breath of relief, Leipziger remarked, "We might have to meet at different times and in various locations. After Pastor left us last time, I fear Mayor might get questioned about his comments. And," he lowered his voice to a whisper, "and this reserved table might already be bugged to spy on us." The farmer, Mayor, and pharmacist nodded and Leipziger changed the discussion by declaring, "Let's face it, we like to forget the past and are willing to work on the restoration of Germany. We want better living conditions."

"You are right," the pharmacist agreed. "All of us want to live even better than before the war. My wife would like a refrigerator instead of our old ice box and I could also use one in our drug store."

206

"A washing machine would be nice," Margret, the innkeeper's daughter mused as she brought a new round of beer to the Stammtisch members.

The farmer wished, "...and I surely would rather plow my fields with a tractor and not with my horses." Margret added dreamingly, "A vacation would be awesome. I'd love to go on a sightseeing tour to look at the wonders of the world. See them on my own and not just read about them." Unfortunately, she, as most of the persons living in the Russian Zone, would encounter ever more stringent travel restrictions instead of having the freedom to experience the wonders of the world personally.

CHAPTER 9

God is our refuge and strength, a very present help in trouble. Psalm 46:1

Hamelin.

New Shelter, Hunger, Border Crossings

In 1947, my mother received permission to cross the Russian/British border with her two daughters and her youngest son. We were glad to finally join my father and older brother. We were the last relatives to leave Family Oemler for the western sectors. Grandma had to stay behind. Oma and Uncle Martin welcomed her to stay with them. She gladly left the rooms which we had occupied and moved downstairs into the old farmhouse, where she could help in the kitchen and knit for the three youngsters (Hermjörg, Lutz and Jochen). I think deep in her heart she did miss St. Bernhard where Paul, her brother, Marlis and Ernst, her grandchildren, and Aunt Ida, her daughter-in-law, resided.

My father had contacted Mrs. Herta Homburg, the widow of his former army major; to see if she could house us, so we did not need to stay in a cellar or camp.[159] She lived in Hamelin with her three children and her younger cousin; she already shared her five-room apartment with Major Frisch, his pregnant wife, and their five-year-old daughter, Wolftraut.

---

159 Usually, displaced people had to stay in a camp until they could find a place to live. Cellars were accepted as suitable living quarters.

Our room was on the second floor. It is the one with the bay windows. This photo was taken after the balcony was repaired and glass panes had been installed in all windows.

Hamelin had seen numerous bombing raids. Our three-floor apartment house, located very close to the railroad overpass, had been damaged. Mrs. Homburg gave us one room in exchange for my father's promise to assist her in taking care of her garden on the outskirts of town. He and Cousin Kappauf took turns guarding the crops, which thieves could steal any time. Father also offered my mother's cooking skills to prepare meals for her family and us. She developed quite a talent in creating meals for twelve people with the little food available, and with only two hours of electricity per day. We shared the kitchen with the Frisch family. They owned a stove but needed to use the sink and part of the pantry that was divided into four sections: Homburg, Frisch, Kappauf, and our family Höfer.

After my mother had to leave our belongings in Thorn in 1945 and now Oma's inherited furniture in Klostermansfeld, we started anew in Hamelin. We were able to bring some dishes with us. We used the doll-dinner set from Oma's attic. They supplemented Mrs. Homburg's china for our meals.

We lived on the second floor, which was on the same level as one of the many railroad tracks passing our windows. Their panes had been broken and only a few could be repaired with glass. We covered the rest with cardboard, old splintering plywood, or blankets. The balcony had lost its railing. The door leading to it could not be locked. After the Frisch's' second child had been born and started to crawl, we constantly had to watch that she did not push this door open and fall from the balcony. The Frisch family lived in one bedroom adjacent to the kitchen, with bunk beds, a small chest, a coal stove, three chairs, and a card table. We had six bunk beds in the corner room, facing the railway where freight trains stopped to fill their steam engines with water. Soon, my father found three small wardrobes for us. They stood in the hallway. That was all the furniture we owned, we were not allowed to bring any of Great-grandmother's bed frames. As long as Mrs. Homburg shared her dining-room (which also served as bedroom for her cousin) and her living-room we did not need more furnishings. We did our schoolwork on the large dining table. She, her daughter and her youngest son occupied her bedroom. When her older son visited, he shared either the dining room or the living room with Cousin Kappauf.

At the beginning of our stay in Hamelin, my father worked for the British guards at a prison camp. He searched for food in their garbage cans; often he did not find any edible discarded morsels, since the British had also suffered food shortages during and after the war. They hardly had leftovers and seldom threw anything away.

After the war, many Germans died of malnutrition or froze to death, especially in the unusually severe winter of 1946/47. Potatoes were a luxury; not many people had bread or vegetables, much less meat. Every Wednesday, my sister and I would go to a place where they slaughtered horses. They boiled the meat and bones. We stood in a long line hoping to get our little bucket filled with that broth, and when we were lucky, a bit of fat might be swimming on top. It was a welcome addition to our ration cards' food allowance. The saying prevailed: "Too little to live, too much to die."

Many European nations received America's help earlier than we in Germany. It was George Marshall who voiced his concern about the war-torn nations facing famine and economic crisis in the wake of World War II.

On June 5, 1947, in a commencement address at Harvard University, Secretary of State George C. Marshall first called for American assistance in restoring the economic infrastructure of Europe. Western Europe responded favorably, and the Truman administration proposed legislation. The resulting Economic Cooperation Act of [April 3,] 1948 restored European agricultural and industrial productivity. Credited with preventing famine and political chaos, the plan later earned General Marshall a Nobel Peace Prize.[160]

≻∙∽≻∙∽≻∙∽≻∙∽≻∙∽

At another meeting of the Stammtisch in 1947, Mayor opened their discussions with a complaint. "Ration cards? Starvation and frostbite cards!" He lamented. "They are worth as much as our money, namely nothing. They have no value. We still had stamps left for some coal and 250 grams of fat. My wife stood in a long line trying to get it, just to find out that the store was all out of butter, margarine, shortening or oil and

---

160   General Records of the United States Government, Record Group 11. National Archives and Record Administration, 700 Pennsylvania Ave. NW, Washington, DC 20408. http://www.archives.gov/exhibits/featured_documents/marshall_plan/.

they had not gotten a shipment of coal for over a week. So she sent the grandkids to get nettles and dandelions to cook it like spinach. Well, they did not bring enough greens, so she had to go on a hamster trip."[161] The pharmacist turned to the farmer with a sheepish grin, "Farmer, you have it made now, with the black market[162] thriving." All of them chimed in with their observations.

"Your drawers must fill up with silver."

"Your wife will sport all kinds of jewelry."

"You probably received first editions of rare books."

"Do you have some paintings, maybe a masterpiece, hanging in your living room by now?"

"How many fur coats can your wife select from, when she visits her friends?"

The farmer took a deep breath and shouted, "Stop, let me get a word in edgewise. Do you think it is easy to figure out how much to give for a silver spoon? You see that poor woman on her hamster trip, peddling her last belongings for bread, vegetables, just anything to eat. I do not have it so easy either. I need to get my grain turned into flour, let the miller have part of it as payment, same with the butcher when he slaughters my animals. And the dairy, when I want some cheese from them, they want cream or milk in return and the blacksmith, when he shoes my horses, rather takes meat than money—and then, there is the new government who wants most of my harvest. I have to be careful not to haggle away any of it."

"Well, farmer, I saw you unloading a centrifuge.[163] Aren't you churning your own cream into butter now?" Mayor laughed.

---

161 So-called because people would travel with knapsacks to the country to barter with farmers. Their knapsacks resembled the filled cheeks of hamsters.

162 As in the Russian zone, when people in the western zones got caught bartering on the black market, they faced the same punishments, namely either fines, losing their jobs, or imprisonment.

163 A centrifuge is used to separate the milk from its butterfat, which then can be used for whipped cream or be churned into butter.

The farmer's face turned red. He went to the bar and ordered schnapps. He was afraid their conversation had become too dangerous for him. The black market was forbidden! Why did they ever talk about it in front of this stranger? Meanwhile, the pharmacist, Mayor and clergyman smiled, silently sharing the same thought: *I know where I can bargain for some extra butter now.* Well, maybe the pastor only tried to make believe that he was thinking about bargaining for butter. He considered mentioning the farmer's "business of bartering" to his brother, the new mayor.

My mother, too, bartered some of her silver flatware for food. She had rescued silver spoons, forks and knives several times, first in Thorn and later from the Soviets in St. Bernhard and again from the "Volkspolizei"[164] at Eisleben in the Russian Zone. Since Mrs. Homburg had lived in the Hamelin area for many years, she was the one who mainly went on hamster trips. She had acquaintances among the farmers near Hamelin who would be willing to trade their food for her goods.

Trying to add to the daily meals, my mother attempted to stay in contact with Uncle Martin and Oma, who would share their victuals, but they lived in the Russian Sector. Although a postal service between the zones was established, it often took too long for perishables to be shipped. They were spoiled before they arrived, or taken by hungry postal clerks or stolen from the postal train wagons. We had no other choice but to cross the British/Russian border to bring back the food we needed to survive. The problem was that it became increasingly harder to get permission to visit Oma as often as was necessary to obtain food for us. We constantly had to find new ways to get to Klostermansfeld and arrive back in Hamelin with the essential provisions. It sometimes meant crossing the border illegally on different routes.

It was not too difficult to enter into the Russian zone. The complications started when trying to get back into the western zones. The Russians would appear out of nowhere and yell, "Stoy!" which means, "stop." We heard it on our way back into the British zone. We had walked

---

164 "Volkspolizei" (folk police) was the name for the police in the Russian zone.

for several miles from the train station toward the sectors' border. My mother encouraged us. She pointed to a sign about twenty-five feet ahead of us.

"Look at that board! It says, 'Now you are leaving the Russian zone.' And see, there is another sign, 'British zone.' We are almost there."

At that moment, what appeared to be a tree stump in the ditch alongside of the road suddenly raised itself up. It was a Russian border guard. "Stoy!" he yelled and pointed the gun at us. He motioned us off the street and onto a field-path that led away from the border. Soon a second soldier joined us taking the rearguard.

After several miles, we saw a barn and a hut. They pushed us into a shed. A tired-looking woman was already sitting there. After an hour, one guard returned and gestured for my mother and the weary woman to come with him. They left us, three very afraid children. What would the guards do to the woman and our mother?

We waited, listening to the cold wind gusts against the dirty, unsealed window. The drafty hut sent chills through us. Hildegard and I huddled down on the featherbed we had carried with us from Klostermansfeld. It did not give us much comfort; we still shivered. Ernst put on a stiff upper lip. I was sure he experienced the cold, too.

My mother knew that the shed would soon be like an icebox. She found a way to persuade the guards to let her return to us and drop a few pieces of wood on the floor. She explained, "The Russians had a party here last night. The lady and I have to clean up the barn. Here is some wood. Ernst, kindle the fire!" The guard motioned impatiently to her to leave. She nodded at us and said under the door, "I will be back soon."

Before long, the little stove provided some heat. After the barn was cleaned, the Russian soldiers released the exhausted woman who had been there when we arrived. We still had to stay in the shed. We awaited our fate. Finally, the guards ordered us onto another field path. There was no escape. One Russian went in front of us and another was behind us with his gun, ready to shoot. We followed. My brother and I had knapsacks filled with food supplies for the next weeks. My sister and I carried the feather comforter between us. We did not know that, among its feathers, Mother had hidden money that my father needed to start his insurance business. My brother lugged a cage with a female rabbit, which was due to give birth soon. We wanted to keep it in the small yard of the apartment house in Hamelin and feed it grass and dandelions, hoping the doe would have many little ones. They would provide fresh meat for dinner in the future.

The Russian guards took us to a makeshift prison and ordered us to descend into a cellar. The door was locked behind us. "Hello, welcome to our abode!" we heard. Squinting our eyes and getting used to the dimly lit cellar room we saw several cheerful fellow "inmates."

"How long have you been here?" my mother inquired.

A young woman with a heavy Saxon accent answered, "Only two days. Every once in a while they let some of us come upstairs to prepare meals for the guards, and then we have to get into the cellar again."

Suddenly, we realized Ernst was missing. I heard my mother's frightful scream. "My son! Ernst, where are you! Where is my son?"

An elderly lady answered her. "He is with the men next door. They separated us from our men. Don't worry, we have a way to contact him."

"How, where, which way?" My mother's anxiety scared me. I had only once seen her like that before, when the Russians were looking for my father in St. Bernhard.

"Wait until the guards are gone upstairs," one woman said. "Listen, some of us have been here for forty-eight hours. We will survive, just keep calm."

Another woman put her ear to the door. After a little while, she nodded, "All clear!"

The young one from Leipzig walked over to the wall and pried a brick out of it. She asked through the opening, "Is Ernst with you guys?"

"Here I am. Do you know where my mother and sisters are?"

Ernst did not quite finish his sentence when my mother stood at the wall and peeped through the hole. "Ernst, are you all right?" she shouted. The young woman pulled her back.

"Lady, don't yell! So far, the Russians have not discovered the hole we chiseled last night. Don't give our secret away."

Mother opened my knapsack, took out a sandwich, and handed it to Ernst through the hole in the wall. "Thank you, Mom!" he said. "Don't worry, I will be all right and the rabbit, too. Somebody here had some cabbage leaves; it ate."

"Hush! I hear the guard." The brick was skillfully replaced, and the young woman stood in front of it, pretending to look at the sky that could be seen through the narrow, barred cellar window just below the ceiling. A Russian entered and selected a few women to come upstairs.

Hildegard and I sat down on our featherbed. The women revealed to us that they had bartered through the hole in the wall. "We even have some salted herring." Mother was not sure if she should share some of our food with the women, but they put her at ease. "We have enough to eat. When we help upstairs, we can get some soup or potatoes. We drop some of the food into our pockets when they are not looking, and then we share with the men in the next room." She added shrewdly, "We organized a regular black market through the hole in the wall. You want to participate?" she laughed.

We heard the key in the cellar door again; the guard motioned to my mother and two other women. Hildegard and I huddled together, waiting anxiously for what would happen next. I do not remember how long we had been detained before we all were ordered to come upstairs. They shoved us among lots of other people who had tried to cross into the British sector and had been caught during the last forty-eight hours. At a border station, the guards asked my mother to pay them fifty RM[165] per person. Then they spurred us on to move fast among the other people. They hurried, they overtook us, and guards bumped us with their gunstocks. We had to watch not to get separated from each other. Finally behind a barrier we saw the sign "You Are Now Entering the British Zone". The Russians

---

165 RM stands for Reichs or Renten Mark, which at that time was the currency used in all four zones.

stopped. British guards lifted the pole and let us pass without checking our luggage or us.

It was late. The next train to Hamelin would not leave until five AM Mother had to get tickets for us. She took me along, while Hildegard and Ernst sat on the featherbed and watched the knapsacks, the rabbit cage, and Mother's suitcase. The Red Cross helped mothers with small children; they were allowed to jump the line. I had to appear as tiny as possible so Mother would be able to receive tickets for us before they were all sold out for the early train. We tried to sleep in the crowded waiting hall of the train station. Not one chair was available. Many people sat on the floor. The travelers across from us at least had a wall to lean on; meanwhile they ate some herring wrapped in newspaper. I watched how the fish oil dripped from a woman's lips and chin. She gave me an icky grin. My siblings succeeded taking small naps. I watched my mother fight the sleep that wanted to overtake her. When it came to sleepiness I seemed to have a tremendous willpower. I could stay awake, humming songs or reciting poems to myself. I told her, "Mom, sleep, I'll stay awake and watch that nobody takes anything from us."

She tenderly smoothed my hair. "Yes, Rosebud, I'll take a snooze. You scream if anyone threatens us."

In the morning we went to the platform and saw full trains coming and going. My brother told us how to jump on a slow-moving train, so we could ride on the outer step of a compartment. "Never run against the direction the train is moving, run with it to jump on it. Grab the handlebar and hold tight." I only needed to jump on a train once, but not this time. We even found room inside a compartment.

Father had expected us two days earlier. He went to every train that came from the little town named Helmstedt, where we crossed the border this time. When we arrived in Hamelin, Father stood at the station to help us.

He saw how tired we were. "I wish I could go and get food from Uncle Martin," he sighed.

"Don't you even think about it," my mother broke in. "You are on their blacklist,[166] you know. I was scared enough when they separated Ernst from us. It is entirely too dangerous for you to cross the border. We just have to see how we get through the winter without hauling food from Uncle Martin's farm."

Of course, the provisions that three children and a woman can carry would not feed twelve people for long. Our rabbit had given birth to nine bunnies. They had just started to open their eyes when the neighbor's cat tore apart the screen of the cage. Cousin Kappauf saw it from the bathroom window. He ran, half-shaven in his underwear, to rescue the rabbits, but he came too late. The cat had killed the doe. We tried to nurse the tiny creatures with skim milk using a baby doll bottle, but only one survived. It never grew big or fat enough to become a roast for all of us. Soon we had no other choice but to go back to Oma and ask for food again.

My parents were always anxious about our schooling, especially for the boys. Their sons had to be prepared for the university. The problem was that in Hamelin, most of the schools had been damaged and still in need of repair. Besides, the town's population had almost doubled from what it was before WWII due to refugees, fugitives, freed prisoners, and expellees from the former German areas that were now controlled by the Soviet Union. There was simply not enough room for all the children in the high school. The town fathers decided that the original inhabitants of Hamelin must have first choice to enter into higher education, no matter if there were more intelligent pupils among the newcomers.

My mother pleaded with the principal to let Ernst continue his schooling. She pointed out his excellent grades, no behavioral problems at his previous schools and his good athletic record. The high school principal looked at Ernst who had accompanied my mother, and accepted him on a trial basis for the next three months after which he could be admitted fully.

For Hildegard and me, it was another story. First of all, my father still had the old precept that girls should become good housewives and raise

---

166   Blacklist meaning a list of politically incriminated persons and their relatives.

children.[167] Yes, a certain amount of schooling was needed, but higher education was not essential for girls. Middle school would suffice for us. Therefore, we were allowed to enter the Wilhelm Raabe[168] School in Hamelin. Since all three seventh-grade classes were full, they registered my sister in a grade below her scholastic standing, and placed me in her class, which was above my achievements.

Every day we went to school in Hamelin, we had to pass the police station. It was set up in a former hotel. We would hold our breath not to inhale the stench caused by decaying bodies. The pictures of the murdered people were displayed on the wall of the building, faces marred by stab wounds, swollen up due to beatings and decomposing. I had horrible nightmares from seeing these posted visages of dead people.[169]

The owners of this hotel had kept a cellar pub. Here, Mr. Nachtigall would look for relief from his pain. He was the father of two girls both at Hildegard's and my age. He had been severely injured in the war, losing both of his legs. Artificial limbs could not be fitted on his hips. He was confined to his wheelchair. Occasionally, when his agony became unbearable, he rolled down our street to the pub. Somebody carried him downstairs, where he met with other veterans and sometimes got drunk. We played with his daughters in their little apartment. Usually, their mother allowed us to use their bedroom, where we acted out fairy tales. If the weather was nice, we went on long hikes together. We sang a lot and looked for secluded spots in the forest where we could play out our fantasies, forgetting the nagging hunger in our stomachs.

In some protestant areas of Germany, children observe Reformation Day on Oct. 31 by going from door to door and singing songs commemo-

---

167   In Germany, the old cliché of the 3 Ks—*Küche, Kirche, Kinder*—prevailed, meaning that women's main tasks in life are to take care of the "kitchen, church, and children."

168   Wilhelm Raabe, a 19th century German author of the Realism movement, was born in Hamelin in 1831. He died in 1910 in Brunswick.

169   The crime rate was high not only because many of the criminals kept in prisons had been released unchecked by the Allies, but also because desperate people would steal and kill for food or clothing.

rating Martin Luther's school years in Magdeburg[170] where he had to sing for his food at the burger's gates as it is told in this well known stanza.

Als Martin noch ein Knabe war,	When Martin was a youthful lad
hat er gesungen manches Jahr	he had to sing some years ahead
vor fremder Leute Türen.	in front of unknown people's doors.
Er sang so jung, er sang so zart	He sang so young, he sang so mild
so recht nach frommer Kinder Art,	just like a deep devoted child
das kann ein Herz wohl rühren	that surely could touch each heart.

Hildegard, the Nachtigall girls and I would walk around our neighborhood and sing the traditional songs. We would put on a real little polyphonic concert with Hildegard's soprano, my alto, the older Nachtigall girl playing the violin and the younger the recorder. We received beautiful grapes and apples from the long established residents who kept well tended gardens. They started to open their hearts to us relocated children. For instance, Mr. Haberland, the vegetable stand owner, discarded his spoiled produce in the tiny courtyard between the railroad bank and our house. My brother Reinhold and Wolftraut Frisch would search for any apples that might still have a spot worth eating. When Mr. Haberland noticed their rummaging he put clean, less affected apples out for them.

Almost instantly after Mr. Nachtigall found out that I knew how to play chess he challenged me, showed me all kinds of neat moves, and sometimes I beat him at his own game. Whenever his suffering became so bad that he wanted to seek the pub, his wife would call my mother, asking if I would be available to come to their place to play chess with him as soon as possible. Concentrating on this game apparently had the same effect on him as the alcohol. It was the better escape from his pain. Since by now I

---

170 Magdeburg is the capital of Saxony Anhalt. It had a boarding school, which Martin Luther attended. He could sleep there but had to find people to feed him supper.

was in a confirmation class[171] and had learned that a good Christian helps others, I honored the request for chess with Mr. Nachtigall. It was not only out of pure Christian motives—I liked chess more than doing homework.

School life became miserable for Hildegard and me. The teachers constantly compared us. Hildegard learned English much faster than I. She could pronounce the *TH* and the English *R*. Miss Sch.—our teacher— called me in front of the class to drill me how to say the English *R*. I had to sound out *"Fdiede, Fdeude,"* and then keep my tongue where I put it for the *D* and say, *"Friede, Freude,"* which in German means "peace, joy." I just could not get the *R* right, as much as I left my tongue on the *D* spot. So much for my peace and joy! I hesitated to pronounce the *TH*. It meant putting my tongue between my teeth, practically between my lips. I thought *that looks like I am sticking my tongue out at people.* That was an outright nasty, offensive behavior I did not want to be accused of.

Hildegard had a beautiful soprano voice. I loved to sing, but I never could reach the high notes my sister sang so clearly. She was selected for the school choir. She told me, "Do not even try out for the chorus." I complied. Anyway, I needed the after-school practice time for my lessons because I still had spelling difficulties, now in German and English.

My mother was called into school often because of my poor grades. Sure enough, she found an old lady who would tutor me. My sister had gotten supplementary rations because she was so skinny. I did not look frail; therefore I received no extra food and was always hungry. The woman, my tutor, dictated stories to me, which mostly had to do with delicious buttered dark bread dripping with honey and whole milk with cream on top. My mind was fixed on the taste of these foods, not on the spelling of them.

In spring of 1947, the catastrophic malnourishment of children in Germany and Austria became evident. The Allies agreed to provide lunch for all schoolchildren in each of the occupied zones. The lunch usually

---

171 At that time, we had to participate for four years in confirmation classes, attend church every Sunday and pass an oral examination in front of the congregation, before we could be accepted into the Lutheran or Reformed Evangelical Church.

consisted of a cup of milk or cocoa and a roll. In Klostermansfeld (the Russian zone), the roll was dark and often under-baked, but later the milk was at least 2 %, whereas in Hamelin (the British zone), the cocoa was made with fat-free milk or water.

At about the same time, American care packages arrived at the churches. The clergy distributed them among the most needy. Hildegard would be confirmed a year earlier than I. She and I went to different pre-confirmation classes, but had the same deaconess for our teacher, who saw me in an ill- fitting HJ coat that my brother had outgrown and selected our family as a recipient of clothing from the care packages. We were given a pullover, knee socks, and some underwear. One sweater had a note attached with an address from Seattle. Our minister, the superintendent, asked Hildegard if she would like to write to this American family. Yes, my sister did, and they answered her by sending packages to us personally. They not only sent dresses for Hildegard, but also food for the rest of us. That was a godsend, for it became increasingly difficult to cross the border into the Russian zone to visit with Oma and Uncle Martin and bring their food back.

Despite the new supply of goods, I sometimes fainted when the teacher called on me and I had to stand up, as was customary. I was still close to starvation, and since it soon became clear that I would have to repeat the seventh grade, my mother decided to send me back to Klostermansfeld for a quarter of a year.[172] She thought, *There Ilse-Rose will have better and enough to eat. Uncle Große can tutor her again and we have one less person at the dinner table.* She needed to wait several months until the school term was over after Easter before we received the necessary papers for a legal visit with Oemlers. Mother was allowed a one week holiday and I was permitted a three months stay.

In the meantime, we celebrated Christmas with Mrs. Homburg's family and the Frisch's. A few days before the holiday, Hildegard, Wolftraut, Ottchen Homburg, Reinhold, and I made paper chains for a

---

172 From 1946 until June 1948, relatives, especially children living in different sectors, still could receive permission to visit each other occasionally.

tree that my father was able to secure. One girl in our class had a wooden candle form. She allowed me to make candles from old wax stumps we collected. We melted them and poured the semi-hot wax into the mold. After the wax solidified, we unscrewed the boxes and could lift the candles out. We had a few of them on the tree, but having neither the right wicks nor the correct mixture of paraffin and wax, the candles burned down rather fast.

We ate what was to us a very delicious meal. Mrs. Homburg had bartered for a can of real "Wiener Würstchen"[173]. We had not seen meat in a long time. Mother made a potato salad[174] using the last ones we grew on Mrs. Homburg's garden plot. Then Mrs. Homburg played Christmas songs on the piano in the dining room, my father and my mother with us four, along with the Frisch family and Mrs. Homburg's children gathered around her and sang. Ottchen had eaten his share too fast. He accompanied our singing with his hiccups; actually, it sounded like he was keeping time. Ernst chuckled quietly at it. A sense of humor did not leave him even in the bleakest times. Mrs. Frisch gave a Christmas present to be shared by all of us. She had drawn a game on a cardboard torn from an old box.

In May, the mailman finally delivered the permission papers for my mother and me to visit Oma. I stayed in Klostermansfeld for close to three months. I did not go to school there, since they had no middle school and the curriculum was already quite dissimilar from that of the western sectors, especially in languages, geography, and history.

Uncle Große tutored me again. He did not care how I pronounced English. He used to say, "Child, if you are in Canada, they speak with a different accent than the ones in Australia, or in Great Britain. In India,

---

173 "Wiener Würstchen" are nothing like hot dogs although they resemble them. In Vienna they make them with veal, and encase them in a delicate, delicious skin.

174 This salad consisted of potatoes swimming in vinegar, water, and a little oil we had extracted from beechnuts. My sister and I gathered these nuts in the woods until one day, the forester forbade us to pick them off the ground. "The animals in the woods need them to survive the winter," he informed us. And we? What about us? Didn't we need them to survive as well?

they pronounce words differently than in the USA, and there it depends if you are in Texas or in Boston." Thus he combined his old-fashioned geography lessons with English. His comprehensive teaching method was avant-garde. When I was younger, he had incorporated history with literature and orthography by dictating stories about Martin Luther to me in an attempt to improve my spelling. Now he put me at ease, saying, "So, do not worry about pronouncing your *R* or *TH*—but you need to spell correctly."

I went to his house only a few times during the week. Between his lessons, I was ordered to help alongside the farm workers, Aunt Ursel included. Under the Soviet regime, she was regarded as being on the same level as any other worker. She still could run the household, but no longer as the privileged owner of it. She had to perform new duties. One of them was to train girls in the skill of preparing poultry and other birds for cooking. It included catching and killing pigeons.

The pigeon coop was outside the second floor of the building on the left between two small windows. Underneath are the windows and the door of the wash kitchen.

Aunt Ursel asked us, "How would you capture pigeons?" We did not know. She continued, "Well how would you... they fly all over the courtyard, the house and anywhere, right?" We agreed. She laughed, "Actually you do not wait until they are old enough to have developed flying skills. Look there is the pigeon coop. You take a long ladder and climb up to it. You reach with your hand into the hole, get a tight hold of the young bird and slip it into the cage hanging from the ladder." We looked at each other: Who of us would like to be the first to climb up and fetch a pigeon? She waved to one of the household workers to bring a cage with a dozen young pigeons from the wash kitchen. Our sighs of relief followed her. Aunt Ursel pulled one of the birds out of the basket. She called on me, "Ilse-Rose, you hold the pigeon in your left hand. Make sure both wings are securely against its body, and then you put your right hand over its head and eyes, clasp your fingers around its neck, twist it, and pull abruptly." She demonstrated. I saw the blood spurting out of the neck and the head in her fist, the beak still gasping. "Don't let go. Pigeons can still flutter around without their heads. You have to hold the bird until it relaxes in your left hand and the blood stops trickling." She gave me a smaller pigeon to acquire this new skill. I learned fast and so did the other girls. After the preparation of the birds, they were roasted in the oven. They are actually very tender and delicious when fairly young and freshly slaughtered. I remembered the delicate taste and 15 years later for my wedding dinner I ordered roasted pigeons for one course. I wanted to impress my American in-laws. The meal was a disaster, because the pigeons had been too old and frozen. They were tough and tasted like straw. On another visit in the Russian Zone, pigeons again played a role for me. At that time it was a rather scary experience.

When I had to repeat seventh grade, we went to Klostermansfeld without any difficulties. My mother had obtained legal papers to visit with my relatives, but three months later leaving the Russian sector became a problem for me. While I stayed with Oma, the currency reform in the Trizone[175] took place. It intensified the disagreements between the western

---

175   The Trizone was created when the French, for economic reasons, finally agreed with the British and Americans, who already had formed the Bizone, to let the

zones and the Soviet sector. The SMAD (Soviet Military Administration) in East Germany countered the financial operations in West Germany by stopping all passenger train and car traffic, and even pedestrians were not allowed to walk between the western zones of Berlin and the Russian part of Berlin. They also controlled the delivery of goods via the waterways.

Just before all Russian borderlines could be fortified more by barbed wire and added guards, Uncle Reinhold phoned Oemlers. Uncle Martin took the call, "Here Oemler!"

"Martin, here Reinhold Seume; Ilse-Rose has to get out of the Russian zone as fast as possible. Her permission documents that she needed to go back to Hamelin are declared invalid." Uncle Martin asked,

"How come?"

"No time to explain. Her mother wants to pick her up at Vienenburg. That is near to us and so far the least secured border, and, as you know, we live close by in Goslar."

"Good. I'll take care of it. My former apprentice Eberhard Fleischer works at a farm, which has a meadow right at the border. He will take her to the Vienenburg station." Uncle Martin assured him.

"That is perfect." concluded Uncle Reinhold and continued, "Give me Fleischer's phone number, so we can instruct him if necessary." After Uncle Martin disclosed Eberhard's number, he told me to pack my things together, but so that none of the household helpers would know what I was doing. "And Illero" that was his endearment for me, "you have to stand at the courtyard door by 5:00AM tomorrow morning. Mr. Probst is bringing pigs to the market; he'll pick you up. Make sure nobody sees you climbing in the truck." I went to Oma's bedroom, which I still shared with her and told her that I had to leave early. She did not ask much and just helped me to pack a small suitcase and my knapsack. I did not sleep well that night. Questions haunted me: What was I to do if the Russian guards caught me? — Well, first meet the butcher, fine and then? Where does he take me, surely not into the British Zone?

---

west occupied zones of Germany unite under one democratic government.

As they so often did, Oma and Uncle Martin assisted me in going back to my family in Hamelin. They knew I needed to slip over the border secretly, so they made sure that no one in Klostermansfeld would be aware of my leaving for the western zones. They asked the butcher, Mr. Probst, if he would be so kind and take me along in his wagon when he delivered pigs and if he would let me off at a certain village's train station. He agreed and the next morning, after an hour ride with the squealing pigs, he stopped at an empty railroad platform to let me out of his vehicle. He left and I looked around. *What now?* I did not have a train ticket. What was I to do? But Oma had contacted her friend, who knew a reliable person to accompany me to the border. Then an elderly man came around the corner of the building and approached me. He stated, "You are coming from Oemlers, right?" I felt uneasy with this stranger, but he knew the Oemlers. Remembering Uncle Martin's advice, I played dumb for five minutes. Finally he concluded, "I am to take you to the village across from the British occupied town Vienenburg." I waited with him for the train and entered it, looking for a place near the compartment door. *If he touches me, I jump from the train.* I thought. We spoke little and arrived near the border at noon. The grey haired person told me, "I'll show you the restaurant where you meet Eberhard Fleischer." Relief flooded over me as I rejoiced. "Eberhard, the former apprentice of Uncle Martin!" But now I felt guilty that I had been so unsociable and I stammered ruefully. "Thank you," and remembering the American cigarettes my mother had given me in case I needed to barter for something, I added, "Would you like some of my cigarettes?" he smiled, shook his head, left me at the door of an inn and went back to the train station. I entered the hotel and right away the owner of it told me to wait in the dining room for Eberhard. He supposedly would meet me at 4 PM. I ate one of the sandwiches Oma had packed in my knapsack. I waited and waited. By 6 PM, Eberhard still had not shown up.

"You have to sit in the kitchen," the lady from the hotel said. "Mr. Fleischer is delayed. You cannot stay in the restaurant. The Russians are having a party tonight. We have to prepare this room for them." I had to look unsuspicious, pretending to be the kitchen help.

At 11 PM Eberhard finally came. He had a bicycle. "Sorry, I had to wait until the Russians were tipsy and changed the guards. Best chance not to get shot," he told me. Pointing to the bike, "Put your suitcase on the carrier seat in back, sit on the bar, and I'll help you to put your knapsack on backwards."

I followed his orders. With one hand I tried to hold my parcel away from the handlebar. It was hanging from my neck in front of me; with the other fist I clasped the middle bar close to the handle's center. I tried to balance myself on the bar and was careful not to interfere with Eberhard steering the bike.

He drove through a park. Every so often, he would hiss "Duck!" to avoid a low-hanging tree branch. Apparently, he was not driving on a path but straight through the close-standing trees. Next we sped over a meadow, there cows lay in the grass. We came to a barbed-wire fence that stretched across a creek.

"Get off the bike," he whispered. "Crawl under the wire."

He lifted the upper strand of barbed wire, stepped on the lower strand, and I slipped through the opening he had created. He hoisted the bike over the prickly barrier. Then he waded through the creek and ducked underneath the fence where the water was shallow. I had picked up the bike and fastened the suitcase onto it again. He swung me onto the bike and started to cycle like a maniac. I heard shots hissing by us. Were they shooting at us? No time to think, just hope they are too drunk, or it is too dark, or they were shooting at somebody or something else. Who knew?

Eberhard drove to the station in Vienenburg. "Stay here until your parents come. They'll pick you up around seven AM. Here are 5 DM[176] if you want to eat something at the station's restaurant." I wanted to give the coin back to him to pay for his help. The DM, the western currency, was the more stable money and —although illegal to possess in the Russian

---

176   The GDR (German Democratic Republic) currency had hardly any value on the world market, whereas the DM ("Deutsche Mark" or "German Mark") of the FRG (Federal Republic of Germany) was becoming a sought-after legal tender.

zone— already very much sought after. One could buy better merchandise in the Russian zone with it—under the table, of course. However, he did not want it. He did take the American cigarettes. He left me in the station's hallway telling me that he had to hurry to make it back into the Soviet sector.

I sat down on the floor and leaned against the wall waiting for the morning when my parents should arrive. Pretty soon, the station emptied; hardly anybody was left. A railroad clerk came and told me that they closed at midnight and that I needed to leave.

"But I do not know anybody here. My parents will come tomorrow morning and pick me up <u>here</u>. I must stay <u>here</u>," I explained to her.

She suggested that I buy a return ticket to Goslar, because there, the station was open all night. "Stay there and take the train back to Vienenburg at 5:25 AM." Was I ever glad that I had Eberhard's DM, how else could I have paid for a train ticket, since the RM had become invalid in the western zones. Only the DM was declared as legal tender in the Trizone. I thought, *Great. Goslar! That is where Uncle Reinhold and Aunt Anne live. If anything goes wrong, I can call on them in the morning.* I would not dare to call them at midnight. Remember, Oma had said, "Sleep is holy, don't wake anybody up."

There were all kinds of unsettled people in the crowded Goslar waiting room. I found an empty place and sat down, clutching my suitcase between my legs; I put my knapsack on the table in front of me, rested my head on it, and folded my arms around it. I could hardly sleep for fear that somebody might steal my parcels. I thought *Maybe this chair was not taken since these individuals around here are so dirty. Phooey, they reek!* Then it occurred to me that I was perhaps not so clean either. After all I had been in a truck for pigs, in a train pulled by a steam engine, at a restaurant's kitchen, on a bike ride through a meadow…through a creek, crossing the barbed wires of the border…and Mr. Probst had picked me up at 5 AM and now it was midnight eighteen hours without an opportunity to wash! *Do I smell bad too? I hope I will not pick up fleas or lice!*

In the morning I took the first train back to Vienenburg. My parents met me around 7 AM and took me back to Goslar, where they had stayed overnight. "Why didn't you call us when you waited in the train station?" Uncle Reinhold inquired. I told him what Oma always said. "It was too late to call. You were sleeping. I did not want to disturb your rest." My father only shook his head and remarked, "You could have saved us a trip by calling when you arrived in Vienenburg." We stayed a few days with Aunt Anne.

Father's youngest brother, Uncle Horst, lived with them. He and his fellow sailors had been imprisoned in Holland and then released. He went to the British Zone heeding my father's warning about going to St. Bernhard where his sister-in-law still resided. He knew better than Uncle Hans to go into the Soviet sector where Ernst Höfer Sr.'s descendants were on the blacklist of the secret police, later Stasi.

Father had also warned his youngest brother and advised him to try to live with Uncle Reinhold in Goslar who was in charge of the grounds around the Imperial Palace. He employed Uncle Horst, who had been trained as a gardener before he was called to join the navy in 1941. Now he was married and his wife had delivered their first child a few months before. Aunt Gertrud asked me to help her with her baby boy, who responded with giggling at the funny faces and animal sounds I made for him.

When I came back to Hamelin, I entered my new class and soon I was so well liked that they made me the class president. Here learning was much better for me. Therefore, tutoring became unnecessary. Math and Biology were my favorite subjects. I still had difficulties with English. That language's orthography and pronunciation just did not make any sense to me. I really liked our Deaconess who taught the Confirmation class so convincingly that I even thought of becoming a Deaconess myself, but my father did not want to hear of it. Memorizing hymns strengthened my faith in Christ. *"O Haupt voll Blut und Wunden"*[177] was the song, which

---

177   In American Hymnals you find this song by Paul Gerhardt (1607-1676) under
        the title, "O sacred Head, now wounded."

impressed me the most. In the English translation it has three verses that incorporate the content of the 10 German stanzas. I would kneel in front of the one chair we had in our bedroom; at my right side the bunk beds hovered over me, as I prayerfully learned the whole hymn by heart.

With the help of our gym teacher, Miss Braun, we put on plays, which were accomplished enough that the school authorities allowed us to act out the fairy tales in the auditorium, which the girls' and the boys' middle school shared. A boy from the upper class, Dieter Fischer, said to me, "Ilse-Rose Höfer sounds like a stage name. I can see it on film posters. You in the lead role! You were born an actress." He was a cute boy with blond curly hair. I think he was my first crush … secretly, of course. He came to Mrs. Homburg's apartment to play chess with me, but having played many times with Mr. Nachtigall, I beat him. I thought I would impress him, but it resulted in the opposite. He did not come again, although he still waved to me and smiled when we chanced to see each other.

In the Brother Grimms' fairytale King Thrush Beard I played the protagonist and my best friend, Sigrid—on the left— had the role of the Lady in Waiting.

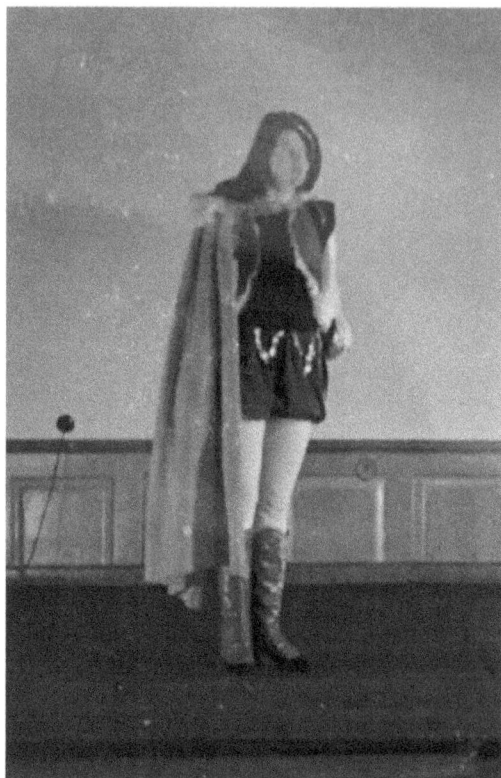

It was amazing how we created our costumes. Our whole class was involved. Miss Braun told us it would be easiest to imitate the fashion of the Rococo[178] times. For the young prince Thrush Beard, I wore somebody's white long stockings and a pair of gym shorts, on which I sewed a little silver trimming. We tacked a feather—cut from on old stole— on my beret and feather trimmings from the same source on my bolero. I do not remember who let me wear the boots, only that they were too big for me and I had to put paper in their toes. The princess and her maids needed long dresses. They were made out of ladies' nightshirts. We fastened

---

178   Rococo originated in Paris in the early 18th century. It followed the Baroque style. It lasted until the French revolution (1789-1791), when it died during the beheading of the aristocracy by a guillotine.

their necklines around the waist, then pulled a summer dress over it, we gathered the front and back of its skirt part in its middle and tucked it up, thus creating the typical Rococo emphasis of the hips. We even strung two small pillows on our waist, one on top of each hip. The camaraderie of the class and the support we gave to each other impressed me.

No wonder that a whole new brighter world opened up for me when I repeated seventh grade. One more factor, which contributed to my new standing between classmates and teachers, was that I was no longer put in competition with my sister. For example: The choir director of the school, Mr. Homann, found that I had an alto that blended beautifully with all the other voices in the school choir. In practice sessions and at performances I hardly ever saw Hildegard who sang in the middle of the soprano section at the far right of the choir and I was at the far left in the second row of our large group.

My classmate, Sigrid, became my best friend. She, her five brothers, her grandmother, and her parents lived in the house next to us. We walked to school together. She was also in my confirmation group. After she and I cleaned their kitchen and took care of her baby brother, I would tell fairy tales and other stories to Sigrid's brothers. Quieted down, they loved to listen to me, which gave their sickly mother her well-deserved rest. She usually lay on the sofa in the living room or in their bedroom. Her husband had worked with my father for the British garrison stationed in Hamelin. I spent many hours at Sigrid's place, where everybody accepted me.

After my father quit his job with the British garrison, he started his insurance business again. He needed an office, so he negotiated with the owner of our apartment building as to whether the attic could be adapted into a living space for the Frisch Family, so we could occupy their room. They were glad when they were finally able to move upstairs into the converted attic. Now with one bedroom for us children available, my father started to set up for his business. The corner room became the office for the mathematician, Mr. Venator, and the secretary, Miss Siepermann. The living room was transformed into Father's office during the day and my parents' bedroom during the night. We sold the bunk beds. Father had designed "sofa beds". They consisted of two mattresses per couch, one functioned as a seat with a box to store the beddings, and the other served as the sofa back. The clientele of Herbert E. G. Höfer's insurance agency had no idea that they sat on mattresses when conducting business with Father. Each morning before we left for school, we had to change these two rooms from bedrooms, one became Father's office and the other served as our family room. I often babysat Wolftraut and her little sister, Diethild, in the attic. Here Mrs. Frisch had her own kitchen, their bedroom and a combined living dining room, all of which had sloping ceilings.

At every Stammtisch in Germany, they liked to anticipate what might be in store for them now, having survived the war. Their conversations might have sounded just the same as the one between our Skat brothers. The pharmacist remembered how he was almost killed in Yugoslavia; either by partisans or his illness, and later when he was transported out of the new Russian areas by force. This time he began their discussion.

"Look at us! We have been spared during bombing raids, evacuation, fleeing, expulsion, starvation, and freezing. I think our lives should make more sense from now on. I always was and now am even more a pacifist. I say, never again war!"

"Never a fanatical ideology either! There must be a reason why we were spared," the farmer added.

The pastor shuffling a deck of cards concluded, "People should live in peace with each other."

Mayor had followed the development of a new German government under the rule of the Allies. He pointed out, "One thing is for sure, the Allies do not recognize our attitude we just expressed: No war! No fanatical government! Only peace! They are positive that all of us Germans are warriors and therefore need to be re-educated."

Leipziger entered the pub and joined them. He had heard the last remarks. Taking off his jacket he commented, "The Americans would love to be able to get into the brains of all the German people and take all the Nazi ideas out of them. They still think all of us are brainwashed Nazis."

The clergyman shook his head, "Leipziger, you are not with it! They gave up their cumbersome questionnaires hoping to lead to a denazification of the Germans. Now—as Mayor just mentioned—it is re-education". Farmer threw in, "Yes, and that with comedies and schmaltzy films." But the clergyman wanted to put in his question.

"What do you think? Did the Allies change their minds after working with German public servants for two years? Do they now finally change their minds about our attitudes?"

The pharmacist replied challenging him, "What makes you think that they changed their prejudice toward us?" The farmer, expecting a battle of words, interrupted, "Must we always talk about the occupational forces?" But the pastor just could not be muzzled; he continued, "I think they might have had their concept of German people wrong right after the war. Then, the Americans, British and French were still influenced by the propaganda and lies distributed through their media, but now, they think differently. Just look, who did the Western Allies call back to govern Germany again? — Men who had been politically active before 1933".

Mayor, siding with the pastor, chimed in. "Yes, these are former politicians who know how to run an administration machine, having been part of the Weimar Republic. In the western zones I would have my job back as mayor, despite having been in the NSDAP. Over there they realize that we had to belong to the Nazi party to keep our jobs. It is different here in the Russian sector." He showed how bitter he had become when he continued. "Here, survivors of the concentration camps, emigrants coming back to Germany, anybody known to have opposed the Hitler regime are installed. I say 'installed'—they are not voted into their civil service. They are rewarded with jobs for having suffered under the Nazis, even if they have no idea how to act to achieve a well-run political organization and have no experience in any economical tasks that has to be dealt with. They just have to claim they are Communists or at least former Socialists and presto they fill the administrative jobs."

Mayor had tried to be placed in his former position, but he was denied any political involvement. Work in the civil service was unattainable for him as long as he remained in the Russian Zone. He had forebodings; he anticipated that all people who had held important positions under the Hitler regime would sooner or later be dismissed from their work. And his feelings proved correct. After the West German sectors united to establish one uniform government and installed a new currency in June of 1948, the Russian zone government under Soviet control did dismiss all former professionals in the civil service of the Russian sector, including industry or economic leaders, heads of banks, lawyers, teachers, and professors. Depending on their degree of cooperation with the Nazi party, these one-time authorities were shipped to Siberia, killed, tortured, or kept in local prisons. Less politically incriminated persons were released from jail but could not go back to their former work. They were allowed blue-collar jobs in mines, on farms, in industry, as railroad workers or in municipal labor. But in 1946 Mayor already had been reduced to cleaning the cobblestones with a broom and picking up garbage. The pastor seemed to disregard Mayor's outburst; he addressed all of the Stammtisch members. "Actually you under the Soviets have it better than the people in the western zones. Here they just will continue to clear all government positions from the Nazis[179] and instead," he fixed his eyes on the former mayor "install people who were persecuted by the Hitler regime". Mayor still embittered remarked ironically, "I can vouch for the new politically educated professionals! Take our new mayor, excuse me, I mean civil servant. He has no idea about working with the police, the fire fighters, or other municipal workers like me, let alone keeping personnel files and learning about new regulations for political voting, for checking the media etcetera!" Suddenly realization struck him, *pastor is the brother of the new mayor; he gasped, what did I say?*

---

179   About 8.5 million Germans belonged to the Nazi party. Many government workers did not agree with the Nazi program, but would have lost their jobs if they did not join the NSDAP. By 1946, the Soviets had ousted all former NSDAP members. It took until the end of 1946 before the governments of all four sectors agreed on a consistent procedure to "cleanse" Germany of Nazis.

The pharmacist had tried to stop Mayor who continued to create a precarious situation for himself by giving him a little kick under the table. Now he covered the lower half of his face with his handkerchief and laid his finger on his lips. The conversation became too risky for Mayor and his friends. They were very uncertain about the visiting clergyman. They had pondered before; *maybe the pastor tries to cajole us into saying things that can be held against us.* Now it had happened and they were sure Mayor would have to deal with repercussions for his words. They should not have voiced their opinions. They knew too well that the secret police arrested anybody who said something against the now established government under Moscow's control. The farmer leaned over and put his hand on the minister's arm smiling lamely, "Pastor, you shuffled long enough. Now let's play Skat." But the clergyman put the cards on the table, stood up and departed leaving three worried Stammtisch brothers in the inn.

One way to re-educate us was to disallow all literature that would evoke any militaristic suggestions. The Allies permitted certain dramas in the German theater as long as they did not have anything warlike in them. In the British sector, part of their re-education was watching their movies, which had been translated, dubbed, and sent to Germany. I saw British films about gypsies camping in a beautiful wooded landscape of England. They did not realize that German people also had romanticized the life of these nomads roaming the countryside. My mother had told us how gypsies had invited her when, as a young schoolgirl, she visited Great-grandmother who had helped the gypsies by giving them hay for their horses. Mother never spoke degradingly about them, only that she refused to eat their special meal consisting of night crawlers, rolled in flour and fried over an open fire. The British did not need to change my mind about gypsies. I liked those melodramatic films, which emerged as a welcome shift from the propaganda films of the Nazi era. American movies with Esther Williams impressed me as she danced in elaborate synchronized swimming scenes in the crystal clear water of the huge swimming pools.

The time when Germans sometimes paid with a lump of coal, wood, or bricks instead of money to see the films ended with the currency reform in 1948. We listened to the music that the Hitler regime had forbidden and now we loved to sing the American songs of the nineteen thirties and forties. In the traditional school for ballroom dancing, Ernst and Hildegard learned the boogie, the jitterbug, the swing, the samba, and the rumba in addition to the usual waltz, tango, foxtrot and polka. This part of our re-education was fun for us. We started to become less critical of the former "enemies". Although I still did not believe what they told us about the horrors the Germans had committed, the Holocaust under the Nazis.

In all four zones the German radio announcers were rather quiet about concentration camps. In the Trizone they focused on the currency reform, the eliminating of ration cards, the rebuilding of cities and railroad lines, the Autobahn and with it the infrastructure to be repaired and expanded. They spoke about the new wonder medication penicillin, which you could get in the form of chewing gum. The reopening of former well known industries was another subject they reported about, including businesses formerly in the Russian zone but now reestablished in various western sectors. Their executives had left the Soviet controlled sector. Now in the Trizone they opened up their businesses—often with their former employees. Many manufacturing plants had been either destroyed or confiscated and needed rebuilding. The former owners built modern factories according to the newest technological standards. Thus, Germany had the most advanced industries after WWII, to the surprise of the Allies who had anticipated that it would take Germany at least thirty years to recover and not just about ten.

After everybody received the DM better merchandise suddenly became available. Better food could be bought in the grocery stores. My mother was surprised how fast certain things were available literally overnight: white flour, butter, sugar, spices, etc. And in the fall, once a week we could purchase fruit and vegetables from the farmers' market. Now we no longer needed ration cards, but money became tight. After all, each German initially received only 40 DM.

My father's business took off. Various insurance companies, for which my father had worked before, employed him and Uncle Reinhold, whom my father had highly recommended. By 1950, my father needed to move into a larger facility. He applied for an office in the newly erected building near Hamelin's center, but he was denied. The town-fathers preferred their own businesspeople to the refugees.

As mentioned before, it was easier to enter the Russian zone than to leave it, especially if one did not get the necessary documents to travel. In that case, one was forced to escape. First, one had to make sure nobody could suspect that one wanted to leave. Second, one needed to get near the border then wait and watch for the border guards to change. Generally, that was the best time to make it across or late at night, when one saw where the searchlights missed a spot and crawl towards it following the rhythms of the sweeping searchlights. One could find persons who would help you to pass into the western zones. They mainly lived in the border regions. They knew when the guards changed, who was a bad marksman, where there was good coverage, and where there might be a hole in the barbed wire. It was dangerous to trust these persons. Some of those who pretended to help were bandits. They stole the few things people tried to bring with them into West Germany, often beating them or even killing them for the few goods they carried.

These criminal acts stopped when in 1948 the Soviets ordered an increase of barriers on their border including a five-kilometer-wide strip. The people who originally lived there were denied visitors, not even by their relatives. Eventually, everyone who occupied a home there had to leave it and find a new residence.

It took not quite one decade to convert this "no man's land" into a minefield; it was hemmed in on both sides with barbed wire. At some stretches the lines were electrified. Intermittently watch towers overlooked the whole sections. The border guards had the command to shoot anybody they saw on the "no man's land". The security guard was never by himself. There were always two or more shooters. The watchman had to be afraid that his buddy might report him if he did not shoot the border offender. The punishment for not obeying the rules could be jail sentences, shipment to Siberia, and definitely losing one's job. Worst of all, his close relatives could also be harassed or tortured. Often, his children might lose the right of high school education and thus to study at a university.

During the almost forty years of Soviet control, those border areas became desolate. They reached from the southern coast of the Baltic Sea all the way to Hungary. This minefield measured 3.11 miles wide and 710 miles long, where no human being interfered, where wildlife could roam freely, birds nested undisturbed, and the fauna and flora reestablished itself. A recuperation of this formerly war-torn environment developed into a "Green Belt". It grew out of a nation divided by alien politicians and their harsh, inhumane harassment of their people who lived in the Russian Zone. Already in 1971, Oma would tell us, "Our songbirds are coming back. Listen! Look, some plants we thought were extinct, reestablished themselves. Take a deep breath, smell the herbs here. It is reassuring that even out of an utter destruction new life emerges. Don't brood over the past but be positive and look for the blessings ahead of us." She might have thought, *isn't this one way our Holy Father shows us that He is faithful and just? After all at the end, He is in control.*

CHAPTER 10

For surely I know the plans I have for you, says the Lord, plans for your welfare and not for harm, to give you a future with hope. Jeremiah 29:11

1948-51, Decisive Years for East and West Germany

The currency reform in 1948 was the final straw that led to the separation of the Trizone (American, British and French sectors) from the "Soviet Occupied Zone," SBZ (Sowjetische Besatzungszone). It caused one of the most important economical impacts of Post-WWII Germany. The division between East and West Germany had already started in 1947 when the Economic Council of the Bizone[180] realized that the inflation induced by the RM[181] became incalculable. Initially, the three western zones combined to form a new democratic government under the guidance of the Americans, British and French. The Russians had been invited to join them as far as a uniform currency reform was concerned, but they declined. They, too, knew that a monetary solution needed to be found, but they refused to work with the capitalistic West Allies.

On June 20, 1948, the Trizone's governing authorities announced the currency reform for all three western sectors. It materialized swiftly. Each person initially received 40 DM. The following day the Deutsche Mark (DM) became the only legal tender in the Trizone. The DM banknotes had been printed in the USA. It took several years to deal with saving accounts and other cash investments by individuals and businesses before the exchange from the former Reichsmark into Deutsche Mark was completed.

---

180   The Bizone was the first cooperation between two zones, namely the American and the British. Later the French joined them, forming the Trizone.

181   At that time RM still stood for Reichsmark and for Rentenmark.

That the reform could take off overnight was the result of two years planning by the Economic Council of the Bizone through the Special Office for Money and Credit, headed by Ludwig W. Erhard[182] as the economic director for the British and American zones. Shortly after the currency reform he decided to lift many price controls, despite opposition from other parties and Allied authorities. His economic guidelines, coupled with financial policies, led to a stunning recovery in the 1950s, overcoming wartime devastation and successfully integrating millions of displaced people from the East.

In the SBZ they also experienced inflation and a monetary reform had been discussed publicly since 1947. It did not reach a satisfactory outcome, because of a veto from the Soviets. By mid-June 1948 the groundwork for a financial reform in the SBZ had not been finished. The necessary legal norms had not been drafted and therefore printing of paper money and minting of coins did not exist.

To prevent an influx of RM from West Germany feeding their inflation, they announced over the Berlin Radio Broadcast shortly before midnight of June 20, 1948, that all pedestrian, passenger train and car traffic between the western zones and Berlin was blocked and freight traffic on the waterways was strictly controlled. There would be a currency reform in the SBZ by June 23, 1948. As a result, in West Berlin two currencies were in circulation. But in East Berlin and in the Russian zone the possession of DM was prohibited.

>⟶⟶⟶⟶⟶

Our Stammtisch had dwindled so much that they had to wait several weeks after the currency reform before they could meet. The clergyman had been absent and Mayor had been arrested once more. At last they gathered again and the farmer called for Margret to bring beer to their table. "You have to pay for it right away, please." She said setting their

---

182   He became the second German Chancellor in 1963, after the first Chancellor, Konrad Adenauer (1876-1967), abdicated.

steins[183] in front of their owners. Mayor wondered, "Don't you trust us anymore, Margret? We have no outstanding debts here. We…"

"No! No it's not mistrust." She tried to put him at ease, "But you must have heard about the currency reform in the western zones? Yes, they have new marks called Deutsche Mark, and we are neither allowed to use it nor to own it. And our Rentenmark is kind of invalid." Mayor was puzzled "What? I don't understand. Could it be that now everybody who still has RM across the border will send it here and we will get swamped with it? Our inflation is high enough. Oh my! I see another 1923 with its uncontrollable devaluation of our money on the horizon."

The minister shook his head and addressing all of them declared, "I might quite as well tell you. I went to Berlin and applied for an extended stay here."

Farmer raised his eyebrows and questioned him, "How did you manage that? Don't we have to apply for a trip like that and wait until we are allowed to go? There are still travel restrictions here, right?"

As usual the minister avoided a direct answer and continued. "On the 23rd of June I saw many people going in and out of the huge hall of the German Economic Commission in East Berlin. There they worked on sticking coupons to the previous Rentenmark notes so they could be used as legal tender for citizens in the Soviet sector of Berlin. After that I experienced a kind of inner city currency trading develop on the black market. It did not last long. The West Allies allocated exchange offices, which opened on August 2. The exchange rate was 1 DM, (Westmark) = 2.20 RM (Ostmark)[184]. You know the one with the stamp on it." Turning his eyes on the farmer he chided, "And Farmer, we are not restricted from traveling. As you said, we just have to apply for a trip and give the reason why and where and when we need to journey."

---

183   When Stammtische or sport clubs meet regularly in the same Pub, the individual members quite often keep their own beer mugs there. These are displayed on a shelf behind the counter when not in use.

184   The Rentenmark with a sticker soon became known as Ostmark (East mark) and the Deutsche Mark as West mark or Westgeld (west money).

"Sure, and you have to have a brother who can give you permission for a voyage," Mayor blurted out, again not being careful and creating a contentious moment. The farmer, to overcome the awkward situation, pulled a 2 RM banknote out of his pocket, "Look here," showing it to Mayor and turning to Margret, "I have money to pay for my beer right away."

A two Rentenmark note with the green adhesive on the designated place for RMs to become legal tender.

Leipziger laughed, "Oh, I see you have the 'adhesive' on your cash."

Mayor leaned over the table "Let's see! Isn't it ridiculous?"

The farmer turned the bank note over, "See there is nothing on this side, only one little stamp on the front."

Mayor muttered, "They had me incarcerated and I had no chance to see the money, although my wife must have used it already for our groceries. Now I know what they mean with a 'wall paper stamp' that makes the Rentenmark legal cash. Okay, but what about our other cash, where do we get that patch? And what about our savings?"

The minister as usual seemed to have the information at hand. "Ah Mayor, you are anxious about money like everybody else in our SBZ who still has the old Reichs- or -Renten Mark in their savings at the bank."

"Or even stashed away under their mattress," the farmer added with a sly grin.

Mayor interjected, "Wherever it is! What really should be discussed is if and when we get new money and who would be in charge of printing it."

The minister added, "One thing is clear, we will not have the DM from across the border. Margret is right. It is illegal to own it. If a westerner sends you some DM, you promptly have to exchange it one to one, and at the same time tell how you acquired it."

Margret collected the tab and glancing at the minister stated, "And there sits the pastor who is a westerner." She leaned forward and asked rather bluntly, "Did you receive your allotted 40 DM already?" She left without waiting for an answer.

The pharmacist, trying to clear up the financial situation for the former Mayor, reminded them of what they had heard about the plans of the Trizone.

"Listen, it is almost two years since the American and British decided to rule their zones together and formed the Bizone, and they established the Special Office for Money and Credit."

The minister added to his report, "At that time they prophesied it would take a currency reform to stop inflation and at the same time get order in the political chaos."

Mayor asked, "Really! Get order in the political mess? Now the west sectors got their currency reform. They even are developing a new government under the scrutinizing eyes of their military authorities. I am sure their inflation stopped promptly. If ours will cease remains to be seen, and the political situation is worse than ever before. Berlin is completely cut off from the western zones ever since all traffic across the border has been prevented."

"Well, Pastor!" The farmer addressed the clergyman, "Now our borders are blocked ever since they got their DM. And you know what? West Berlin would have starved and would have been forced to give in to become completely controlled by the Russians. But right away the

Americans and British flew their bombers over the airport Tempelhof[185] and dropped everything the West Berliners need to build, to heat, to eat, to wear and medical supplies for the sick."

With some glee Mayor interjected, "and they have not stopped getting all living essentials into Berlin and …"

"Essentials! Mayor?" The pharmacist exclaimed, "No, not only that. Our former Skat-brother, Berliner, tells me in his letter that there are a few American pilots who, after delivering their load of goods, fly low over the fence of the airport, wiggle the wings as a sign that more is coming and drop candy for the children. They call them candy bombers."

Berlin Tempelhof Airlift Memorial. Photo by Torsten Lüth, Aug 2019
https://get.google.com/albumarchive/117753700194048076333

Three sculptures were built to commemorate the Airlift. One at the Frankfurt Airport (built 1985) one in Celle at the British military airport (built 1988), both commemorate the take off flights to Berlin. At Tempelhof (built 1951) it commemorates where the goods were dropped.

---

185   See the map of divided Berlin in chapter 8.

The minister replied, "I wonder how long they will keep on doing this? It costs them a tremendous amount of fuel, planes, and pilots. Yes, and pilots! They had mishaps. I heard that some planes crashed on this mission[186]. I tell you, it could have been easier for the West Allies. After all, the Russians delivered everything needed for the people in their Berlin sector. They would have extended the freight traffic into West Berlin, if…."

Mayor had the urge to counter, "Be realistic, Pastor, they closed the borders for anybody or anything from the west. Only they could cross from east to west. Soon they would have controlled all of Berlin."

Surprisingly the pastor agreed, "You are right and I am not unrealistic, Mayor. Then Berlin would be one capital under Soviet control and Germany would not have to face separation but rather stayed connected."

The farmer could not hold back, he had to speak up, "Oh yes, under Soviet control! And soon Communism!"

Leipziger shrugged his shoulders, "Alright let's not get into politics." Turning to the minister he asked, "Tell me, Pastor, could you go freely into West Berlin to get your 40 DM when you were there?"

" I did not want to go, but after a few days, West Berliners could come and visit. They had to exchange their DM for RM with a patch on it. As I have mentioned already the exchange rate was 1 DM to 2.40 RM."

Mayor listened before voicing his opinion, "I really do not care what they do in the west or even Berlin for that matter. I want to know what will happen here? "

The farmer had started to shuffle the cards, "It is useless to speculate. It is a dilemma. We are still here. Let's enjoy each other's company as long as we can and play Skat. Pastor, you are not leaving us again are you?"

"No, I won't, Farmer. I'll cut the cards and Mayor deals."

---

186   For more about the Airlift, see the article by Mathew Noblett under Academy for Cultural Diplomacy, The Transatlantic Relationship The Berlin Airlift. www.culturaldiplomacy.org/academy/index.php?en_tar_the-berlin-airlift

The minister hoped that he would hear some more remarks from Mayor to finally have him arrested for good. His wife, both sons and his daughter were already under surveillance.

In 1948 the military governors of the USA, Great Britain and France suggested the formation of a German state. After the vast majority of citizens had approved the constitutional law for the proposed Federal Republic of Germany the occupational authorities accepted it as a basic legal system on May 12, 1949. On the same day, the Soviet Union ended the Berlin blockade and thus the airlift stopped. On October 7th they announced the German Democratic Republic (GDR = "DDR") as the second German state.

Frau Homburg's apartment slowly became less crowded. First Family Frisch had moved upstairs. Then Cousin Kappauf left. He had met his future wife, a native Hamelin resident, and in 1949 they married. They chose me to carry her veil and take care of the long train flowing from a

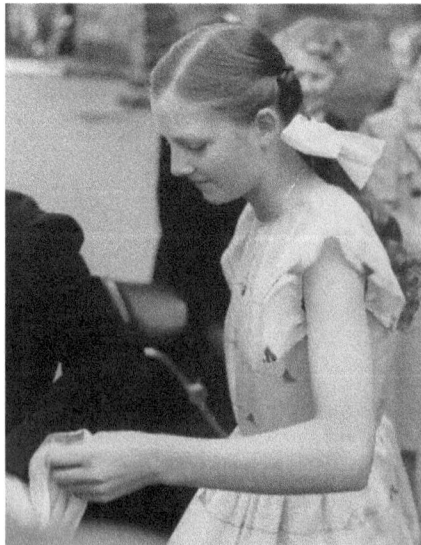

beautiful American dress that had arrived via a care package. Another parcel reached us from Seattle with dresses for Hildegard. My sister graciously allowed me to wear one of them on the occasion. After the wedding celebration the young couple moved in with her parents.

In the meantime my father, Herbert Edmund Gottlob Höfer, started his own business by selling truck insurance. It was a hampered, slow beginning with not enough office space and only a lady's bike to visit his clientele. After he insured a vehicle, he would put a round metal plate, nails and a hammer on the carrier seat, cycle to the truck owner and nail the blue-white sign onto the back of the freighter. Sometimes, when he went on foot, I would accompany him carrying his tools and helping him fastening those plates. Uncle Reinhold had connections to the forestry, sawmills, and wood businesses, all of which used trucks that needed insurance. Father hired Uncle Reinhold as the second agent for the direct contact to the customers. It took until February 21, 1948, when his business was catalogued in the Commerce Registry. He had initiated his insurance venture with the Reichs- and Renten–Mark. We had hidden the money in featherbeds and the fur collar of my mother's jacket to be able to bring it secretly over the border.

Four months later, the currency reform took place in the western zones. Many former corporations started anew, among them the insurance companies who remembered my father's expertise. Consequently, when he contacted them they gladly welcomed him back as their agent. Now his enterprise grew rapidly, chiefly since he soon concentrated on his specialty—life insurance and pensions. Ernst and Hildegard mentioned Father's business to their classmates and they in turn told it to their parents. This way, even the native population of Hamelin heard about this accomplished insurance agent, who would not wait for people to come to his office (remember he really did not have one) but instead went to potential clients, and in his knowledgeable, friendly manner convinced them to insure themselves—later their employees, too—through his agency.

Father's business grew immensely. As a sign of his success he was one of the first representatives of several insurance companies to own a VW cabriolet[187] in 1949. He had only one problem; it was exceedingly

---

187   Cabriolet is the term Germans use for cars with convertible roofs.

difficult to find office space in Hamelin. He applied again and again for it but to no avail.[188]

Father was often away from home to negotiate with different companies and to open up new areas for life insurance, i.e. one that at the date of maturity could be converted into a pension. He discussed this type of insurance with the Minister of Economy, Ludwig Erhard, of the newly founded Bundesrepublik Deutschland,[189] and suggested that people who took out life insurance should get a tax exemption; after all, they would not become a burden for the Social Security later on in their life. So, life insurance became a tax write off in Germany and the premiums could be deducted from the annual taxes. Father also helped older citizens recover at least part of their life insurance, which they thought was lost after WWII, despite having paid faithfully for years with their RM. He could assure them that their insurances were not wiped out; although they seemed reduced, but when changed into DM policies their value actually could increase.

Since my father could not find adequate room in Hamelin for his expanding agency, he looked westward to the Ruhr-district, where the heavy industry of the FRG established itself again and the economic boom took off.

The treatment of the western people stood in stark contrast to that of their relatives in the East. Under the more and more relaxed rule of the British and Americans, the West German government worked towards rebuilding their cities, their infrastructure, their factories, and international trades, which resulted in the "Wirtschaftswunder"[190] (economic miracle).

---

188 In all German cities and villages housing was so very scarce that housing authorities assigned apartments or houses to people in need. One could not just go looking for a place to live.

189 BRD, in English known as FRG (Federal Republic of Germany), founded in May 1949. In October 1949 the Russian Zone became the DDR, in English GDR (German Democratic Republic). From 1949-1991 history has to consider two Germanies.

190 Wirtschaftswunder means economic miracle. The western Allies thought it would take 30 years for Germany to recover, but the restoration only took 10 years.

One thing became clear to all Germans—in the west, you could travel freely, choose your profession, and establish your own business. In contrast, in the east, although the word freedom dominated the Communists' propaganda, people were restricted in traveling, had to meet high production quotas and give up privately owned firms or factories. The youth had hardly any choice of careers. They had to go where jobs needed to be filled. The control of Moscow over the GDR continued well into the 1970s.

⚜ ⚜ ⚜ ⚜ ⚜

The Volkspolizei followed the Soviets' command to monitor all meetings of civilians. Nevertheless, our Stammtisch continued their get-together for Skat, beer, and discussions, but their numbers dwindled because the lure of the western zones was too strong for the less privileged East Germans. They could not, and did not want to resist the appeal of the unfolding Wirtschaftswunder across the border. They met as usual; hoping some authority would not ask them to join one of the many politically manipulated new groups that had been established. They played their card game and drank their beer. From now on, they abstained from discussing any political, economic or even cultural issues. They never knew who would listen in on their conversation, or worse, if one of their members— Pastor maybe— might be an informer for the secret police.

One evening Mayor was missing. The farmer asked, "Why is Mayor not coming? Does anybody know?" The pharmacist, looking rather thoughtful, remarked, "Maybe he will not come anymore."

"At all?" cried the farmer in simulated surprise. "Tell me, why? Did they incarcerate him again?"

The pharmacist leaned over the table and whispered, "I think he left for the western zones. He could not get employed here in his capacity and always had to fear being arrested once more."

At that moment the minister entered and the pharmacist waved to him cheerfully. "Hello, Pastor. How is it going?"

"Fine, thank you." He looked at the farmer and inquired, "Why are you so gloomy? Our pharmacist is friendly enough."

251

"I am afraid we will never see Mayor again. He might be shipped to Siberia by now," the farmer replied.

The minister exclaimed, "Siberia! Don't be so sure about this. He might just be detained again so he can inform about people here who committed crimes during the Nazi time or, on a too familiar but newer scale, they hope he can tell about those people in our village who have relatives or associates in West Germany. Those might plot against the GDR regime. I myself had to convince the authorities in Berlin when I applied for staying here in your village that I am not a spy. My brother had to vouch for me."

Leipziger looked at him ponderingly but then picked up where the conversation had left off. "Or most likely Mayor is getting tired of being apprehended by the police. They know where to find him, namely here on Thursday nights at 8:00 o'clock. He probably wanted to avoid being booked in front of us."

Margret came to their table to bring their steins with their usual round of beer. She had overheard their conversation and remarked, "He took some vacation."

"From what?" The pharmacist asked, "Ever since the Red Cross had to let him go, he could not get any suitable position anywhere. I would not blame him for leaving. All he was allowed to do was clean our streets and pretend to be happy about it."

The minister nodded at the pharmacist, "You know one thing! We have to be aware of the Socialist Communist movement in the GDR. We belong to the Worker and Farmer State of Germany and the Soviet government oversees everything. Differences between blue-collar or white-collar workers must disappear. We should act united for the common interest of the entire Communist nations." He paused, searching in their faces if any of them could not be trustworthy. Silently he stipulated, *Farmer is too down to earth to get politically involved and he still barters on occasion—secretly, of course—with people desperate for food. Pharmacist? He is cunning. Didn't I hear about his escape from the partisans in Yugoslavia and how he made it to Poland through enemy*

252

lines? True to his profession as minister, he instructed them. "From now on it would be better to belong to one of the many government supported organizations if we want to gather for card games."

"Unless," the pharmacist interjected, "we meet privately in one of our homes."

Leipziger added. "But we cannot meet regularly. That would be suspicious. Before you know it, our homes are bugged and our conversation is overheard by the secret police. We would need to gather at different times, days, and places."

The farmer grew tired of their speculations. He suggested, "Let's not puzzle over meeting places and times, and even not over reasons why Mayor hasn't shown up tonight. We have enough people to play a good round of Skat."

Actually, the farmer felt uneasy. He knew that their Stammtisch member had left for good. Mayor had confided in him and asked him to plow under a few documents that could cause trouble for his friends in the village if they were found. He had hidden them under the floorboards in his kitchen and so far the Volkspolizei did not find them when they had staged a sudden raid a few weeks ago.

He had tried to get permission to move to West Germany, even suggested that the new mayor could take possession of his house, where Mayor's family still lived on the second floor, which was wired. Downstairs the new mayor and his assistant could hear what was said upstairs. But Mayor's request was denied. The authorities were not willing to let him go. As the minister stated, the secret police hoped to press him for more information on former Nazi affiliates and increasingly more about people with connections to the FRG. Since the police were regularly informed by the clergyman about Mayor's outbursts and his detestation of Communism, Mayor feared it would not take long before he would be in prison for good. They had found one document in his apartment that told about the teacher, a devoted Nazi. Although this man left even before the village had been under Soviet control, they suspected Mayor to have been instrumental in teacher's successful escape to South America.

Mayor, now a blue-collar worker, had left his family behind under the pretense of attending the Labor Day celebrations in Berlin[191] on May 1. But instead of watching the elaborate parades he went to visit Berliner, who helped him to get an airplane ticket into the FRG.

My father drove a car by now, that we understood, but why a cabriolet? Mother felt he had gone so long without his passion for cars that he deserved a special automobile. Sometimes Father would take us on a ride.

One day I was allowed to invite Sigrid to join us. My mother sat in front. Father had stopped to pick up Helga G. My girl friend sat in the middle of the back seat between this young woman and me. Father had asked me if I would part with my amber pendant and its silver chain. He wanted to give a special present to Helga. I gladly helped him out. Mother had rescued Hildegard's and my jewelry that he had given us when we lived in Thorn. Each of us received the same. Later he bought coral pearls for us. When I was four years old, he gave me a set of brown amber. It consisted of a ring, bracelet, a brooch, and matching pendant as reward for my endured sufferings during an operation. He had heard that the doctor had removed a growth in my throat without anesthesia.

Now, to thank me for handing over the yellow pendant to him, he drove us all to an exclusive new café for cake and ice cream. The next day I visited with Sigrid and innocently asked her what she thought about Helga G. She seemed upset answering, "I certainly do not like her. Where I sat in the car I could see how your father made eyes at her. He probably thought I was too exited to have a ride in his cabriolet that I would not notice." I was devastated and did not want to believe it. My father making eyes at strange women? She could not have been a stranger. He gave her my amber pendant and she was a friend of Mrs. Sieperman, his secretary. Maybe Sigrid was a little jealous and made up that story.

---

191 Many DDR citizens went to Berlin to escape into the FRG. If they did not have the money for hotels they usually had to live in West Berlin's barracks before they could fly to the FRG.

In 1949 I received permission to visit Klostermansfeld again. Oma shared her room with me as always. Although the Soviets frowned upon owning a Bible, Oma had a small version of it in her nightstand. In the evening I would take it out of its hiding place and read it. My Aunt Ursel passed me on her way to retire, "What are you reading?"

"The Old Testament in the Bible."

" Really? Do you understand these chapters? I don't believe you do."

I nodded. She remarked, "You are too young to understand this book, find something else to read." I did not react, just wished her a "Good Night!" and kept my nose in the book. She left muttering, "This is not the right reading for you. It is over your head."

I thought, *man, I will be confirmed soon. I had an excellent religious education by our Hamelin deaconess and now I was too stupid to read the Bible.* I was glad she did not take it from me.

Uncle Martin had to make sure I would go with Aunt Ursel to all the places the Communist authorities directed her for community work. Oma was spared the—in her eyes—degrading procedure lowering her from the higher estate owner class to mere fieldworker. So far even Aunt Ursel still had a higher status by teaching young girls the rudiments of farm household care.

Before, when we lived with them in 1946 and went to school in Klostermansfeld, I was among all the schoolchildren who collected– actually killed—the potato beetles on the plants of Uncle Martin's fields. In late summer Hildegard, her friend, Helga, and I had to walk around the poppy field and clap our hands to discourage the sparrows picking on the seedpods and destroying much of the crop. At noon we would crawl under a bale of poppy stalks to get some shade. Helga had the idea to see who could swallow all the poppy seeds that filled a whole pod. She was the winner, having the biggest mouth. In the end, we neglected our job by falling fast asleep due to the opium in the raw poppy seeds. That was the last time Uncle Martin asked us to shoo the sparrows away.

This time my visit was too short to get involved with fieldwork. The potatoes had been harvested. There were only sugar beets to bring in.

Now Uncle Martin could use a machine to plow them out of the ground. I think I might have refused to work with the field hands. I was neither a DDR citizen nor a Communist. If I would have been old enough, I would have voted for the CDU (Christian Democratic Union), which by now hardly existed anymore in the GDR where they had forced the KPD (Kommunistische Partei Deutschland) and SPD (Sozialistische Partei Deutschland) to combine and form the SED (Sozialistische Einheitspartei)[192]

My nine-year-old cousin, Hermjörg, had a hard time with a fifteen-year-old boy who harassed him on his way to and from school. The teenager would shout, "Hey, you! Sell me some of your pigeons. And don't you tell anybody about it." Hermjörg had neither access to the birds, nor would he be allowed to sell them. He was afraid to tell his father about the boy's demand.

It was masquerade time again. Oma asked her seamstress to sew a chimney-sweep costume for Hermjörg and a female pirate one for our doctor's daughter. I wore a male pirate outfit. I really felt a little too old for this, but they wanted me to look after the two during the children's "Fasching"[193]. When we had to walk in a circle for judging of the best costumes, some older boys and girls sat on the windowsills of the gymnasium and watched us. I overheard their comments about me. "That is no boy; she is a girl trying to be a pirate." It really made me very uncomfortable all the time.

The mother of the girl pirate came and claimed, "We have a birthday party for my son." Turning to my cousin she said, "Hermjörg, you are invited. But Ilse-Rose, you can stay here as long as you like." I did not want to go to the "Fasching" to begin with, and now ... I was ready to leave and go home.

---

192 KPD=Communist Party of Germany, SPD=Socialistic Party of Germany, SED=Socialistic Union of Germany. See also chapter 8 Footnote 13.

193 Fasching is one of the expressions for masquerade festivities. They are held mostly in the Rhine region and throughout southern Germany from November to Ash Wednesday. They are also called Fastnacht, Carnival or Maskenball.

I had to walk through a narrow alley between walled-in gardens. A teen- aged boy cornered me. "You better get the pigeons for me!" he demanded. I answered, "They belong to my uncle." "Liar! You are an Oemler, just like the rest of them. I'll teach you to be bigheaded." With this, he slapped me on my cheek. I did not flinch, just stared in his face. *Would he hit me again? What should I do? How could I get out of this remote alley where nobody seems to come and help me?* Suddenly, he turned.

The gate to the courtyard with the entrance door to its right.

I slipped past him and walked briskly away, expecting to be clobbered from behind any minute. When I arrived at the courtyard entrance door, there he stood again, now he had a stick to threaten me with.

"What do you want now? I told you I am not an Oemler. I only live here."

"But you were a Nazi. So, you are a liar!"

Wasn't there anybody who would come to help me? Inside, the dog started to bark. I called, "Here Karo, come here!" The dog's growling must have scared my molester; he turned away and I had free access to the door of the courtyard. "Karo, good dog," I whispered under tears. I knew from now on, I had to be on my guard. I took comfort in the thought that I had to leave soon for Hamelin. Klostermansfeld was not as wonderful as it used to be.

I never told my parents about this incident, and not being aware of the predicament I might be in, in January they applied for a visa so my brother Reinhold and I could visit with Uncle Martin and Oma in our summer vacation. I hoped the request for our holiday in Klostermansfeld would be denied. In the meantime I prepared for my confirmation on Palm Sunday.

One morning—I was still at school—the doorbell rang at Mrs. Homburg's apartment. My mother opened the door, expecting one of Father's clients. She looked at the pale, tall man and then in sudden recognition, she clasped her hand in front of her mouth, shouting, "Major Conn! Is it really you? What brings you here? Come in! Come in! How did you find us?" He took both of her hands and shook them heartily. Entering, he followed Mother into the dining room and greeted Mrs. Homburg, whom my mother introduced. He finally answered her question. "Well, I work in Hamburg with somebody who has connections to Herbert's business. When I heard Roselett is going to be confirmed soon I wanted to talk to her. May I?"

"Of course, you may." My mother told him.

Uncle Conn visited with Mother and Mrs. Homburg until school was out. I hardly recognized him. Six years of imprisonment and work in the lead mines in Siberia had left their mark on him. He invited me to a little café not far from the St. Boniface Minster, a beautiful church resting on a Romanesque foundation that, in the 13th century was enlarged and topped by a big Gothic cathedral.

Major Conn told me about his daughter and what advice he had given her. Now he wanted to relate it to me. "Roselett," he said, still using the diminutive of my name as he had called me in Thorn, "Whenever you feel something for a man, and might even think you love him, look at that fellow closely. Always consider if you would like to have him as the father of your children, before you get into a relationship with him." I listened, wondering why he would tell me this. I did not even have a boyfriend. Hildegard did but not I. He continued counseling. I felt a little awkward but also very important that he took the time to discuss guidelines for my future life.

I have no idea how much he knew about my father and the changes he had gone through because of the war and its aftermath. I cannot explain what happened to him. But so much was true; Father had little time for us children. He worked hard and found his relaxation away from Mrs. Homburg's crowded apartment. Therefore, it was especially meaningful for me that Major Conn talked to me in a way none of the grown-ups ever did before.

I told him about my four years of confirmation classes. How I had learned many Bible verses and hymns and how I had memorized my favorite Easter song "O Haupt voll Blut und Wunden". When I mentioned this to Uncle Conn he could not relate to my Christian belief. I kept quiet from then on. I did not tell him that I would have liked to enter the deaconess's school. What hindered me? I needed parental permission to access the institution. My father did not like my decision and threatened to abandon me. If he threw me out on the streets, I had no place to go.

I must have stated to Uncle Conn, "It does not matter to which denomination I belong, as long as I go to a Christian church." At the end, Uncle Conn gave me a small package to be opened on the day of my confirmation. It contained the third edition of Theodor Storm's *Meisternovellen* (Master novellas)[194]. The Georg Westermann Publishing Company had reissued the 1918 version of the book, keeping the gothic script of the original publication. When I opened the little volume, I found a dedication on the flyleaf. Major Conn had written it in Sütterlin script[195].

---

194   Theodor Storm was born 1817 and died 1888 in Husum, Schleswig Holstein. He is considered one of the great masters of the genre Novella.

195   "Sütterlin" also see chapter 4 footnote 7.

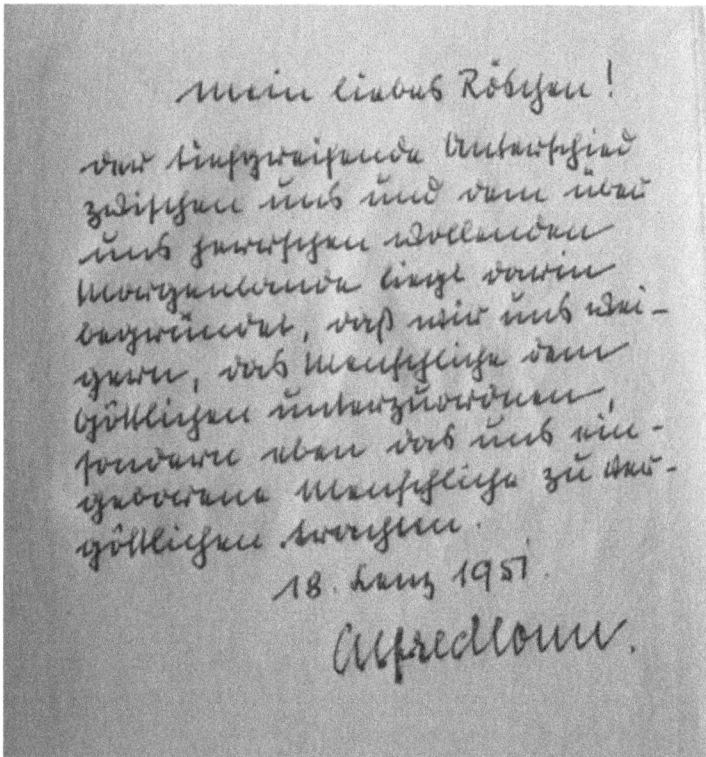

Mein liebes Röschen! der tiefgreifende Unterschied zwischen uns und dem über uns herrschen wollenden Morgenlande liegt darin begründet, daß wir uns weigern, das Menschliche dem Göttlichen unterzuordnen, sondern eben das uns eingeborene Menschliche zu vergöttlichen trachten.

18, Lenz 1951

Alfred Conn.

I never had learned to write these archaic characters; still, I was able to read them, because Oma used a mixture of Latin and Sütterlin letters in her correspondence to me. For a long time I did not understand the meaning of Uncle Conn's inscription. Years later, after I had studied German literature, had learned about Storm's attitude towards religion, and had read about the difficulties for postwar authors[196] to overcome

---

196 Wolfdietrich Schnurre said about the German language, "The Nazi and war years had contaminated the language. Painstakingly, the author has to knock

the Nazi language, I realized that the Major still used the jargon of the Nazi time and expressed his perception of godliness with mythological undertones, so prevalent in the Nazi ideology.

We celebrated my confirmation in Bad Pyrmont, a well-known spa with good hotels and extensive parks. My father had selected it for us to spend the weekend there. He wanted to find out if my mother could register for a prolonged therapy at that long established hot spring resort during our summer vacation.

On Palm Sunday[197] I slipped on the same black dress Hildegard had worn the year before, which belonged to Mrs. Homburg's daughter.

My father thought his daughters did not look good in black and therefore would not spend money on the traditional confirmation garb. If we absolutely had to have a new outfit, we still relied on Oma's help for textile goods. All of Hildegard's dresses from the care packages were second-hand and some showed wear.

---

off the dust (mud) from each word, before it can be used." The Nazi propaganda and ideology alongside the military jargon had changed the meaning of words. Many of the postwar authors experienced this phenomenon. In: K. Wagenbach's edition *Das Atelier* 1963, page 149. Translated by Dr. Ilse-Rose Warg.

197 Palm Sunday is traditionally the day for confirmation in the Protestant church in Germany.

Confirmation class of 1951. Sigrid and I are in the front, on the far left, next to the girl in the lighter colored dress. I am the one wearing pearls.

Most of the money Father earned needed to go back into his business, although he did hire a cleaning woman[198], Lisel, from a nearby village, after Mrs. Homburg's living room became his office during the day and my parents' bedroom at night. Lisel lived in the country. Once a week she took the train to come and help us. In the beginning of our stay with Mrs. Homburg, Hildegard and I, under Mother's supervision, had taken turns with Family Frisch in cleaning the kitchen, hallway, bathroom, and the stairs leading to the apartment, and the cellar staircase. These were especially dirty, since everybody in the house used coal stoves to heat each individual room. The coal dust from carrying the briquettes or the egg shaped coke upstairs was tough to get rid of. We needed several pails of water to wipe everything clean. After Lisel came, we could devote more time to our schoolwork, friends, and Ernst and Hildegard to their dance school.

---

198   At that time in Germany it was still customary that the middle class people had servants. My parents hired help as soon as they could afford it.

In 1950, Mother needed a lengthy treatment at a spa to recover from the stress that had accumulated in her over the last six years. My father chose Bad Pyrmont for her, because it was close to his center of business in Hamelin. In order for her to relax and not worry about her children, so she could concentrate on her therapy, my parents sent us four children to places where they thought we would be safe.

Father planed a business trip to Karlsruhe and on his way he took my sister with him to her godmother Aunt Hilde in Heidelberg. Ernst stayed near Hamelin in Aerzen with the family of his friend Hermann from the Adolf Hitler School. His parents were very glad to repay my brother for taking their son to Klostermansfeld when all boys had to leave the school but were not allowed to return home if it was in a battlefield. Aerzen is near Bad Pyrmont. Ernst could visit with Mother often. And my younger brother and I finally received legal papers for the bus trip from Hannover to Magdeburg in the Russian Sector, where Uncle Martin would meet us at the station and take us with his black stallions to the farm and to Oma.

I knew that this time my visit would be different than the many stays before. I was fourteen and therefore considered another work force to be added to the household. They had to incorporate me into their system. Just as the clergyman of the Stammtisch had said, "… We have to be aware of the Socialist Communist movement in the GDR. This side of Germany is now 'the Worker and Farmer State'. The Soviet government controls us." They controlled all farms, firms, factories, in short the whole workforce. "Differences between blue-collar or white-collar workers must disappear. We should act united…" I wasn't about to act united for the common interest of the entire Communist nations. But Aunt Ursel had no choice. As in the year before, she took me along when she had the order to shell peas with all the farm workers, who had been her employees. Now she was just one of them. I, too, had to go to the big hall where a Communist overseer, a woman, regulated who would sit with whom. She let me sit with Aunt Ursel and several women in a circle of six to eight around a big tub for the peas and another for the empty pods. Pointing at them I asked,

"What are they for? Compost?"

"No, they get cooked and fed to pigs," a former field worker for Uncle Martin answered. They started talking about meetings that Aunt Ursel had to attend. In the evening she was required to show up at several informative assemblies. I seldom saw Reinhold who played with her three boys under the care of Christa Rahbel. I had to work along all the others in her household but when it came to going with her to the hearings, I acted as before and refused. I was a visitor not a DDR citizen, and I would leave soon. After all I was not finished with my higher education. I needed to go back to Hamelin. I did not need to go with her, get indoctrinated and long to become a "Thälmann Pionier" of the FDJ.[199]

When the time came to go back to Hamelin, the remarkable recovery in the western sectors prompted my Aunt Ursel to ask a rather daring task of me. She requested. "Take Hermjörg with you; he has his school vacation now. He would like to eat some chocolate, which we cannot get over here." She did not listen to my reservations about her plan. She just packed his suitcase. It was twice as big as Reinhold's and mine together. It was made from yellow leather, and heavy. I was not sure how I would get a 10-year-old boy across the border without the legal documents.

But when I waited for the bus in Magdeburg, the driver hardly looked at our papers. He might have thought, *they are kids, why bother?* Although he did not like the extra heavy luggage from Hermjörg. *They will have a hard time crossing the Russian control with this suitcase,* he might have thought.

He had a good heart, but he was right. My trouble emerged at the border when the Russian guards searched our luggage. I told the boys to go to the outhouse and I pushed Hermjörg's suitcase with my foot in front of me below the long table where they searched the luggage. They questioned me about my brother and I told them he is at the toilet. I had only our suitcase and knapsacks on the counter. Slowly I shoved the big

---

199   Ernst Thälmann Pioneer Organization. "Freie Deutsche Jugend" (Free German Youth). Just as under the Nazis the DDR had their organizations for young children, and teenagers.

suitcase alongside the table wondering what I should do at the end of it. Suddenly the bus-driver came "time to get in the bus," he called, grabbed the suitcase and threw it into the luggage compartment. It happened so fast that the Russian custom officer did not realize it belonged to my party and had not been searched.

"I have to get my brothers," I whispered to the driver.

"Hurry!"

I ran back, fetched the two boys, and scampered with them behind the outhouses to the backdoor of the bus, which surprisingly was left open. I hustled them in and climbed after them. So, the Russian checkpoint was behind us. I made sure we three sat on the last two seats in the back of the bus.

"I know it is tight but we have to see how we make it through the British checkpoint." The boys understood. The British guard checked all papers, then counted the people in the bus and asked, "Is somebody here who took the wrong bus?" I was quiet, we were in the right bus, but we were the party with the extra person. He spoke to everybody in the bus.

"I cannot let you continue your journey until I know who the additional traveler is. All of you have to leave the bus and enter again as I count and check your tickets."

"No officer!" I yelled, "You counted the two boys as two persons, but they count only as one." Everybody looked at me questioningly. I stood up. "Sit down!" he shouted, "don't you dare get up again, my comrades might think you want to do something awful. Stay seated!" I had to give my papers to be transported from hand to hand to the front of the bus until the officer received them. He looked them over thoroughly and said, "One young female, one younger boy, her brother. Who is your brother?"

Pointing to Reinhold I answered, "Yes, Sir here are two boys, whereas my documents only shows one male. But let me explain. I received permission for two people on this bus, apparently for two adults. The two boys take only one seat on this motor coach like one adult would. That makes one adult seat for them and the other for me. I am even not really a grown-up, since I am only 14 years old." I do not know if they let me pass with Hermjörg and Reinhold because I was so young or if it was high time to move on, because a traffic jam started to build up behind us; or, I kind of like to think, they might have been impressed by my 'clever' answer.

This was the last trip I was able to make to Klostermansfeld. I was not allowed to see the old farmhouse I grew up in —with the attached eyesore as the adults called the yellow brick building—until 1992 when I showed it to my husband, but only for a short visit. It was too painful to see the old main house and stables converted into unfamiliar apartments. Where the Victorian garden house once stood, there ugly cement block garages blocked off what had been the garden. We could not enter the courtyard. My husband and I left disappointed.

After my Uncle Martin died, the Treuhand[200] granted my cousins Hermjörg, Lutz, Jochen, and Martin Jr. the inheritance rights to the farm. In 2009 Hermjörg took us inside the old farmhouse. I could not show the former layout of its rooms, not Oma's rooms, not my favorite hangouts to my husband; all of them had been turned into the apartment complex. However, we walked up the steep stairs to where the two rooms had been that we occupied when we had to hide my father—and wouldn't you know it—the old key to the door leading to the roof still hung on its nail. But the access to the barn across the gate had been torn down. A slight dizziness befell me and I declined to walk over the roof again as I had done so often as a child.

But back to Hamelin! In late 1950, the walls of the Wilhelm Raabe School had just been repaired and whitewashed, when the art teacher selected me to help create colorful aquarelles for our hallway walls. I always liked to draw or paint pictures. Now my flowers and landscapes had found approval by the commission for adornment of our middle school. Besides being a good enough "artist," one had to be free of

---

200   The *Treuhand* was created in Germany after 1990. It is the administration of restoring lost property to the original owners. It came into existence when the states belonging to the Russian zone were incorporated into the Federal Republic of Germany, the "Bundesrepublik Deutschland".

acrophobia and not mind climbing on scaffolds. I spent afternoons with the other chosen students. We had fun working together. Unfortunately I could not continue to enjoy their company long enough to see the finished product, because my father moved us to Mülheim on the Ruhr in 1951.

CHAPTER 11

For we are what he has made us, created in Christ Jesus for good works, which
God prepared beforehand to be our way of life. Ephesians 2:10

The Cold War

Germany Divided Into Two Countries

As stated before, in 1949 occupied Germany became politically divided. The three western zones were combined to form a new democratic government under the guidance of the Americans, British and French. The Russians were invited to join them but they declined; in fact, they opposed the capitalistic Federal Republic of Germany (FRG) by promptly setting a Communistic regime against the west in October 1949. It was called the German Democratic Republic (GDR) under Moscow's management. In the following forty years the two separated German states—or should I say nations or countries—drifted more and more apart politically, economically, culturally and their language changed along with it, resulting in different interpretations of word and speech. Two new vernaculars developed, colored by their contrasting political and socioeconomic use.

It became clear to all Germans: in the west, they could travel freely, choose professions, establish their own businesses and rebuild the destroyed factories and cities. In the east, although the word "freedom" dominated the Communist propaganda, people became restricted in traveling, had to give up privately owned properties, and had hardly any choice of careers. They had to work where they were needed. The control of Moscow over the GDR continued well into the 1970s.

This division explains why nowadays one finds different abbreviations, names and symbols for Germany. Since 1949 there were two

German nations, the <u>FRG</u> (West Germany) and the GDR (East Germany). On November 9, 1989, the quiet revolution started with the fall of the Berlin Wall. In 1990, naming the reunified Germany posed a problem. To adopt FRG as it was used by the English speaking countries, caused concern, since in the 1970 the Federal Republic of Germany tried to hinder the use of this abbreviation, which reminded them how the Communists used the name since the late 60's as an insulting term. In West German school books this terminology was widely taboo. BRD was preferred instead. The reunification of Germany and the advances in technical communication put an end to this dilemma; for German e-mails, websites and other ever newer means of communication, "de" or "DE" (abbreviation for Deutschland) was now widely used since the 1990s. When mentioning the BRD in English writing, one just says Germany.

⋙⋙⋙⋙⋙

In the later half of the 1950s, our Stammtisch in the "Green Heart"[201] of East Germany slowly ceased to exist. On a small scale it resembles the political impact on the German people from the 1920s to the late 1950s. You remember that the first one to leave had been the shopkeeper, Mr. Schumann. He had decided to depart in 1934 before the Nazi Nuremberg laws came to effect, since his wife was of Jewish ancestry. His family went to France, then to Spain and finally to America, where he could find a job in a clothing factory. I imagine him as a good reliable employee who worked his way up the ladder and eventually became their best salesman.

The next one to leave the Stammtisch was the former pastor. He was drafted and lost his life at the Russian Front. The pharmacist, too, had to follow the call to arms. He was missing in action when his unit had to leave him to die in Yugoslavia, but he survived and came back in the late fall of 1945. He had been forced, along with millions of expellees from Eastern

---

201 Thuringia has extensive woods and it lies in the middle of Germany, therefore Germans named it "Das Grüne Herz Deutschlands" (The Green Heart of Germany).

Bloc Countries[202] to settle in the Russian Zone, although he was lucky to be able to come back to his former village and run his pharmacy again.

By 1944, evacuees replaced the three unavailable Stammtisch members. They were simply named after the towns they originated from – Berliner, Leipziger, and Hamburger. Then in 1945 before the end of WWII (May 8) the teacher and later headmaster fled to Chile[203]. He left before the four occupied sectors of Germany received their distinct borders, July 1, 1945.

In 1946, in the course of relocation, Hamburger, Berliner, and Leipziger, as evacuees, had been ordered back to their respective hometowns. All three could not move back right away, as it depended on finding shelter and/or jobs for them in their cities.

Hamburger was old enough to retire and collect a pension. After this great harbor town rebuilt housing for returning evacuees, he and his wife received an apartment and enjoyed living in the cultural atmosphere of the restored arts and science centers in Hamburg.

After Berliner and his family were assigned to go to the French zone in his hometown, he left the village but stayed in contact with the rest of the Stammtisch. He was still able to visit the American, British, and Russian sectors in Berlin until 1953.

By early 1950, the mayor knew he had to leave in secret without his family and cross the border into one of the western zones illegally. His family would have liked to accompany him, but the police were already spying on them. They would have been forcibly stopped in any of their moves. Nevertheless, he and his wife had quietly made plans that they would meet at Berliner's apartment as soon as possible. His wife did not reveal anything to their children; she only hinted that they might go on a

---

202   Eastern Bloc Countries, the Communist Bloc, or Soviet Bloc were terms used to denote groupings of states aligned with the Soviet Union, even states outside Central and Eastern Europe.

203   Countries of South America and Egypt became a refuge haven for former Nazis.

trip during their summer vacation. She intended to file for permission to visit the GDR's capital.[204]

The chance of receiving the coveted stamp of approval for traveling to Berlin grew dramatically for the East Germans if they declared they wanted to experience the excitement at the international meetings that Eastern Bloc countries performed there under Moscow's mandate, or if they liked to witness the spectacle of military parades, which usually accompanied these political ceremonies. Another way to apply was to state they wished to see major sport events where young athletes collected laurels for the GDR. It helped if the applicant belonged to one of the mass organizations, e.g. "Freier Deutscher Gewerkschaftsbund" FDGB (Free German Trade Union Federation). Her oldest son, Erich, had been killed at Normandy but her second had entered the "Freie Deutsche Jugend" FDJ, and she herself had joined the "Demokratischer Frauenbund Deutschlands" DFD (Democratic Women's Federation/League of Germany) shortly after it had been formed in 1947. At that time she thought belonging to this organization would assist her husband in being reinstated to his former position as mayor of their village. It did not benefit him, but now she was successful. She held the papers that gave her and her children access to Berlin.

They met Mayor at Berliner's place; only they could not stay in his tiny apartment. They had to live in barracks at the overcrowded reception camps in Berlin and wait their turn to fly into the American Zone. The inhuman conditions there became too much for their older son. One day he declared he wanted to go back to their village. His parents were surprised. Mayor asked him, "Why? We just left their oppression and spying on us." And his mother added, "After all I went through to get permission to take every single one of you. And then were able to meet Father at Berliner's. You know they helped us to find shelter in this barracks."

---

204 From 1949 to 1991 Berlin was the capital for East Germany (GDR). Bonn, close to the French border, was the capital for the FRG. After 1991, it took several years before all departments (especially the foreign embassies) of the FRG could resettle in Berlin.

"You are right to call it shelter and not living quarters." Spreading out his arms touching their bunk beds, he continued, "Here we live in confinement."

His father tried to persuade him. "Son, just think clearly. Here the school system will honor your Abitur. You can apply for a place at a university. Or, if you like, enter an academy."[205]

"I know that, except what you say about my high school diploma. Remember, I was only allowed to enter higher education since I joined the 'Pioniere' and, when I turned 14, the FDJ."

Mayor interrupted him, "Oh, how I disliked all of this catering to the Communist regime. Here you can chose a profession. You cannot do that in the Russian zone. There the higher education institutes are not allowed to accept you anymore since we never left our church. They might consider you a traitor."

Their son listened carefully and then countered, "First, Mom, I am not ungrateful, but the conditions in these barracks compounds are degrading. All those rules about when to use the shower stalls, when to stand in line for food, where to go for medical help, on which day may I apply for a job, etcetera." He took a deep breath, "And when I tried to apply for work they told me that my Abitur —yes Dad—it does not meet their standards. I would need to take another language, different history courses, and, depending on what I wish to study, other preparatory programs." He walked toward the barracks door muttering, "I am homesick for our village." Opening the door he half turned to his family and shouted, "I am in love with Margret." And ran through the barracks' lanes.

Reluctantly his parents let him go. Their daughter and youngest son stayed with them until his father found a job as mayor in a small town near Munich. Here their daughter was able to enter the university and study chemistry, an opportunity that had been denied her in the

---

205 Germany has many Academies. They specialize in particular professions. One of the oldest is the "Königlich-Sächsiche Forstakademie" (Royal Saxon Academy of Forestry) founded 1811.

Russian Zone and their youngest son was accepted into the eleventh grade "Obersekunda" of the high school nearby.

When the Stammtisch met in the spring of 1950, Leipziger, still teaching at the elementary school, was with them. He, the farmer, the pharmacist, and the clergyman were all that were left as Skat players. Margret, the innkeeper, would occasionally join them if her duties allowed it, but she never played their favorite card game with them. Nobody else asked to join their circle. Nonetheless, the Stammtisch came together again.

It might have been in April, when the "show trials" took place, during which over 3,000 Nazis, war criminals, and political prisoners, even some KPD comrades and close to 150,000 SED members, who were marked as unreliable elements, were disposed of. The SED had insisted that they needed a Ministry for State Security, and the still provisional "Volkskammer" (People's Chamber) in Berlin complied by establishing a secret service branch of the State Security Service (MfS)[206], known in the vernacular as Stasi.

The pharmacist opened the Stammtisch's conversation with, "What do you think? Was the SED complaining to the People's Chamber that they needed protection, because of spies from the Western Powers?"

"And maybe deceptive agents from there." The farmer added, "I heard about this on the radio for quite some time now."

Leipziger agreed, "And not only spies but also delusive saboteurs. They, with the spies and agents, supposedly try to undermine the productivity of our factories, heavy industry, and farms."

The clergyman raised his eyebrows, "Deceptive, delusive, supposedly, you say? Why these adjectives? What I could gather from my brother, the new mayor, the Stasi was announced in February after the SED declared that they needed a 'shield and sword' against spies, saboteurs and agents from the western powers, mostly the FRG."

---

206 "Ministerium für Staatssicherheit" founded 2/8/1950 by the provisional "Volkskammer" (People's Chamber) in Berlin GDR. Soon referred to as Stasi. See chapter 7, footnote 23.

The farmer took a deep breath and gasped, "Sure! Yes, of course! We need something like the Nazi Gestapo to double check on everybody if our five year plans are fulfilled. They are geared to productivity, no matter if the land, factories and workers can produce the quotas they unrealistically set in those plans."

The pharmacist tried to interrupt his torrent of words by changing the subject, "Did you know that the apartment in Mayor's house is empty?"

Leipziger turned to him, "You mean his family did not return from their trip to Berlin? Well, thanks for letting us know. I'll apply to move there, my room being kitchen, bedroom, and workspace all in one is getting too crowded. I would love to have my own bathroom for once and not need to share it with others. I'll apply for it tomorrow morning. Pastor, is your brother available?"

The clergyman looked at him pensively, "I guess I could put a good word in for you. The housing department might just like you to move in. Parents could visit with you there and discuss their plans for their children with you in private." The farmer listened and thought. *Of course, and overhear their conversation. I know their place is wired. How convenient for the IM[207] who could just fabricate a story for the SED, who tries to get rid of unfaithful members in their party!* But Leipziger beamed at the pastor, "That would be great. I have to let my wife know about it. Neither beer nor Skat for me tonight!" He left and the clergyman suggested they depart for the evening and meet on another Thursday for cards. The regularity of each Thursday at 8.00 PM Beer and Skat had been disposed of long ago, ever since they suspected that their corner in the inn was wired and the minister might be an **IM**.

Our family already lived in the British zone when many East Germans fled to West Germany during the 1950s. Life started to become unbearable in the Russian controlled East Germany. At that time we started to be glad

---

207   IM stands for "Inoffizielle Mitarbeiter" (unofficial secret informers), who overshadowed suspected citizens, like church members, or people with relatives in West Germany.

that our farm had fallen under the land reform, not because of its acreage, but for political reasons. In 1951 my father's business had excelled and more rooms for an office were required. He had tried to convince the town fathers of Hamelin to let him move out of Mrs. Homburg's apartment, but every time they refused to accommodate him, thinking that the available offices should be given first to the original firms of their town. They were just as immovable when we requested to rent an apartment. They insisted, "First we supply our people, then come the displaced persons." Since half of Hamelin's occupants were refugees, evacuees, or expellees, we had hardly any chance of receiving suitable living or office space.[208]

Consequently, Father looked for other towns that were more hospitable. Southwest of Hamelin, at the largest most densely settled industrial district in West Germany, he found Mülheim on the Ruhr River. This city had been bombed more extensively than Hamelin, but its town fathers saw potential growth for their city by encouraging new businesses to settle here. They granted my father the whole upper floor of an office building downtown and an apartment on the fifth floor of a dilapidated, but partially repaired house just across from the bank.

Some weeks before the movers came to haul our few belongings to the Ruhr-district, Hertha Homburg reminisced with my mother about their life together since 1947. She started their conversation. "Your husband surely convinced me that your family would be decent folks. He told me about your cooking skills and what you could do with the little food available for us all. That sold me on his plan to share my already overcrowded place."

My mother smiled at her 'decent folks', and then said,

"Yes, Mrs. Homburg[209]. We were very glad to have a roof over our heads, but now you will finally have the whole place to yourself."

---

208 Housing all the people created headaches for the German authorities even into the 21st century. Germans still need to apply for apartments or for building permits, even on their own properties.

209 Although Hertha Homburg shared her apartment for over four years with us, living in tighter quarters than relatives usually do, both ladies did not address each other by their first names. At that time in Germany it still took a very long time before grown-ups would consider being on a first name basis.

275

"Hum, it will be nice not sharing my bedroom with my two children. Each of them can have their own room now. We will have the living room again, and can roll the piano out of the dining room into it. The landlord will even send a contractor to rebuild the barely fixed balcony."

"It was better for us when family Frisch moved upstairs. We did not need to share the kitchen anymore. And what is best, we finally have electricity almost all the time," my mother threw in.

Mrs. Homburg nodded and recalled, "Remember when my Cousin Kappauf moved out after he married?"

"That was when Herbert extended his office. He got rid of the bunk beds, and designed a kind of sofa bed."

Herta Homburg had to laugh. "Your husband's clients never knew they were sitting on beds."

Mother joined her cheerfulness and concluded, "Luckily we found material to cover them, so that each of them would look like a couch."

"Are you taking all of them with you?"

"Yes, we need them in Mülheim. We have only Herbert's big desk, these box beds, and the three wardrobes."

"What will you do for chairs and a table?"

"Herbert's secretary, Miss Siepermann, is moving with us. She'll bring all of her furniture. She will have one room in our apartment. We'll divide the biggest room with her hutch and our closets. In front of this partition will be our dining area and behind it the children and Lisel will sleep. Herbert and I will have our own bedroom."

"You have such a talent for organizing things." Mrs. Homburg mentioned.

My mother nodded, "Thank you, you noticed! In return for Miss Siepermann letting us use her furniture, she will join us for breakfast, lunch and dinner and I will do her laundry as well." Mrs. Homburg thought, *this woman never stops cooking for others. Her husband is fortunate that she always agrees to his arrangements.*

My mother took a sip of her coffee and, changing the subject, she mused. "Aah, this coffee is good. Remember when the mailman brought a letter from my mother that contained enough grounds for just one cup of coffee?"

Mrs. H. responded mirthfully, "Suddenly the whole apartment smelled delicious!" She also took a swallow of the dark brew and interjected, "That reminds me of 1948, when our money changed from Reichsmark to DM. It was amazing how we suddenly could get all the basic food, even real coffee and without ration cards." Mrs. Homburg chuckled. "Good bye, hamster trips!" but then she thought back to what this currency reform meant for the Berlin population in the western sectors and continued. "We recovered fast, but Berlin was cut off from all basic necessities to survive hunger and the hard winter. If it wasn't for the American and British pilots flying everything into the western sectors of Berlin, the people of the French, British, and American zones of Berlin would have starved or frozen to death."

My mother, contemplating about divided Germany, stated, "I saw it coming. Already in 1946 Churchill had called the border between the Russian and the western zones 'The Iron Curtain'. The Cold War started then. It pushed Germany into two countries or should I say nations? Here we formed the FRG in May 49 and the Russian Zone received their supposedly independent government but under Moscow, in October of the same year."

Mrs. Homburg took up the train of thought, saying, "That means now politically we are separated."

"Yes, and they have a different currency."

" So, economically we are separated."

"Communism is taught like a religion to the young people."

"So, culturally we are becoming detached as well." My mother sighed long and deep, saying, "And visiting my mother and brother has become an impossibility." Both women sat quietly for a few moments until Mother reminded our landlady, "Herbert worked for several insurance companies.

First he just sold truck-and-car-insurance. Remember how he went to his clients?"

"Oh my! He took the one bike that all of us shared. It was my ladies bicycle. He did not care. Nobody cared, and now—he owns a nice VW."

"When he added life insurance to his agency, he needed a car. That's when our business took off. He hired Uncle Reinhold and several others as sales representatives. Mr. Venator and Miss Siepermann took care of the office here. She can take shorthand faster than anybody I know and holds a speed record in typing."

"And your bookkeeper, Bob Venator, is fantastic. Wasn't he employed by German ship companies before the war?"

"Yes, he was their paymaster."

"When will you leave?" Mrs. Homburg asked.

"Pretty soon after Ilse-Rose's confirmation." Remembering that Hildegard had worn Gerlinde's (Mrs. Homburg's daughter) traditional black dress she exclaimed. "Oh, I wanted to thank you for the dress Hildegard and now Ilse-Rose could borrow to wear for their confirmation."

"Don't even mention it. We are glad that this faded old thing is of some use again. Will you celebrate Ilse-Rose's confirmation at the same location where you had Hildegard's feast, at the 'Ratskeller'[210]?"

"No, for Roselett's confirmation we have reserved a special room in a great hotel in Bad Pyrmont."

"Bad Pyrmont! The spa for the misunderstood women!" Mrs. Homburg exclaimed.

My mother did not want to talk with Mrs. Homburg any longer. She did not want to get into a discussion about women's attitudes and she knew that the conversation soon would repeat itself. Sometimes this dear owner of the apartment showed signs of senility. Mother felt she'd better see Mrs. Frisch and say good-bye to her. She wished to stay in contact with her and

---

210 Usually, the town halls in Germany have a restaurant located in the cellar of the building. Here, the town fathers like to take a break during their meetings. The "Ratskellers" are known for excellent food and service.

give her our new address. We had become good friends with them. Later on, no matter where they or we moved, we continued to see each other whenever possible. But it became impossible to keep in touch with Mrs. Homburg. Many years had passed when my brother Reinhold found out from Ottfried Homburg, her youngest son, that she had to enter a home for mentally unbalanced people and succumbed there to her illness.

When we left Hamelin, our household helper, Lisel, went with us to Mülheim. By now she was part of our family. Hildegard befriended her. Those two would sometimes sing and dance in the kitchen. Nevertheless, she was rather shy when it came to running errands in Mülheim. I told her that I, too, had to get used to the big city. For an example, I told her about my encounter with the blind clerk selling stamps at one of the windows in the post office. I disclosed to her how bewildered I was about him.

"I greeted him politely, but he would not answer. He probably did not know if the voice he heard was directed towards him. I wished I would know his name, then I could call on him directly, but so, I said louder than necessary, 'Could I please have a stamp for a letter to St. Bernhard?' He promptly said, 'You do not need to shout, girly, I am not deaf.' And then he asked if St. Bernhard is in the Russian Zone. After I told him that it was close to Hildburghausen in Thuringia, he asked for the envelope. He took it, felt its size, weighed it on a scale for the sight impaired, and gave me the correct postage."

Lisel asked, "How does he handle money? I mean coins and paper money?" Before I could answer her she exclaimed, "I know! You can feel money; the coins and paper notes are cut into different sizes according to their value. The 5 DM bill is the smallest and five hundred the largest[211]. A blind person can tell the value of a bank note or coin by feeling it. I understand now how he can touch the money and know how much it is,

---

211   Coins came in one, two, five, ten, and fifty-penny pieces, followed by 1, 2, and 5 DM coins. Each was, according to its value, bigger and heavier than the lesser one. The paper money followed the same pattern. They came in 5, 10, 20, 50, 100 and 500 bills. When the Euro was introduced in 1999 the European Union agreed to keep this manner of sizing for coins and paper money.

but what about the stamps? They do not come in different sizes according to their worth."

"He has a folder" I explained, "that has pockets with Braille written on top of it, so he can feel the money value of the different stamps organized inside of each pocket". Lisel nodded thoughtfully and typically for me, I continued ready to teach her more about handicapped people.

"You see, we have so many injured soldiers, they do not just want to sit in homes and do nothing. Here in West Germany the government designed many different ways, so that veterans and injured civilians can fulfill a job. I think their goal is to get all physically or mentally challenged humans back into the work force."

Lisel had listened patiently but now she suggested, "Could you, please, always mail the letters for me?" Her reaction was understandable. It was more complicated to send parcels to the GDR. We had to fill out declarations, use the right paper for packages and have it wrapped with string—no tape or glue—so a parcel could be opened and checked by the IM among their postal clerks to inform the Stasi.

Lisel never got used to Mülheim. She only stayed a short time with us. One day she asked my mother if her sister Annie would be allowed to take her place. "The many steps to your apartment on the fifth floor are too much for me." She claimed. "My sister likes to come and clean for you while I go back to my parents. Anyway, when washing Miss Siepermann's clothing, I feel I never do it good enough for her." My mother had noticed how pale Lisel had become since living with us in the big city. She said. "Well, Lisel, I think you might be homesick. Call your sister. She can stay here and share your bed when she visits." Lisel's face flushed, as she shyly declined, "No, Mrs. Höfer, let me go home and let her come after I leave. She will be alright." My mother agreed to this arrangement.

Soon our young helper left and her older sister, Annie, subsequently arrived. She was much stronger than Lisel but had been working on a farm and knew practically nothing about a city household. Mother groaned often. After a few weeks, Annie received a letter from home and broke down in tears. We stood around her wondering what made her cry so hard. Wiping her eyes, she sobbed, "Lisel is dead."

My mother went to the funeral and found out that Lisel had contracted syphilis during one of her train trips from home to Hamelin and back. Now we understood why Lisel did not want to share her bed with her sister. She knew her sickness was contagious and did not want to infect her or us. Her parents wanted to keep Annie at home and my mother did not object. I think my mother was actually glad that Annie liked to stay with her family and work on a farm again. From now on Mother made sure that we did not share our living quarters with any household helpers again.

The town fathers of Mülheim worked diligently and thoughtfully to rebuild the ruined town center. One of the first houses they deemed irreparable was our residence. It had to make room for a commercial building in the shopping district. We were allotted a rental in a huge apartment complex near the beautiful Ruhr River Park. Mr. Venator's family lived there already. They occupied an apartment on the second floor catty- corner from us.

We gladly moved from Victoria Street's bomb-damaged house and the noise of the city center. My father had opened a second office in a town closer to Frankfurt/Main. There he found a suitable place for Miss. Sieperman. She moved with all of her belongings and my parents finally bought furniture for themselves and us. And now Grandma could live with us in Luisental. But first she had to leave the Russian zone.

She had left Klostermansfeld and went back to St. Bernhard after she knew that Uncle Martin could not fulfill the quotas that the GDR government had imposed on him and he had to decide how to survive best. Grandma stayed in her little village for a while until my father sensed that the Soviets had fortified their East German border more and more and an escape became impossible. He sent her urgent messages to leave and to meet him at the Russian/American border near Coburg[212]. I do not remember the exact date when she left the Soviet Sector. The no-man's strip must not have been completed. She walked across the border without

212   Coburg is a town close to the border and easy to reach from St. Bernhard.

any interference by the guards. My father picked her up on the American side and drove her to Goslar, where she found shelter with Uncle Horst's family. We assumed the police did not stop her because she was old and of no more use to the workforce in the GDR. From then on Grandma took turns living in Goslar with her youngest son, Uncle Horst, and my parents in Mülheim.

As soon as we settled into our new home, she came to visit with us. Grandma kept in contact with Aunt Ida, her daughter-in-law, and her grandchildren, Marlis and Ernst who did not want to leave St. Bernhard, although my father encouraged them to move as well, promising to support all of them and pay for Marlis' and Ernst's education.

But Aunt Ida owned the house she and her daughter lived in, though only in the upstairs apartment. Early on she had been forced to allow the secret police with his family to stay in the downstairs rooms. He was the very man who had arrested her husband, Uncle Hans, and had transported him to the concentration camp Buchenwald. The Stasi wanted to keep a close eye on this little family, knowing that through them they might get hold of my father and Uncle Horst. Therefore, they soon had wired the upstairs living quarters. Another reason why Aunt Ida hesitated to follow my father's advice was that her bother, Uncle Tosse, still lived just up the hill from her. She could not know that in a few years her son, Ernst, working a double shift in the steaming hot factory, left on his motorbike into the cold night and collapsed. He died instantly and was buried in the churchyard near her house.

In September 1951, we had to get used to yet another school. Hildegard and I continued in the secondary school, called simply "Realschule"[213]. It was geared towards practical education, not much emphasis on art or music. I missed the latter the most. They did not even have a choir. In Hamelin our school was named after a well-known author of the 19th century, Wilhelm Raabe. But in Mülheim we entered "die Realschule in der Stadtmitte" (the middle school at the town center), whereas the Lyceum

213 Realschule stands for a school with a secondary education of realistic subjects that pupils could use in everyday life, e.g. gardening, cooking, needlework, stenography and typing.

(high school for girls) had the name "Luisenschule" after Queen Louise of Prussia[214], the middle school had nothing in its name to remind us of an honorable German person.

Since our school's curriculum was tailored to practical applications for life, I chose bookkeeping, shorthand, typing, garden work, cooking, sewing, alongside of the mandatory subjects, math, biology, geography, history, art, music, sport, German, English (required in the British Zone), and French. Somehow the latter language suited me much better, I had good grades in it, but because my grades in mandatory English were poor I had to drop French. I thought, *too bad we are not living in the French Zone, then French would be compulsory instead of English.* Every Wednesday morning our teachers separated Catholics and Protestants to go to our respective church services. Religion was another subject we had to take. Pastor Busch was one of my favorite teachers. We learned hymns and poems that complemented Bible passages.

My brother Reinhold did not need to adapt to any new school. He entered first grade in the elementary school, but Ernst had to finish his education in the Otto Pankok School, the name of the "Humanistische Gymnasium"[215] where he received his high school diploma, the Abitur that enabled him to enter any university. After his graduation he soon left us and lived in Frankfurt/Main where he studied law.

My classmates told me that Miss Westrup, our classroom teacher, had something against us five refugees. All the other girls in my class came from indigenous Mülheim families. Sometimes we felt like outcasts; that we came from a well-educated background supplementing our schooling did not count for her. She just did not have an open mind for originality, different perspectives or opinions. But she did take us on excursions, which the school committee had assigned. I still remember a visit to a

---

214 Louise of Mecklenburg-Strelitz became Queen of Prussia by her marriage to King Frederick William III of Prussia, (1776 - 1810).

215 "Gymnasium," is the German name for the boys' high school. Mülheim has two of them. One is the science and math oriented "Oberrealschule" and the other is the "Humanistische Gymnasium" with emphasis on literature, history, and languages.

gothic church and in the last month before we graduated, Miss Westrup and a retired science teacher accompanied us on an eight-day tour along the famous stretch of the Rhine River from Cologne to Bacharach and Koblenz.

Our class on an overnight excursion to a cave. Front row second from the left my best friend, Gisela Meißler, and on the far right, Miss Westrup (nicknamed *Wespe*) our classroom teacher. Above her third from the right in the back row Ilse-Rose Höfer.

We stayed at youth hostels, once even in a castle along the River. Our class was the last she taught before retiring from the responsibilities of a classroom teacher.

Later at class reunions, my classmates told me that they always looked forward to hearing me read my in-class or homework essays or to listen to a speech mixed with humor, which was apparently not to my teacher's liking, but they loved it.

I did not dislike her; I respected her belief in God and how she tried to teach us important life lessons, which we could rely on for our future. Only with what we had already experienced, be it bombing raids, evacuation and relocation or in the case of us five refugees, loss of our homeland, displacement, flight from the Soviets, she used her former utterly obsolete teaching methods. She tried to be nice, even have understanding, but did not realize that we had seen and lived through more of the world's evil than children should have been exposed to. She clung to her books and read from them, oblivious to our reaction towards these old fashioned stories. At the end of the lessons she always wound them up by warning us not to become pregnant before we were married in a church, preferably by a Catholic priest.

About a year after our graduation, Gisela, Hannelore, Luise, and I decided to visit her, bringing her a big bouquet of flowers. I do not remember too much about this encounter, except that we told her where we went to further our education for jobs we hoped to receive, and that she was surprised that I chose to become a physical education teacher.

Hildegard was much luckier with her educators. Her classroom teacher, Miss Vandelack, had an open mind and my sister became acquainted with a much wider spectrum of German literature, especially the more modern authors' writings. Both of us had the same art teacher. She and my math teacher were fantastic educators. They shared a small apartment not far from the school. We admired them so much that, on our way to school, we tried to pass by the house where they lived. We hoped we could offer our help by carrying their bags or folders and thus walk alongside of them. We could tell them everything, be it happy events or concerns. They understood and did not talk about it to others.

Hildegard and Ernst had taken ballroom dancing lessons in Hamelin. Now it was time for me to enter this part of my education, having reached the age when, in the evening, teenage girls and boys received training in the proper steps of popular dances, alongside a thorough teaching in correct social behavior. Since the school system still believed it best to separate boys and girls in our schools, it was here that we had a chance to meet the other gender.

It only took a few minutes to walk from our new location to a privately owned school for ballroom dancing. I went alone. Some of my classmates could not afford the classes, but that was not the main reason why I went by myself. My mother did not want me to get acquainted with those sons of blue-collar workers. She thought we were in a more educated higher class than they.

It was a little awkward for me to be the only one from the middle school. Some of the Lyceum's girls treated me as an intruder. But despite the way I used to walk with my feet facing inward instead of outward—my siblings called it "walking over the great Uncle," uncle meaning big toe—I learned the steps easily and developed enough grace to be asked to take a second course free of charge, since they did not have enough girls for the next high school class.

My partner (in black) for the performance of *Swan Lake*.

At the end of the dancing lessons we had a grand ball. Our parents were invited and sat at the outer walls of a huge square surrounding the dance floor, where we showed our skills. As an intermission between the dances, our instructors selected some of us girls to perform a short intermezzo of *Swan Lake* by Tchaikovsky. I was one of these elite students.

After visiting the dancing school a second time when the instructor sometimes chose me to demonstrate the new steps, my relationship with the girls from the high school changed for the better.

Now I suddenly had the desire to go to the Lyceum. I needed the Abitur, like Ernst. I wanted to become a veterinarian. I loved animals and they seemed to like me. But my mother had experienced my failures and doubted if I ever could accomplish the demanding curriculum of a high school. She discussed my wish with my classroom teacher, old fashioned Miss Westrup, who told her that although I had good grades in Math and Biology and, well, even German (not in spelling, but good essays), I would never be able to learn English satisfactorily let alone tackle still another language as required for the Lyceum. My mother believed her and discouraged me from applying for the 10th grade. She told me I would not pass their entrance exam. It did not occur to me that Ernst had gotten permission in Hamelin to stay in the Gymnasium for three months to prove he had what it takes for the high school. But then he did have good grades to begin with. To show Miss Westrup that she did not know my abilities I, for the first time, studied my books and in the last school year advanced from 30th place to fourth in our class with an A- overall. But it was too late for me to try out for the Lyceum.

In Mülheim I had made a new friend, Gisela Meißler. Finally, a friend for life! I passed her apartment house on my way to school and met her, as well as Hannelore, and Luise who waited for us at the next crossing. I admired Gisela's mom. She had lost her husband during the war. He had been employed by the "Krupp Konzern" (Krupp Concern/company). Being left with two girls to support, she received a pension from them. Still, to supply her daughters with the best possible upbringing, she sewed all of their dresses and even some of my outfits that I needed after I graduated and entered the Medau School[216]. She called me "Röschen" (little Rose). Although I did take sewing and knitting, she was the one who taught me how to cut material using a pattern, even how to alter it, so the

---

216 The Medau School—teaching gymnastics and dance—was involved in the bombastic events the Nazis staged. At the 1936 Olympics in Berlin, Medau students performed for entertainment.

garment would fit me correctly. Sometimes I ate at her place, especially when my mother was recuperating at a spa again in Baden Baden or Wörrishofen[217]. In our summer vacation I was sent with Reinhold to a retreat, which originally had belonged to the SA leader Ernst Röhm.

I called Gisela's mother "Aunt Mei". We had quite some fetes at her apartment, where we changed the hallway into the dance floor. In the living room we served food and drinks. There Aunt Mei met her neighbors whom she had invited to join her. This way we need not fear occupants who—living below her—might be annoyed by our dancing and music above them.

All girls and boys pictured were pupils of the Realschule, not one went to the Humanistische Gymnasium or to the Oberrealschule. Gisela in the center of the upper right photo, flanked in front by Luise and myself. Lower left picture: One of the boys with me. Lower right photo in front from left to right: Luise, Gisela and myself.

---

217 Both spas are in southern Germany, "Schwarzwald und Allgäu" (Black Forest and Allgovia).

I liked these get-togethers in Aunt Mei's apartment. At my home I did have birthday parties, albeit without those boys. But young men visited us here, too. All were from the higher education institutes or nobility. Konstantin Sossin Arbatow came often. He was the only son of aristocrats who emigrated from Russia in 1919. He was 6'5" tall and had a great appetite. Mother knew that his parents did not have much money for food. Here and there she invited him to join us for the evening meal. Well, Grandma would always say about him, "He has quite long sides." Meaning he was so tall and therefore needed to feed his length at our table. He reciprocated by bringing his violin and playing classical pieces for us. Konstantin liked me a lot and wrote poems for me. He tried to interest me in appreciating classical music by doing more than just listening to it. He told me about the backgrounds of composers and the different styles or instruments they preferred.

I favored folksongs over symphonies, so Konstantin introduced me to Franz Schubert's version of Goethe's *Heideröslein*[218]. Although I knew its popular folk tune, I soon learned to sing Schubert's version. He promptly told me that quite a number of composers wrote melodies for this poem. When I left Mülheim, my tall friend took it and transposed his thoughts onto it. He stretched it into nine verses instead of the original three.

Somehow my mother instilled into us that we belonged in a higher class of society. Consequently when Dr. H., an employee of my father and a former university student belonging to the "Landsmannschaft"[219], invited Hildegard and me to come to their special annual festival, which included a social dinner, boat trip and dance, she eagerly agreed.

When meeting the guests in Bonn, the capital of West Germany since 1949, I felt absolutely like I had in Thorn when Hildegard had taken me to her girlfriend's house. I was constantly anxious about my behavior. *How do I act properly in this distinguished group?* I asked myself. *They talk about*

---

218 Most students studying vocal music know this poem about a "wild rose" blooming at the edges of meadows by Goethe (1749-1831) and Schubert's version.

219 Landsmannschaft Suevia academic fencing male fraternity.

these art movements, expressionism, cubism, and Wassily Kandinsky's[220] paintings. Sigh! *Never heard of it.* I had no idea that this artist believed shades resonated with each other to form a symphony, as colors did in his paintings. Miss Westrup did not give me the education I needed for this group. Hildegard had a better teacher, more avant-garde, more geared to new, trendy movements in art and music. The two students who were our assigned gentlemen during the social gatherings tried their best to involve me in a conversation. Hildegard knew what they were talking about. I was oblivious to their parley. Yes, I had heard about Paul Klee, but not about the Bauhaus movement[221]. And I liked Franz Marc's "Die großen blauen Pferde" (Blue Horses). But that was it.

Hildegard knew more about modern literature, I about Romanticism and Goethe. My history lessons were scanty, since I did not pay attention when my classroom teacher was reading from her teacher's manual: meanwhile I played Skat under the table with the girls beside and in front of me.

In the evening we attended their traditional ball. My cousin Ingrid had outgrown her wardrobe and Aunt Magda sent a huge package to Mülheim. The clothing was not fashionable enough for Hildegard but I was glad to have a tartan skirt, blouses and a soft rose-pink dress for the evening.

---

220   Russian painter, born in Moscow 1866 and died 1944 in Neuilly-sur-Seine, France. He is credited with starting abstract art and Expressionism.

221   Paul Klee and Kandinsky were teachers at the Bauhaus, a movement in architecture, furniture and household utensils that started about 1910 and lasted well into the 1960. Most of this movement was regarded as degenerate art by the Nazis.

At dinner: Ilse-Rose at left, looking at my sister, past the student assigned to me in our middle. The assigned student for Hildegard took the photo.

When the band called for "Damenwahl," it meant the women could get up and select the man with whom they wanted to dance, I went straight to Johannes Steinhoff[222] and asked him for this round. "No, my girl, you would not want to dance with me, look at me." He said. I looked at him, I knew he was disfigured but I declared, "I am sure you know how to dance this slow waltz better then the younger men," and smiled at him. He shook his head but his wife turned to him, "Go ahead, Macky, she will not step on your foot." Yes, this man with dripping eyes, since his eyelids had been burned out, with the scars in his face and a slight limp did dance with me. And I did not mind the salty drops from his eyes on my dress. He told me that he was surprised that I would choose him as dance partner. We slowly waltzed and I led him back to his table, where his wife looked at me pleased, maybe thinking *Macky should know now that he does not need to shy away from the younger generation after this teenager asked him for a dance.*

---

222   Johannes Steinhoff (1913-1994) was one of the famous German pilots during WWII.

A picture of participating guests after a boat trip on the Rhine

Front row L – R: a student, Dr. H., his wife Charlotte, her brother J. Steinhoff, his wife, Ursula. Hildegard is in the top row near the left window in front of a male and I am right in front of her.

Little did I know that this war-marred man was one of the most distinguished pilots of WWII. What made me decide to go to this terribly disfigured man? There must have been many thoughts that crossed my mind. I knew he was a soldier from WWII and I always liked to care for wounded veterans, as in Thorn's veterans' hospital, or in Hamelin the double amputee Mr. Nachtigall, or Uncle Conn in Thorn and Hamelin, or the blind postal clerk in Mülheim. These brave soldiers were not always respected by the occupational forces or even by our younger generation, so I at least wanted to pay them my homage. Another reason was not so noble. I felt uncomfortable around those educated university students. I feared being left alone on the dance floor with that knowledgeable student, assigned to me. I anticipated embarrassment by not knowing how to make conversation with him. Or maybe I just followed God's prompting without even knowing it. *For we are His Handy-work, created in Christ Jesus for good works, which God previously prepared for us so that we should live in them.*[223] In retrospect, I like to entertain the thought that God trained me for this very moment, in which it was my purpose to approach J. Steinhoff as a representative of my generation.

After his Jet fighter accident (1945), J. Steinhoff endured many operations. During his long hospital stays his pilot friends visited him often. They tried to inspire him to offer his knowledge for rebuilding Germany's air force. Maybe through me, a young German girl, he received just one more encouragement not to shrink back from society thinking he is incompetent for the West German military under American and English supervision.

Known to be a great teacher, he was asked to train pilots for the Lockheed F-104 Starfighter—nicknamed the Widowmaker—of the new Luftwaffe[224]. Right from the start he was surprised to find out about unexplained accidents with this particular aircraft. After researching each casualty thoroughly he concluded that it was not flaws in the plane, but the insufficient training of the pilots that caused so many crashes and numerous enlisted men to die. Now he rigorously trained the new pilots with the result that the accidents diminished considerably.

Steinhoff would become instrumental in helping to rebuild the Luftwaffe in 1955. He agreed to use his expertise, and served later as Chief of Staff and Acting Commander Allied Air Forces Central Europe in 1965– 1966. From 1971–1974 he held the position as Chairman of the NATO Military Committee.

---

223 Ephesians 2:10, quoted from The Modern Language Bible: The New Berkeley Version in Modern English, Rev. ed. Grand Rapids, MI, Zondervan Publishing House. 4th printing 1976.

224 German Air Force founded in the BRD in 1956 when NATO wanted a West German military because of the Cold War between the Soviet Union and the western Allies.

Steinhoff frequently gave interviews and speeches, especially in front of young people. Quite a few books have been written about him. He became so internationally well known that The New York Times published a large article titled: "Gen. Johannes Steinhoff, 80, Dies; Helped Rebuild German Air Force"[225].

---

225 Wolfgang Saxon. *The New York Times* February 23, 1994, Section A, Page 16. The New York Times Archives.

CHAPTER 12

But we know that for those who love Him, for those called in agreement with His purpose, God makes all things work together for good. Romans 8:28

West Germany's Recovery
East Germany under Soviet Control

In 1951 we left Hamelin and settled in Mülheim on the Ruhr at the beautiful Luisenthal apartment complex. My father's employees secured living quarters for their families in or near this town at the western part of "Nord Rhein Westfalen" (North Rhine Westphalia). Uncle Reinhold, one of his longest employed agent, left Goslar and moved into a new place between Duisburg and Mülheim.

New Year's Eve 1952/53, from left to right: Uncle Reinhold Seume, Ilse-Rose, Reinhard (the eldest son) his fiancée, his middle brother Hellmut, Hildegard, Aunt Anne and Fritschi (Friedrich Wilhelm, the youngest son), who—for this photo—had set up a tripod with an automatic flash for the camera.

He continued to work as one of Father's insurance representatives. Just like his boss he, too, was often away from home. Then Aunt Anne would lock the door and give the key to me, so she could spend some time with her sons, knowing I would check on the apartment, water her many flowers and make sure the heating was functioning. I also put grain out at the bay window for the birds. Hildegard and I liked to visit with Seumes at special events. Aunt Anne was my godmother[226], just like Aunt Klärchen and Aunt Ursel, but she had the most influence on me. Every one of us four Höfer children liked to recall the pleasant weeks with the Seumes. As long as they lived in Goslar, I spent several short school vacations[227] with them. I liked that here we thanked God for His blessings before the main meal at noon.

Aunt Anne taught me how to preserve berries, make apple sauce and tomato juice without wasting any of the pulp. She would look into the sieve and say, "It still is too moist, press it a little more through the mesh." They had a garden in the woods near their house. Uncle Reinhold made all kind of devices to scare hares and deer away from their crops. These animals were not as abundant as before the war. They, too, had died in bombing raids.

During my last Easter vacation in Goslar, Uncle Horst and his family still lived with Seumes in that old forester's house. At that time, Grandma shared her bedroom with me. She and Aunt Anne were glad that I was one more person to watch Aunt Gertrud and Uncle Horst's first son Hartmut. Now they were expecting their second child.

Back in Mülheim, Hildegard and I became good friends with Arwed Venator and his brother Otto Erik. We often came together to walk on

---

226 In our family the duties of godparents included caring for the child, giving thoughtful presents, and advising them in choosing a profession.

227 We had about 14 days of Easter Vacation, four to five weeks in summer and 14 days for Christmas and New Year. We had several holidays off. Ascension Day (Thursday, 40 days after Easter), Pentecost Sunday and Monday, "Buß und Bettag" (Repent and pray day) happens on the Wednesday before "Totensonntag" (Death Sunday) in November; which was the last Sunday in the church calendar.

the well-groomed path alongside the Ruhr River. Sometimes we planned outings. But mostly we discussed our schoolwork, our teachers, and the dance lessons for high school students, which Arwed attended this semester, and in which I helped out by guiding the new comers through difficult steps.

On winter evenings Daisy and Bobs Venator, the parents of our two friends, liked to play Rummy with their children and welcomed us to join them. We devised more elaborate rules for the game. Even Juliane, their youngest child, was able to adhere to these. We laughed a lot. Daisy Venator put a bowl of caramel candy in the middle of the big round table. At the end of each round the winner received one or two pieces of the sticky morsels depending if they won a plain Rummy or Grand Rummy. When the Venators went to events in which Otto Erik or Arwed were involved, they asked me to stay with Juliane, sometimes even overnight. Again I was chosen to "babysit". Juliane invited me to her birthday parties. I altered games for all of her guests in such a way that nobody was left out. God had given me the skills to teach children without them knowing that they were learning social behavior, i.e. to have patience with and respect for one another.

In contrast, back in the Soviet Zone, my older cousin, Marlis, missed out on such friendly games with neighbor children. She did not join the FDJ. She went through the educational system that was geared to train pupils as obedient citizens, defying the older generation and their Christian faith. Marlis faced practically no freedom of choice when making decisions. For instance, she could not enter into higher education for several far-fetched reasons. Her father was imprisoned in Buchenwald, her uncle Herbert had fought on the Eastern Front in WW II, had escaped from prison and now was a successful business man in West Germany, her grandfather had been the president of the Thüringer Landbund, which became later the anti-communistic Farmers' Party. None of these arguments against her further education had anything to do with her intelligence or physical abilities.

~~~~~~~~~~~~~~~~~~~~

In January 1953 at the Stammtisch, the pharmacist opened the conversation with a question.

"Can you imagine this? Joseph Stalin got in contact with the FRG and suggested forming an independent and politically neutral Germany by uniting the FRG with our GDR."

"That would be great!" rejoiced the farmer. The pharmacist contradicted him immediately. "Really? Not in your wildest dreams! Do you think Moscow would abstain from politics, its form of Communism, so that the <u>proposed</u> united Germany could stay neutral?"

Leipziger voiced his opinion, "I think West Germany's economical success—the 'Wirtschaftswunder'—got to Stalin. He is jealous now after siphoning out all we had to give. You know what I think—he would love to profit from the western achievements, which we, despite all our diligent work, could not accomplish, since the SED's five year plans failed miserably."

The minister listened carefully and, as he so frequently did, decided to inform them. "Well, it will not come to an unified Germany, because Konrad Adenauer rejected that proposal."

The farmer took a sip from his stein before turning towards the clergyman, "Can you blame him, I mean them? Adenauer is an old fox. Under his governing the FRG enjoys prosperity but we struggle over even more stringent rules and regulations. Ulbricht[228] will think up more ridiculous ways to boost higher production. I heard he had training in Moscow. He doesn't look to the West anymore for help. No! Walter feels the Soviet regime is our only chance for recovery."

Leipziger added to the farmer's future outlook for the GDR. "Yes, ever since Stalin's proposal of unification was denied, old Walter tries to accelerate socialism. You listened to his speech over the radio last year

---

228 Walter Ulbricht (1893-1973), since 1953 first secretary of the Central Committee (ZK "Zentralkomitee").

in July. They put the emphasis on heavy industry. There, Ulbricht said, should lie the beginning of a better economy."

The pharmacist continuing the theme remarked, "Well, we'll see. At least there is a beginning, although it would be better considering consumer articles like washing machines or cars than heavy machinery, which will end up as war reparations in Russia anyway. At any rate, our factory workers are overburdened with constantly requiring higher product outputs from them. And they'll hardly get paid for it."

"You are right. I also heard that workers in those factories do not get better pay, instead they have to fill quotas, which are impossible to achieve," the farmer added.

"Hmm," the clergyman mused, "Pharmacist, you have a point. Automobile production could help our economy. Who would not want to drive their own car?" He pulled out a newspaper article and pointed at it. "Here, look at this paragraph! In Eisenach they converted the former BMW[229] factory into a VEB[230]?"

"Was there anything worthwhile left after the Soviets dismantled it?" the farmer asked.

The pastor answered, "As far as I know not much, but the buildings lend themselves to that type of industry. I think the SED's next five year plan will include cars."

The pharmacist retorted, "Of course, form another VEB! Pretty soon nobody will own anything. They put me with my pharmacy, and the few others who still possess their own businesses, under exorbitant taxes, so we will soon give up and let the SED succeed in turning everything into a VEB."

The farmer, scratching his head, looked at the pharmacist, "Your business to be combined with all the other drugstores in the district? I hope it does not come to this, Pharmacist. At your store we still feel like human

---

229 "Bayerische Motoren Werke." BMW had established a subdivision in Thuringia.

230 "Volkseigener Betrieb" (folk owned business).

beings. You care. Nobody in a VEB does that. But I know what you go through. I also feel the political pressure as far as my farm is concerned. I think they want to eradicate us old agriculturists. First, it was the infamous land reform right after the war. And now eight years later, they find new means to get rid of us so they can incorporate our farmland, animals and machinery into another form of their VEB, namely a Kolkhoz like they have had in Russia since 1917. But for the GDR they call it LPG."

Leipziger smiled, "Landwirtschaftliche Produktionsgemeinschaft[231], another of those long German combined words. We never can call things just by a short name; it always has to be a conglomerate of meanings strung together. That's why the less educated man likes to abbreviate everything."

"Thanks for the lecture, Leipziger. Never mind, but I think abbreviations have nothing to do with more or less education." The pharmacist winked at him and smiled changing the subject, "By the way, Leipziger, did you get permission to move into Mayor's apartment?"

"Oh no! We will have new teachers in our village. That meant they had to let me go. As a semi retired librarian, I am looking for a half-day job in Leipzig. I applied for a place to live and I am waiting for their assignments." All of them looked at him and knew, once he left, it would mean the end of their Stammtisch. Soon their concerns about VEBs and LPGs took a new turn.

In March 1953 Joseph Stalin died. In the months following this dictator's death, the political and especially economic stress from Moscow seemed to lessen. However, the GDR government officials, having experienced no profits in the heavy industry, hoped, by demanding even higher quotas from the workers in their factories, to see better economic results, and that without even raising their income. That led in June 1953, in Berlin and other cities, to an uprising of most workers, not only in the heavy industry but also in construction. The SED had the folk police, heavily armed but untrained, as a standing army. They could not squelch

---

231 "LPG" Agricultural production cooperatives.

the revolting masses. Promptly, the Russian occupation pulled rank and rolled into Berlin with tanks against the demonstrators, who could only defend themselves with sticks and stones[232].

Nevertheless, some changes did take place. After the uprising was crushed, the GDR government took back the unrealistic quotas for heavy industry, raised the hourly earnings of the workers, and turned to manufacturing consumer supplies, which had been neglected for a long time.

Even the Soviets curtailed some of their demands. In 1954 they reduced the cost for the occupational forces to 5% of the GDR's budget, and they cancelled all war reparations. Instead, they sent grain to East Germany. They also released confiscated private establishments that they had claimed as Soviet possessions since the end of WWII.

You might wonder how our Stammtisch members fared after Stalin died. In their little village they saw no significant changes. The Soviet Union did not crumble. The grip on the Russian Zone lasted. You know the mayor had left, as mentioned in the previous chapter. I'll touch on his son and his family again later on.

Keep in mind that, while they are fictional characters, their fate is based on true facts. Let me begin with the leaving of Farmer. For him, the changes after Stalin's death came too late. Before the June uprising of the workers, he had to abandon his land. His fields, livestock and buildings became part of a huge LPG in the area. He had been unable to supply the demanded produce. The board of the SED, who governed the LPGs, offered him a little parcel of his own fields and also employment in the new LPG. To him this felt like a slap in his face. He just had to leave. Under the pretense of visiting an exhibition of farm machinery, he went to Berlin, where travel from the east to the west inside of the GDR capital still existed. He looked up his one-eyed friend, Berliner, who gave him shelter until he could secure an airplane ticket from the Tegel Airport (located in the French Sector) and fly to Hamburg. Here he visited

---

232   The West German government declared June 17th as "Tag der Freiheit" (Day of Freedom). For about 30 years it became a national holiday in West Germany.

Hamburger, who helped him to find a job in the "Lüneburger Heide" (Luneburg Heath) trucking farm goods, including livestock, especially the "Heidschnucken"[233]. He never farmed again, but he found a little house in the Luneburg district. Later his family was permitted to join him in West Germany.

Our Stammtisch met for the last time in March 1954. Leipziger proposed a toast, "Things will get better now! Although I did not get permission to move into Mayor's bugged apartment, I landed a job in Leipzig at the Gewandhaus Orchestra. So tonight the tap is on me." The pharmacist, being familiar with this distinguished 200-year-old musical establishment, lifted his glass and shouted. "A Votre Santé[234], Leipziger! It calls for more than just our usual 'Prosit!'" Leipziger smiled, "Pharmacist, come and visit me and you, too, Pastor. Maybe I find a few of my old friends at home and we can play some Skat when you see me."

The pharmacist had been tempted to leave for the FRG. However, he was allowed to function in his profession in the collective VEB. He continued to care for the villagers. Sometimes he had to interrupt his daily routine when he was called by the SED to attend their mandated meetings, although he did not belong to the party. Somehow he was exempt from becoming a member, perhaps because he was the only pharmacist in the district who knew how to fill certain prescriptions, and the governing office could not afford to lose his expertise in the surrounding communities.

As for Margret, she had stayed with her mother and married Mayor's son in the late 1950s. He had been in the FDJ and became a leader for the "Junge Pioniere". Both appeared to be dedicated Communists, knowing their decision to belong to the SED party would open up the future for their children, especially if they left the church. They continued to run the pub as well as they could under the political circumstances.

---

233 The "Heidschnucke" is a collective term for moorland sheep in northern Germany.

234 A French toast meaning "to your health," mostly used when drinking wine, "Prosit!" is mainly used when drinking beer.

Leipziger returned to his hometown as the last of the evacuees. He had filled in as an elementary teacher in the village, but when new communistic teachers were available and he declined to join the SED party, he had to leave his post and return to Leipzig. Although his leg had been amputated, he adjusted well enough to the artificial limb that he was able to work at the Gewandhaus. He loved his new position since it allowed him to be in touch with West Germany. After all, the world renowned Orchestra and its director toured in many countries regardless of whether they were in the West or East. He remained in the GDR to the end of it in 1991, when the GDR and the FRG reunited to form the BRD (Bundesrepublik Deutschland). He had taken part in the peaceful, quiet revolution of 1989, which had started with church gatherings in the early 1980s.

The leader and conductor of the Gewandhaus, Kurt Masur[235], had opened the building for discussions about reforms and the future of the GDR. These conversations, which reached their climax in the 1980s, opposed the politics of the GDR, including the hated travel restrictions for the East Germans[236], which was another point added to the grievances against the closed borders between the GDR and FRG.

Leipziger did meet with some of the former Stammtisch members in his hometown. Mayor's son and his wife, Margret, came with the clergyman who had in the 1980s agreed with most pastors and priests to emphasize peaceful demonstration. They joined the thousands that marched every evening, holding a burning candle in one hand and shielding the flame with the other, so no one had a free hand if tempted to pick up a stone or other item to throw against the hated "Polit Büro"

---

235 Kurt Masur (1927-2015) was called an "old-style maestro." He conducted many of the principal orchestras in his era in a long career as the Kapellmeister of the *Leipzig Gewandhaus.*

236 Dr. Horst Strohbusch describes the beginnings of the Peaceful Revolution in his book *Das Licht kam aus der Kirche, Die Wende in Meiningen* 1989-1990 (The Light came from the church, The Turning Point in Meiningen 1989-1990). Börner: Meiningen, 2nd ed. 2009 Meiningen, ISBN 3-930675-19-6.

(political office). Instead, the people fastened candles on the iron fences that surrounded the office buildings in many GDR cities.

The clergyman was allowed to preach as long as he supported Communism and condoned the Jugendweihe that had been established in 1954. He could have tried to form a new Stammtisch, but people stayed home rather than exposing themselves to spies who listened in on conversations. In the 1960s many East Germans had the opportunity to buy televisions. Now they preferred to spend their evenings in front of the screen instead going to a pub. They were able to receive western channels and by watching these, their hunger for the western world with its opportunities grew.

In the 1980s, when news about Glasnost and Perestroika[237] reached the village, the clergyman took part in the Peaceful Revolution by starting meetings for young adults. He encouraged the pharmacist, Margret, and her husband to attend discussion groups in his church where they talked about changes for the future of the GDR.

In early 1953, the same political regulations that forced the farmer to leave pushed Oemlers to abandon their fields and house, which had been in the family for over 400 years. In 1525 the Graf (Count) of Mansfeld gave Nicolaus Oemler—a close friend of Martin Luther—the right to own the confiscated cloister's buildings and part of the land, a settlement that was confirmed at the Peace of Augsburg in 1555[238].

But now, four centuries later, my uncle saw no future for his sons under the Soviet controlled government in the GDR. Although his farm had not been confiscated, the demands to deliver goods became unreasonable. And, since his family did not withdraw from the church, his sons would be denied a high school education. They certainly would not be allowed to study at a university. He and Aunt Ursel knew there would be no freedom

---

237 Mikhail Gorbachev promoted the reform of Glasnost (openness) for the Communist Party; it led to Perestroika, an attempt to restructure the party.

238 That burghers were allowed to own land and keep it as inheritance was one of the many changes brought about by the Reformation.

for their children to choose a profession and eventually his farm and his family would be absorbed into an LPG.

Like so many other citizens of East Germany, the Oemlers had applied for permission to move to West Germany. After much run-around and endless degrading behavior from officials, even threats from the Stasi controlled Administration for Travel; they were not allowed to leave. Now they had to secretly devise a plan to escape. There was no other way for them to cross the borders. They had to flee. They also went surreptitiously by traveling to Berlin. Here they could—just like the Stammtisch farmer— get to Berlin's western sectors from the Russian zone.

They left in stages. First, Oma and Jochen took a train to the GDR capital to visit one of Oma's friends of the Luisenbund. Then Uncle Martin, Aunt Ursel, and their other sons, Hermjörg and Lutz, followed. They did not have to live in barracks at the overcrowded reception camps in West Berlin. Uncle Martin had enough means to stay in a hotel. They remained there until my father secured a job for Uncle Martin and an apartment for them in Mülheim on the Ruhr. Now we were finally able to repay the generosity they had shown us ever since we had lost all of our possessions. We remembered very well that without their continuous help we would not have survived starvation in 1947.

As soon as we found a suitable place for Uncle Martin and his family, we gave our box beds to them. Oma slept on the low mattress. She, being in her seventies, had a hard time getting up from it, but she neither complained nor succumbed to her fate. Oma told us, "Yes, it hurt when I lost my homeland, my possessions and that I may not tend to my husband's grave anymore, but I'll get over it. I would be ungrateful to mourn and brood." Then she smiled and looking lovingly at us she said, "Didn't God grant me to be with my son and now with all of my children and my ten grandchildren?"

For a short time my father employed Uncle Martin until Uncle Richard, found a farming position for him. He, working for Austrian aristocracy, had connections to the nobility in Heidelberg and had heard that a baron in the area was looking for an experienced former landowner to farm his estate.

The main entrance of the hunting mansion.

In front: a water trough and pump

The Baron was delighted to employ Uncle Martin and offered his "small" former hunting castle for their new location, although its right wing was still occupied by a displaced family. Their and Oemler's children were about the same age and soon became good friends.

Family Oemler—it always included Oma—moved into the converted hunting mansion near Zuzenhausen, a little village about 16 miles east of Heidelberg.

Worn stone steps led from the large courtyard to the spacious entrance hall. On either side of it two huge rooms—formerly used for the bagged animals after a royal hunt—now had their extensive floors covered several inches high with grain, stored there for fermentation. When the rye, wheat, oats or barley reached the desired ripening phase, the farm helpers poured the mush into huge kettles to be heated. From there it was filtered and the liquid brought to a distillery tower located on the right wing of the main house. The remnants of the fermented grain served as pig and cow fodder. Each month a government agent came to open the sealed container for the high proof alcohol and oversaw the loading and delivery of the distilled liquid.

In 1953 life in the FRG was already very different from that in the GDR. My father's business grew. It soon extended into the southern parts of West Germany. Whereas in the former Russian zone people had a hard time applying for a car, and then, when granted a petition, they needed to wait for years to receive it, despite having paid for it in advance. In contrast, my father owned several vehicles for his office. In the meantime he had bought a big Mercedes for himself. Occasionally, when he was home, he would drive Gisela and me to school. My girlfriend never forgot how elated she felt to sit in this plush car. It did not happen often. One year Father bought a Jaguar, but was not very satisfied with it. He left British cars and went back to Mercedes. This time he purchased a racing green convertible with tan leather seats. Soon we named it the wedding car. My father designated it for driving every one of us four children on our wedding day to the registry office, then to church and back to the place of celebration with food, music and dance. But Father also used it for his business.

Another person who enjoyed the luxurious vehicles was Käte E., his very accomplished private secretary. She had followed Miss Siepermann, who now was an assistant in one of Father's new offices in southern West Germany. His main office stayed in Mülheim. But he moved it several times. When the upper floor of the bank building in the city center needed to be remodeled, he was offered a second floor in the Commerzbank not too far away from the first office. Soon it became too small and he rented all six floors of an office building near the Schloßbrücke (castle bridge) at the River Ruhr. Later, an architect designed an enormous office building, which he could rent. It boasted three floors and stretched out along a whole block of the major road to Essen and Düsseldorf. Here parking was more abundant for his clientele than in the crowded downtown district and he had a big underground garage for the office vehicles. Yes, Father's business had become extensive.

Sometimes, if we were let out of school early, I walked to his new place. I would try to see Father in his large elaborately furnished bureau with heavy chairs, sideboards and wardrobes in the New-Baroque style. His desk was impressive. I took the elevator to reach him on the third—the top—floor that was completely surrounded by a balcony. He had a small kitchen, restrooms, one with a shower stall, a long conference room, a waiting room and at one end of the balcony a cocktail lounge for private festivities like his birthday party. His employees ate in shifts in a bright dining room below Father's "realm". Hollerith machines tabulating complicated insurance mathematics filled the whole first floor. These apparatuses were forerunners of our computers.

Father gave company parties, not only for the employees but also for their spouses and children. Mr. Venator or Father's secretary, Ms. E., would organize the festivities. Sometimes they rented the ballroom in Schloss Hugenpoet[239] that could accommodate all of his 200-300 in-house and external workers and their families. Hildegard as princess, and I as her Rococo admirer, would dance a minuet for entertainment. At the Christmas parties, he always gave presents accompanied by humorous speeches to his employees and their spouses. Some of the gifts were a pretty pearl for each woman and a silver beaker with Father's initials carved into it for the men, or a glass on a silver base for everybody engraved with his

---

239   A castle between Mülheim/Ruhr and Essen.

firm's insignia **HHH**—**H**erbert **H**öfer **H**ameln (Hamelin). Sometimes I wondered, *does Father like to live like a Baroque Duke of the 17th century?*

His business had several new offices especially in the south of Germany. He had employed nobility—barons, counts, and even a prince. In my sight they belonged to a different class of humans. I still was under the influence of fairy tales and also 12 years of the "Reich"[240] under the Nazis, where aristocracy belonged to Hitler's staff and military, like many a Prussian general.

West Germany continued to rebuild. Among the numerous things to reconstruct was a new military as is mentioned in the previous chapter. In a few years my brother Ernst left his studies of law and not only joined the army, but choose it for his profession.

After I graduated from the middle school in 1954, I would have liked to study to become a veterinarian. But without an Abitur it was out of the question. So, I announced I wanted to become a manager of a hotel. Again this was not possible either, the school doctor discovered a vertebrae problem on my spine. He frankly said, "You will not be able to carry heavy stacks of bed sheets or pots and pans as an apprentice. You ought to look for another vocation". He ordered therapy for my back three times a week and swimming at least twice a week.

Since physical therapy was essential to straighten out my posture, my mother suggested I go to the Medau School for a year. There they taught rhythmical, therapeutic movements combined with music. I told her, "Mom, if I am to spend money for a whole year just to learn how to play the piano, do body training, and sing in their choir, I might quite as well stay for two years. Then, I can receive a certificate from the Bavarian Sport Academy, Grünwald, near Munich, and teach physical education at high schools."

My mother admired my assertiveness and said, "If that's what you desire for a profession, I will talk with Father and see if he is willing to pay for your education." She probably thought, *'this girl knows what she*

---

240 Reich meaning realm, as the 1,000 year lasting Holy Roman Empire of Germanic Nations was called "Kaiserreich" (Caesar's empire)

wants. She is so different from her sister. I am glad I do not need to choose an occupation for her as I did for Hildegard. I sent her to a household school. After graduation she was so unhappy at her first job in Kempten.

After my sister changed her "career"—which really wasn't one, namely just a preparation to be a good housekeeper and cook—she went through a business school in Mülheim. With Father's help, Hildegard entered the insurance business at the "Alte Leipziger" (the name of an insurance company) in Frankfurt. Mother agreed with her husband's attitude that girls did neither need a higher education nor a driver's license. They should marry, have children, and lead good family lives.

As was often the case, Father did not have much time for us, but he let me enter the Medau School, where his daughter could become strong and athletic. He did not even know that I already possessed these qualities. He had nothing against me becoming a teacher, especially choosing Hinrich Medau's school, which had been involved with entertainment during the Olympics in 1936.

Mr. Medau had worked under the Nazis in their "Kraft durch Freude" program KdF (Strength through Happiness). After the war, he started his school again in Flensburg but moved to Coburg, where he could secure a royal mansion, called "Schloß Hohenfels" (castle on the high rock). So, Father made arrangements with his accountant, Mr. Venator, to pay for the schooling. My mother, accompanied by Ernst and myself, went to Coburg. Here I applied and was accepted after I clearly expressed my desire not to stay for just the "Musische Jahr" (one year of education in the fine arts) but intended to become a physical education teacher in two years.

Before entering the Medau School in Bavaria, I visited my brother Ernst who still lived in Frankfurt pursuing his studies of law. I spent one week with him, sleeping on a cot that a friend lent him. I cherished this time with my big brother. He took me to some of the huge lecture halls. After a while I refused to go with him. I had no idea what they were talking about. Neither the students' rapping with their knuckles on the tables in front of them when they approved of the professor's statement or a student's essay, nor the shuffling of their feet to express their disapproval of the presentation could hold my interest. Ernst understood. He often used his bicycle to ride from one lesson to the other.[241] We agreed that I would either meet him somewhere to eat in a restaurant, or cook for us. I had saved up some money and Mother had given me D-Marks as well, so I could pay for our outings, or the food I prepared. I was surprised that Ernst did not reject my generosity but rather gladly ate from my budget. Before I left, Ernst took me to a typical student bar and restaurant. On Saturdays, they had a live band and played jazz but also popular dance music. I never had been in such a place and thoroughly enjoyed being there with such a good-looking young man who knew how to dance very well. I thanked him afterwards, but he told me that he was grateful for the meals I had supplied and disclosed that Father quite often forgot to send the money he needed for his studies. He told me, "for too long I have been living with Dad's unreliable behavior. I am seriously thinking about joining the army, although so far they only talk about a new military for West Germany."

Autumn came and with it my entrance into the Medau School. In my second year, I had an opportunity to learn how to drive, but I needed the money for twelve driving lessons (the minimum to be accepted for testing driving skills). As it was with Ernst, Father simply had no time for sending extra money and his accountant, Mr. Venator, just paid for my schooling. It was in spring and a nearby farmer looked for helpers to weed his carrot field. I used every free minute working and had enough to pay for driving lessons. I passed the test and received my driver's license without my parents knowing it. They actually should have given their permission for me, but the gentleman who conducted the tests realized that I had been born in Gera and he himself coming from my birthplace in Thuringia was so elated to meet somebody from across the border, that he talked to me in the vernacular of middle Germany and I answered him in the same familiar tone where *P* sounds often like *B*, most *Ts* sound like *Ds*, and some *Gs* sound like *J* or *K*. Who would have known that the P,

---

241   The Frankfurt University has very diversified studies. They were not conducted on a campus. The lectures were held at different buildings often quite far from each other.

T, and some G, converted into the soft B, D and J, which hindered me in spelling during my school years, would help me to pass the driver's test.

I knew I would soon obtain my sport and gymnastics' teacher certificate for older children at high schools. However, I broke both elbows during a training session for my final exam. Now I had to wait until my arms healed before I could graduate.

Nevertheless, I was fortunate that a few months earlier Mrs. Luzi—a former Medau student—had visited the Medau Schule looking for an assistant among the more advanced students. She observed me as I conducted our School choir. She liked the song and how I directed the chorus. At the end, she chose me to be her assistant in Zurich, Switzerland for four months until the next round of examinations were given for the Medau graduates-to-be. I had the opportunity to be an intern in a foreign country and even assisted with teaching a rhythmic course at the ETH[242].

After I received my teacher certificate, I worked for one and a half years at a vacation home for underprivileged teenagers. Then a job at a Lyceum was offered to me. When after one year of teaching there, the opportunity arrived to go to the USA as an exchange teacher at the Moravian Prep School in Bethlehem, PA. I eagerly took it.

All the privileges I had by being able to choose a career, getting the job I liked and having the advantage of being an exchange teacher, my cousin Marlis was denied. She had no choice in selecting her profession. She never left the Russian Zone. She had to become a Care Center helper and assisting nurse in Themar, a town about five miles from St. Bernhard.

In November of 1955 the Bundeswehr[243] was founded with 101 volunteer soldiers. In the beginning, young Germans were reluctant to join the newly established army. Attempts to persuade more young people to join fell short. The Parliament saw itself forced to introduce conscription

---

242   ETH Zurich University. "Eidgenössische Technische Hochschule" (Federal Institute of Technology Zurich) Switzerland.

243   The Bundeswehr was, by law, a purely defensive entity. The FRG was not allowed to declare war, but its army could be called on through the North Atlantic Pact (NATO)

in 1956. Ernst turned twenty-four when choosing a military career instead of completing his studies in law. Now he was independent of Father, who actually was proud of his oldest son. Ernst had met Hildegard's new girlfriend, Hannelore G. Both girls worked at the same insurance company in Frankfurt. He promptly fell in love with that pretty girl and married her in the late 1950s.

1958 Ernst in uniform at his wedding behind of bride and groom: my father between Reinhold and me.

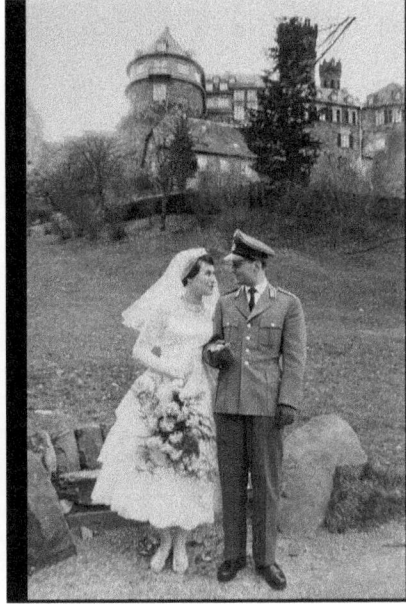

Ernst and Hannelore in front of the castle where the wedding was celebrated.

Weddings and Oma's birthdays were highlights for everybody. Oemlers, Töttlers, and Höfers knew how to be cheerful hosts. They entertained their guests with witty commentaries, little sketches and songs aimed at the celebrities. Children were part of the festivities, but when the drawn out meals and the speeches became boring for the little ones, sitters would take them away to play after they also had enjoyed delicious foods and drinks.

At all festivals good meals were customary. Oma enjoyed her special birthdays with her four children. Aunt Ursel and helpers from the village prepared a long table for everyone at her 80ᵗʰ birthday with lots of cakes, tea, coffee, and hot chocolate. Later the guests were invited to salute and honor Oma with a glass of champagne.

1962 at Oma's eightieth birthday, her four children stood in Front of the main entrance to the hunting mansion in Zuzenhausen: from left Aunt Magda, Paula—my mother—, Uncle Martin, Aunt Hilde.

On November 2, 1967, when Oma turned 85, she was again privileged to invite all of her still living relatives and friends to Zuzenhausen. But this time there were not so many guests. Aunt Hilde and Aunt Magda had lost their husbands. Oma's dear friend Mrs. Heinroth had passed away. We just rented an events room in a restaurant and celebrated her special day there. We had ordered one of Oma's favorite meals. It always included white asparagus, goose, plus another roast, and "Leipziger Allerlei"[244].

Oemlers had to leave the hunting mansion. The Baron sold his estate and the new owners converted the house into a restaurant. Uncle Martin had reached the age of retirement anyway. The baron gave him a plot of

---

244   A vegetable dish made from cauliflower, carrots and peas in a Béchamel sauce.

land on a steep embankment above the hunting castle. Oemlers stayed in Zuzenhausen and built a house there. Oma was allowed to still occupy two rooms on the third floor of the former hunting mansion. Aunt Hilde had moved to Zuzenhausen to be closer to her family and now she was often with Oma whose eyesight had failed several years ago.

In 1972 Oma passed away as she always hoped, to part from this Earth during the night. My Aunt Hilde told us, "I sat in Oma's easy chair at the foot of her bed. Oma was asleep, then at 2AM she opened her eyes, waved to me and clearly said "Leb' wohl" (goodbye), then she took her last deep breath.

In most places in Germany they do not have a viewing. When observing the funeral custom in other countries, for example, passing by an open casket, I often think, "I rather like to remember them when they were still alive."

Oma's funeral gave us the last occasion for a big celebration. First, all of us went to the cemetery hall where her closed coffin stood covered with flowers and wreaths. The minister held the service based on Bible verses that Oma had selected long ago. We sang two of her favorite hymns. She had played them on the piano for me when she was still living in Klostermansfeld. A few designated persons gave short speeches honoring our beloved Oma. Then we walked behind the pallbearers to the churchyard where they laid her to rest. Everyone paused in front of the open grave for a moment of silence and then either took a little spade nearby to scoop up some soil and drop it on the casket or to send a flower into the grave.

Then we went to the restaurant where, for her funeral, Oma had prearranged a delicious meal for everybody. She had written down the different specialties that she had served at numerous festivities. And there was also a list of wines and beers to choose from. We reminisced about our times with Oma and told many an anecdote. We had cried at her grave but now we laughed, although sometimes with tears in our eyes. Oma's burial was typical for funerals in the countryside.[245]

All of us remembered how we had to go through hard times, how we had lost most of our belongings that included valuable forests (my father) and rich fields (Uncle Martin, Aunt Magda, Aunt Klärchen, Uncle Wilhelm Schulze) and first class animals, especially Uncle Richard's thoroughbred horses, and Uncle Martin's selected cows and bulls. We survived and now thought we could live in more security than before in spite of the Cold War.

For my father it was only possible since his business took off in the wake of the "Wirtschaftswunder" that started with the new currency for the FRG and lasted well into the 1950s. By 1958 my father was able to buy a thatch-roofed mansion in the country surrounded by a sloping park-like garden with fruit trees scattered throughout and a huge linden tree near the garden veranda. He talked to my mother about the purchase. She stated with a sigh, "Herbert, the only drawback is, this house happens to be rather far away from your office in Mülheim. Does your work allow you to come and visit often?" But he, as always, could convince Mother to move there by saying, "Of course, I will love to come and stay here. We will be able to entertain our children and later our grandchildren here. We can invite our relatives and have wonderful festivals with them. I'll cherish having a house of my own. This one reminds me of St. Bernhard, with the fresh water spring in the back of the house and," he pointed with his hand to the tree in front of the dining room, "this big linden tree—isn't it like the one at your parents' house in Klostermansfeld?" After a short pause he added, "And, Paula, here in the village people are looking for work. We will hire enough household helpers and a ground keeper you can over see."

Father might have had our family in mind when buying this lovely property in Erbach[246] as the village was called when they moved there.

---

245 In big towns when they need vehicles to get to the cemeteries it is different. But most of the time it includes a good meal.

246 Erbach and Büdingen, located in the Westerwald Mountains, are now called Nistertal.

But we had gone our own ways. In Mülheim, only Reinhold still lived with them, but needing to finish his high school education, and my mother, not wanting him to change schools so close to his Abitur, stayed in Mülheim. Ernst had married, as did Hildegard. I worked in the south of West Germany. Nevertheless, for many years Mother and Father did have many guests. It was self understood for my mother that she kept the home open for all relatives, friends and acquaintances to visit and enjoy her hospitality. She had experienced that warm welcome growing up under her mother—our Oma—and later through her brother's family, especially during the war and its aftermath when many evacuees, homeless refugees and displaced people needed shelter, and found it in many German homes.

Do not neglect to show hospitality to strangers, for by doing that some have entertained angels without knowing it. Hebrews 13:2.

SELECTED BIBLIOGRAPHY

American history about medicine disease prevention in occupied areas.
http://www.archives.gov/exhibits/featured_documents/marshall_
plan/.
General Records of the United States Government, Record
Group 11. National Archives and Record Administration, 700
Pennsylvania Ave. NW, Washington, DC 20408. Aug. 2010.

Baale, Olaf: *Abbau Ost: Lügen, Vorurteile und sozialistische Schulden.*
München, Deutscher Taschenbuch Verlag, 2008.

Draeger, Hans, PhD. Foreword. *Der Vertrag von Versailles (The Versailles*
Treaty) Berlin: Heinrich Beeken Verlag, 1933. Print.

Fechter, Paul, PhD, *An der Wende der Zeit. Menschen und Begegnungen,*
Gütersloh: C. Bertelsmann Verlag, 1950.

Goethe, Johann Wolfgang von. *Goethe's Poems,* selected by James Boyd,
PhD. Oxford: Basil Blackwell, 1965. Tenth impression. Print.

Complete Fairy Tales of the Brothers Grimm. Trans. Jack Zipes. Expand.
ed. New York: Bantam Books, 2002. Print.

Reitsch, Hanna: *Fliegen: Mein Leben.* Stuttgart: Deutsche Verlags-
Anstalt, Nd.

Strohbusch, Horst. *Das Licht kam aus der Kirche: die Wende in Meiningen,*
1989-1990. 2nd ed. Meiningen: Verlag Börner PR, 2009. Print.

Wagenbach, Klaus, ed. *Das Atelier: Zeitgenössische deutsche Prosa.* Frankfurt a. Main: Fischer Bücherei, 1963.

Selected List of Works Consulted

Arnold, John. History: *A Very Short Introduction,* New York: Oxford University Press, 2000. Print.

Detwiler, Donald S. *Germany: a Short History.* 3rd Rev. ed. Carbondale: Southern Illinois University Press, 1999. Print.

Elton, Geoffrey. *Political History: Principles and Practice.* New York: Cambridge Basic Books, 1970. Print.

Ewen, David. *Encyclopedia of Concert Music.* New York: Hill and Wang, 1959. Print.

Fulbrook, Mary. *A Concise History of Germany.* In the series Cambridge Concise Histories. 1. Vol. 2nd ed. Cambridge: Cambridge University Press, 2004 Print.

Hagen, William W. *German History in Modern Times: Four Lives of the Nation.* New York: Cambridge University Press, 2012. Print.

Hamberger Wolfgang. *America — my fascination, Biography of a friendship from the Nazi era to the present.* Trans. Joan Clough-Lamb. Fulda: 2009. Print.

Kettenacker, Lothar. *Germany 1989: In the Aftermath of the Cold War.* Harlow, England: Pearson Education Limited, 2009. Print

Kitchen, Martin. *A History of Modern Germany: 1800 to the Present.* Chister, West Sussex: Wiley-Blackwell, 2012. Print

Koeltzsch, Hans. *Der neue Opernführer.* Verlag Deutsche Volksbücher, Stuttgart, 1961. Print.

Lixl-Purcell, Andreas. *Stimmen eines Jahrhunderts 1888-1990: Deutsche Autobiographien, Tagebücher, Bilder und Briefe.* Boston: Thomson, Heinle, 1990. Print.

Makos, Adam with Larry Alexander. *A Higher Call.* The Berkley Publishing Group. Penguin Group, Inc. New York, 2012. Print

Metaxas, Eric. *Bonhoeffer: Pastor, Martyr, Prophet, Spy.* A righteous Gentile Vs. the third Reich. Thomas Nelson Inc. Nashville, Tennessee, 2010. Print.

Pothorn, Herbert. *Baustile: die Anfänge, die grossen Epochen, die Gegenwart.* München: Südwest Verlag, 1968. Print.

Reinhardt, Kurt F. *Germany: 2000 Years.* 4th Rev. ed. New York: Ungar Publishing Co. 1965. Print.

Schulze, Hagen. *Germany: A New History.* Trans. Deborah Lucas Schneider. London: Harvard University Press, 1998. Print.

GRAPHICS

Herman Georg Oemler supplied most photos of Klostermanfeld, which were taken in 1953 before Family Oemler had to leave their farm. The photographer of these is not known. This also is the case for most other family photos, which were selected from the albums of Ernst Höfer, Reinhold Höfer or Ilse-Rose Warg. Photos of personal objects were taken by Ernst Bernhard Warg, 2019-2022. All other photos and maps are recognized in the order they first appear in the book.

I am grateful for the permission to print maps and pictures from the Internet for educational purposes.

Map of Germany after 1991 with permission from https://www.germany-insider- facts.com/german-staates.html

Map: GERMANY after the PEACE TREATY of 1919 with permission from https://www.google.com/search?q=germany+map+treaty+of+ver-sailles&client=firefox- b-1-e&

MAP: THURINGIA Large Thuringia Maps for Free Download and Print High- Resolution and Detailed Maps, orangesmile.com

Photo: Toruń's Town Hall, with permission https://www.torun.pl/en/turystyka/zabytki/old_town_hall

Photo: Ilse-Rose 6 years old, taken by Anton, a Polish civil worker, @1942

Map: Germany reduced to 4 zones, with permission from IEG-Maps, Institute European History, Mainz/ ™A. Kunz, 2005 GHDI – Map

Map: Divided Berlin inside of the Russian zone. Courtesy of pinterest. com, History | Berlin, Berlin wall, German history

Photo Berlin Tempelhof Airlift Memorial. Photo by Torsten Lüth, Aug 2019 https://get.google.com/albumarchive/117753700194048076333

GLOSSARY

AD   Anno Domini (after Christ)

AM   ante meridiem (before noon)

AHS   "Adolf Hitler Schule" (Adolf Hitler School for especially gifted boys)

BC   Before Christ

BDM   "Bund deutscher Mädchen" (League of German Girls)

BMW   "Bayerische Motoren Werke" (Bavarian Motor Works)

BRD   "Bundesrepublik Deutschland" unofficial abbreviation for the Federal Republic of Germany, used in scientific and political contexts, analog to DDR during 1949-1990)

D   "Deutschland" (Germany)

DDR   "Deutsche Demokratische Republik" (since 1949 the Sowjet controlled part of Germany in the East)

DDT   Dichlorodiphenyltrichloroethane was a synthetic pesticide. It was banned after discovering that it harmed any living and breathing being.

DFD   "Demokratischer Frauenbund Deutschlands" (Democratic Women's Federation/League of Germany) DDR

DM   "Deutsch Mark" (Federal Republic currency since 1948 until Euro took its place in twelve EU countries in 2002)

Displaced persons could be

a) evacuees: people who were asked to leave their city, since the government expected bombings of factories and military places.

b) expellees: those Germans who still lived in Russian bloc states that were expelled by the Soviets into the four occupied zones.

c) refugees: people who left their homes before the Soviet Army entered their city in eastern Germany.

ETH "Eidgenössische Hoch Schule" (Zurich Swiss Federal Institute of Technology ETH) ETH Zurich University

EU European Union

FDJ "Freie Deutsche Jugend" (Free German Youth)

FDGB "Freier Deutscher Gewerkschaftsbund" (Free German Trade Union Federation)

FRG Federal Republic of Germany "Bundesrepublik Deutschland

GDR German Democratic Republic "Deutsche Demokratische Republik"

Gestapo Geheime Staatspolizei (secret police)

GI a nickname for the US army soldier, especially for the army police; GI later stood for government issue or general issue.

HHH "Herbert Höfer Hameln" (The original name of Herbert Höfer's insurance agency)

HJ	"Hitlerjugend" (Hitler's youth)
ICC	International Criminal Court
ICRC	International Committee of the Red Cross
IM	"Inoffizielle Mitarbeiter" (unofficial secret informers)
IMT	International Military Tribunal
Jungvolk	boys under 10 years of age belonged to this organization, which was a preparation first step towards HJ. 8-14 years old
KdF	"Kraft durch Freude" (Strength through Joy). It was a Nazi controlled organization connected to the German Workers Front.
KPD	"Kommunistische Partei Deutschlands" (Communistic Party of Germany)
LPG	"Landwirtschaftliche Produktionsgemeinschaft" (Agricultural Production Cooperatives)
MfS	"Ministerium für Staatssicherheit" (Ministry for State Security)
NATO	North Atlantic Treaty Organization, established in 1949.
NSDAP	"Nationalsozialistische Deutsche Arbeiterpartei" (National Socialist German Workers Party)
Nazi	generally referring to members of the NSDAP
PM	post meridiem (after noon)

POW	Prisoner of War
RM	"Reichs or Renten Mark" (monitary currency in East and West Germany till 1948)
SA	"Sturm Abteilung" (Hitler's storm troopers, an army for his protection)
Stasi	a nickname for the "Ministerium für Sicherheit" (Ministry of State Security) Secret police in the GDR
SBZ	"Sowetische Besatzungszone" (Soviet Occupied Zone)
SED	"Soziale Einheits Partei" (Social Unity Party of East Germany) Under Russian control the KPD and SPD had merged to form the SED in 1946.
SS	"Schutz Staffel" (Protective squadron as Hitler's personal guard)
SMAD	Soviet Military Administration in Germany
USSR	Union of Soviet Socialist Republics
VEB	"Volkseigener Betrieb" (a business owned by the people)
VE	Victory of Europe, celebrated May 9th, 1945
V-I	"Vergeltungswaffe," (retaliation weapon) first rocket built in Peenemünde on the island Usedom in the Baltic Sea.
V-II	Second stage rocket, also called "Wunderwaffe" (wonder weapon)
VoPo	"Volkspolizei" (folk police)

WWI   World War I (originally called the Great War) 1914-1918
                WWII   World War II, 1939-1945

ZK   "Zentralkommitee" (Central Committee in the GDR)

Zirkel Mine   Name of the copper mine near Klostermansfeld

www.ingramcontent.com/pod-product-compliance
Ingram Content Group UK Ltd.
Pitfield, Milton Keynes, MK11 3LW, UK
UKHW050926280725
7099UKWH00048B/1160